BLUE RIBBON
DESIGNER SERIES™

200 EXPANDABLE
HOME PLANS

Design GG2682

Stylish Designs with Bonus, Flexible or Finish-Later Space

HOME PLANNERS, INC.
TUCSON, ARIZONA

Published by Home Planners, Inc.
Editorial and Corporate Offices:
3275 West Ina Road, Suite 110
Tucson, Arizona 85741

Distribution Center:
29333 Lorie Lane
Wixom, Michigan 48393

Rickard D. Bailey, President and Publisher
Cindy J. Coatsworth, Publications Manager
Paulette Mulvin, Senior Editor
Jan Prideaux, Project Editor
Paul Fitzgerald, Book Designer

Photo Credits
Front Cover: © Andrew D. Lautman
Back Cover: © Laszlo Regos

First Printing, January, 1995
10   9   8   7   6   5   4   3   2   1

Printed in the United States of America

Library of Congress Catalog Card Number: 94-079100

ISBN softcover: 1-881955-21-4

On the front cover: This lovely traditional home, Design GG2682,
captures all the charm of a Cape Cod dream, featuring a basic plan
as well as an expanded plan version. For more information about
this design, see page 6.

On the back cover: A 1½-story classic, Design GG2563 presents the best in expanded Cape Cod design. For more information about this design, see page 129.

TABLE OF CONTENTS

EDITOR'S NOTE

Imagine building a home that offers expansion without growing pains. Resourceful planning that utilizes and enhances existing space to its full potential can bring a great sense of satisfaction and pleasure to today's homeowner (not to mention the added benefit of keeping costs at a minimum by working with the originally built structure.) Therefore, it is with a great deal of pride that we present the following portfolio of innovative designs which offer a creative development of space—providing floor plans with immediate livability, partnered with expandable portions that combine effortlessly for future use. With upper stories to finish later, basements that accomodate growth, separate spaces for extended livability and much more, these plans provide options that are certain to meet your individual needs for the present—and fulfill your dreams for the future.

ABOUT THE DESIGNERS

The Blue Ribbon Designer Series™ is a collection of books featuring home plans of a diverse group of outstanding home designers and architects known as the Blue Ribbon Network of Designers. This group of companies is dedicated to creating and marketing the finest possible plans for home construction on a regional and national basis. Each of the companies exhibits superior work and integrity in all phases of the stock-plan business including modern, trendsetting floor planning, a professionally executed blueprint package and a strong sense of service and commitment to the consumer.

Design Basics, Inc.

For nearly a decade, Design Basics, a nationally recognized home design service located in Omaha, has been developing plans for custom home builders. Since 1987, the firm has consistently appeared in *Builder* magazine, the official magazine of the National Association of Home Builders, as the top-selling designer. The company's plans also regularly appear in numerous other shelter magazines such as *Better Homes and Gardens, House Beautiful* and *Home Planner*.

Design Traditions

Design Traditions was established by Stephen S. Fuller with the tenets of innovation, quality, originality and uncompromising architectural techniques in traditional and European homes. Especially popular throughout the Southeast, Design Traditions' plans are known for their extensive detail and thoughtful design. They are widely published in such shelter magazines as *Southern Living* magazine and *Better Homes and Gardens*.

Alan Mascord Design Associates, Inc.

Founded in 1983 as a local supplier to the building community, Mascord Design Associates of Portland, Oregon, began to successfully publish plans nationally in 1985. With plans now drawn exclusively on computer, Mascord Design Associates quickly received a reputation for homes that are easy to build yet meet the rigorous demands of the buyers' market, wining local and national awards. The company's trademark is creating floor plans that work well and exhibit excellent traffic patterns. Their motto is: "Drawn to build, designed to sell."

Larry E. Belk Designs

Through the years, Larry E. Belk has worked with individuals and builders alike to provide a quality product. After listening to over 4,000 dreams and watching them become reality all across America, Larry's design philosophy today combines traditional exteriors with upscale interiors designed for contemporary lifestyles. Flowing, open spaces and interesting angles define his interiors. Great emphasis is placed on providing views that showcase the natural environment. Dynamic exteriors reflect Larry's extensive home construction experience, painstaking research and talent as a fine artist.

Larry W. Garnett & Associates, Inc.

Starting as a designer of homes for Houston-area residents, Garnett & Associates has been marketing designs nationally for the past ten years. A well-respected design firm, the company's plans are regularly featured in *House Beautiful, Country Living, Home* and *Professional Builder*. Numerous accolades, including several from the Texas Institute of Building Design and the American Institute of Building Design, have been awarded to the company for excellence in architecture.

Home Planners, Inc.

Headquartered in Tucson, Arizona, with additional offices in Detroit, Home Planners is one of the longest-running and most successful home design firms in the United States. With over 2,500 designs in its portfolio, the company provides a wide range of styles, sizes and types of homes for the residential builder. All of Home Planners' designs are created with the care and professional expertise that fifty years of experience in the home-planning business affords. Their homes are designs to be built, lived in and enjoyed for years to come.

Donald A. Gardner, Architects, Inc.

The South Carolina firm of Donald A. Gardner was established in response to a growing demand for residential designs that reflect constantly changing lifestyles. The company's specialty is providing homes with refined, custom-style details and unique features such as passive-solar designs and open floor plans. Computer-aided design and drafting technology resulting in trouble-free construction documents places the firm at the leading edge of the home plan industry.

The Sater Design Collection

The Sater Design Collection has a long established tradition of providing South Florida's most diverse and extraordinary custom designed homes. Their goal is to fulfill each client's particular need for an exciting approach to design by merging creative vision with elements that satisfy a desire for a distinctive lifestyle. This philosophy is proven, as exemplified by over 50 national design awards, numerous magazine features and, most important, satisfied clients. The result is an elegant statement of lasting beauty and value.

Home Design Services, Inc.

For the past fifteen years, Home Design Services of Longwood, Florida, has been formulating plans for the sun-country lifestyle. At the forefront of design innovation and imagination, the company has developed award winning designs that are consistently praised for their highly detailed, free-flowing floor plans, imaginative and exciting interior architecture and elevations which have gained international appeal.

EXPANDABLE DESIGNS

*Building
Toward the Future*

Necessity became the mother of invention for early Colonial settlers. From rustic, box-like beginnings their homes adjusted in proportion to events that took place in their lives. As family size and prosperity increased, the size of the house increased also, often telescoping from one or both sides to meet varying requirements. This concept has evolved into truly flexible designs, uniquely planned to meet the needs and lifestyles of today. In this chapter, an array of expandable homes in various sizes and styles are enhanced with distinctive textures, rooflines and decorative trim sure to offer favorites for everyone.

Thoughtful design allows expanded portions to combine gracefully with existing structures. Considering the cost of purchasing land today, utilizing an existing site and modifying the floor plan is a budget-smart choice. On the following pages, you will find many styles that lend themselves particularly well to finishing in stages. Consider the charm and style of Cape Cod homes and Country Cottages. Often begun as simple, economical dwellings, these homes are both attractive and easy to expand. Fine examples of basic and extended plans are illustrated by Designs GG2682 on page 6 and GG9187 on page 18. If a more formal appearance is desired, many traditional-style homes borrow design elements from winged Colonial houses that present a symmetrical expansion using corridors to connect appendages to the initial home. In the finest Colonial tradition, Design GG2665 on page 10 displays a stately courtyard created by additional two-story wings connected by galleries.

Maybe a separate guest suite or mother-in-law suite is a consideration for the future. Designs GG9159 and GG9096 (pages 20 and 21) create exceptional exterior appeal with the inclusion of these additions. Designed to take advantage of maximum privacy, these separate suites allow a pleasing marriage of style and livability.

Whatever your preference, you'll find plenty of options in this chapter. The designs on the following pages offer a variety of alternatives certain to fit special needs. Accommodating floor plans provide room-to-grow interiors filled with amenities for homeowners today as well as in years to come.

Expanding the Half-House

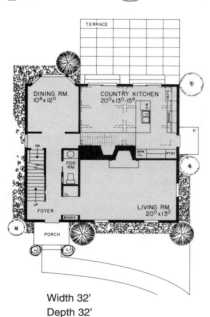

Width 32'
Depth 32'

Design GG2682

First Floor (Basic Plan): 976 square feet
First Floor (Expanded Plan): 1,230 square feet
Second Floor (Both Plans): 744 square feet
Total (Basic Plan): 1,720 square feet
Total (Extended Plan): 1,974 square feet
Expandable Features: Study, Garage & Attic

L **D**

CUSTOMIZABLE

Custom Alterations? See page 237 for customizing this plan to your specifications.

● Here is an expandable Colonial with a full measure of Cape Cod Charm. For those who wish to build the basic house, there is an abundance of low-budget livability. Twin fireplaces serve the formal living room and the informal country kitchen. Note the spaciousness of both areas. A dining room and powder room are also on the first floor of this basic plan. Upstairs three bedrooms and two full baths.

QUOTE ONE™

Cost to build? See page 232 to order complete cost estimate to build this house in your area!

Design by
Home Planners,
Inc.

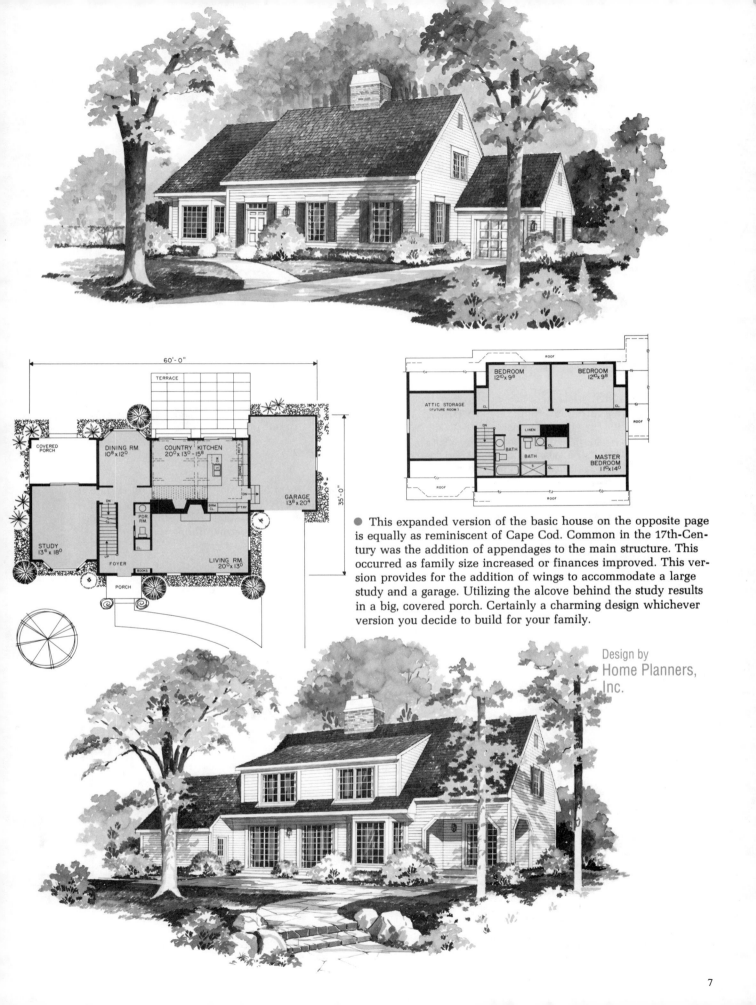

60'-0"

TERRACE

COVERED PORCH

DINING RM.
10⁸ x 12⁰

COUNTRY KITCHEN
20⁰ x 13⁰ -15⁸

GARAGE
13⁸ x 20⁴

35'-0"

STUDY
13⁶ x 18⁰

DN

PDR. RM.

CL.

BRM. CL.

PTRY.

FOYER

UP

BOOKS

LIVING RM.
20⁰ x 13⁰

PORCH

ROOF

BEDROOM
12¹⁰ x 9⁸

BEDROOM
12¹⁰ x 9⁸

ATTIC STORAGE
(FUTURE ROOM)

ROOF

DN

LINEN

CL.

BATH

CL.

BATH

MASTER BEDROOM
11⁰ x 14⁰

CL.

ROOF

ROOF

● This expanded version of the basic house on the opposite page is equally as reminiscent of Cape Cod. Common in the 17th-Century was the addition of appendages to the main structure. This occurred as family size increased or finances improved. This version provides for the addition of wings to accommodate a large study and a garage. Utilizing the alcove behind the study results in a big, covered porch. Certainly a charming design whichever version you decide to build for your family.

Design by
Home Planners,
Inc.

Expandable Cape Ann Cottage

Design GG2983

First Floor (Basic Plan): 776 square feet
First Floor (Expanded Plan): 1,072 square feet
Second Floor (Both Plans): 652 square feet
Total: 1,428 square feet (Basic); 1,724 square feet (Expanded Plan)
Expandable Features: Dining Room, Study & Garage

● This charming gambrel-roofed Colonial cottage is reminiscent of the simple houses built and occupied by seafarers on Cape Ann, Mass. in the 17th and 18th Centuries. However, this adaptation offers a new twist. It is designed to expand as your need and/or budget grows. Of course, building the expanded version first will deliver the bonus livability promised by the formal dining room and quiet study, plus the convenience of the attached garage.

Design by
Home Planners,
Inc.

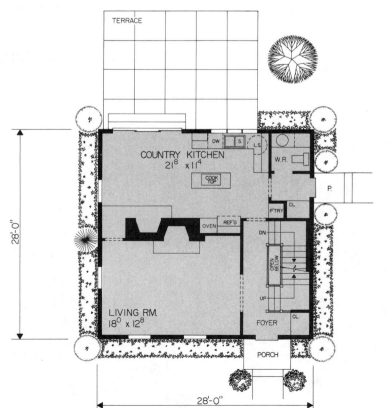

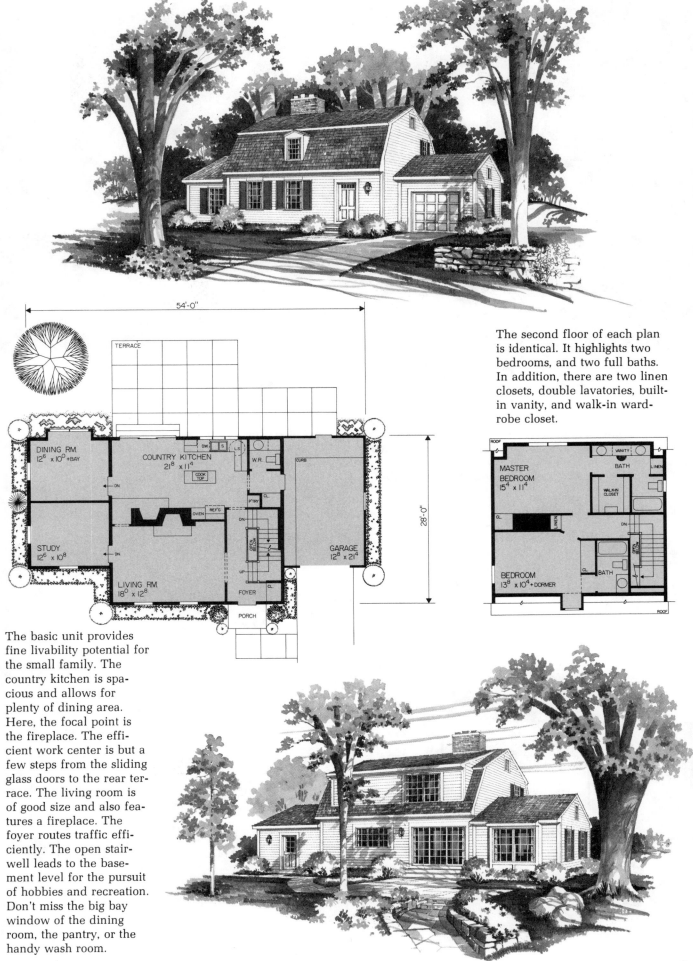

54'-0"

TERRACE

DINING RM.
12⁶ x 10⁰ +BAY

COUNTRY KITCHEN
21⁸ x 11⁴

DW. S

W.R.

CURB

COOK TOP

STUDY
12⁶ x 10⁸

OVEN   REF'G

P'TRY   CL.

OPEN BELOW

DN.

GARAGE
12⁸ x 21⁴

28'-0"

LIVING RM.
18⁰ x 12⁸

UP

CL.

FOYER

PORCH

The second floor of each plan is identical. It highlights two bedrooms, and two full baths. In addition, there are two linen closets, double lavatories, built-in vanity, and walk-in wardrobe closet.

ROOF

VANITY

MASTER BEDROOM
15⁴ x 11⁴

BATH

LINEN

WALK-IN CLOSET

CL.

LINEN

DN.

BATH

BEDROOM
13⁸ x 10⁴ + DORMER

CL.

OPEN BELOW

ROOF

The basic unit provides fine livability potential for the small family. The country kitchen is spacious and allows for plenty of dining area. Here, the focal point is the fireplace. The efficient work center is but a few steps from the sliding glass doors to the rear terrace. The living room is of good size and also features a fireplace. The foyer routes traffic efficiently. The open stairwell leads to the basement level for the pursuit of hobbies and recreation. Don't miss the big bay window of the dining room, the pantry, or the handy wash room.

Appending A Magnificent Manor

● What a grand presentation this home makes! The origin of this house dates back to 1787 and George Washington's stately Mount Vernon. The underlying aesthetics for this design come from the rational balancing of porticoes, fenestration and chimneys. Flanking wings—which may be added later—create a large formal courtyard. The rear elevation of this home features six two-story columns, along with four sets of French doors. This home, designed from architecture of the past, provides an amenity-filled floor plan sure to please today's homeowner.

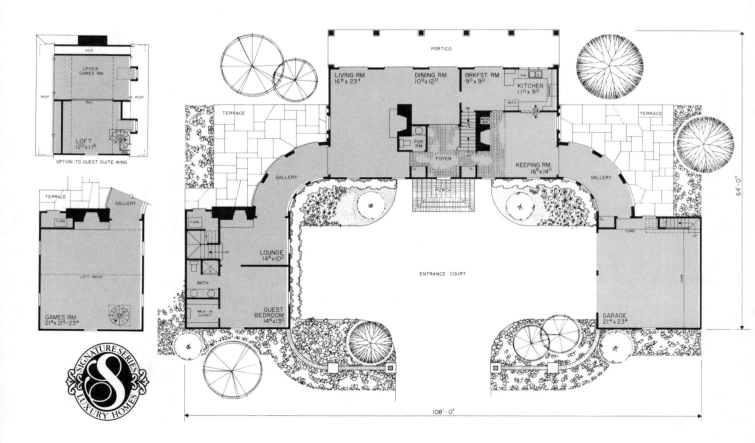

Design GG2665

First Floor: 1,152 square feet; Second Floor: 1,152 square feet
Total: 2,304 square feet (guest suites and galleries not included)
First Floor Guest Suite: 562 square feet; Second Floor Studio: 331 square feet
Expandable Features: Guest Suite, Studio, Gameroom, Loft & Garage

● Versatility and planned use of space are key factors in this courtyard mini-estate. A keeping room (with a pass-through to the kitchen and a fireplace with a built-in wood box), formal dining room, breakfast room and formal living room (with fireplace) on the first floor allow plenty of social areas. Four bedrooms with two full baths are found on the second floor. Separate guest quarters with a full bath, lounge area and upstairs studio (connected to

the main house by a gallery) may be completed later to further enhance livability. A complementary gallery is located on the other side of the house and leads to the garage with a storage room or hobbies room situated above. The guest bedroom/lounge with an upstairs study can be optionally designed as a game room with a spiral staircase and a 162-square-foot loft area.

Design by
Home Planners,
Inc.

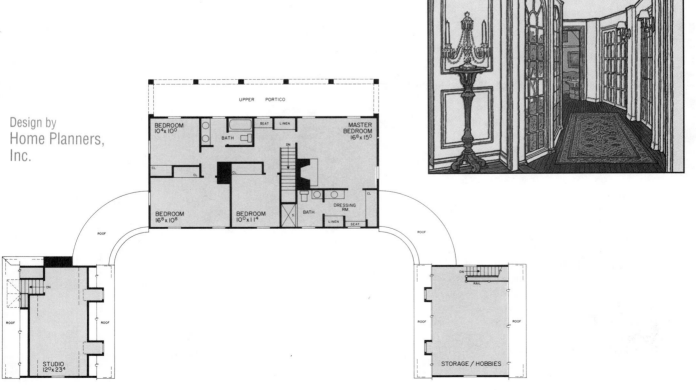

Extending The Folk Victorian

Extending The Folk Victorian
Design GG8970
First Floor: 1,213 square feet
Second Floor: 535 square feet
Total: 1,748 square feet
Expandable Features: Guest Room, Morning Room & Garage

● This charming Folk Victorian home may start as a small cottage, but if all expansion options are used, it grows to a sizable 2,166-square-foot home. The basic plan is well-designed and provides fine livability with a living room, dining room, kitchen, three bedrooms and two baths. Of special note is the private master suite which invites relaxation with a pampering tub, a separate shower and a compartmented toilet, accessible from the hallway as well. Plenty of storage is available in the huge walk-in closet. The addition of the sunlit morning room is a welcome space for casual dining, while the guest room, with a private bath, enhances livability and offers room to stretch. A two-car garage may be completed at the same time or later if you prefer.

Design by
Larry W.
Garnett &
Associates, Inc.

Width 30'-8"
Depth 51'-8"

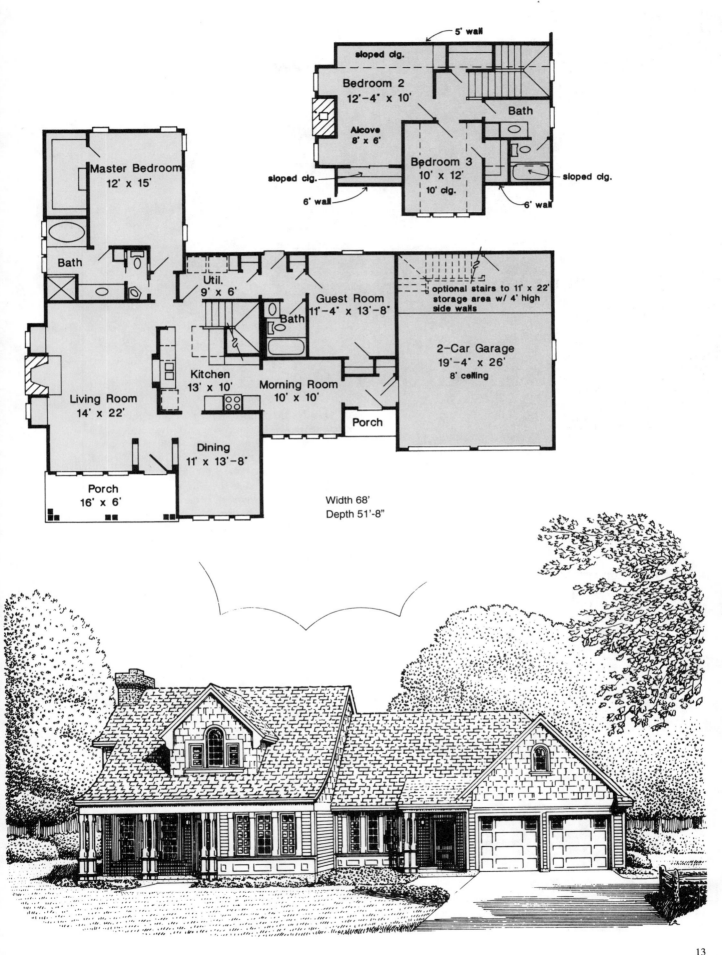

Bedroom 2
12'-4" x 10'

5' wall

sloped clg.

Alcove
8' x 6'

Bath

Bedroom 3
10' x 12'
10' clg.

sloped clg.

sloped clg.

6' wall

6' wall

Master Bedroom
12' x 15'

Bath

Util.
9' x 6'

Guest Room
11'-4" x 13'-8"

Bath

optional stairs to 11' x 22'
storage area w/ 4' high
side walls

2-Car Garage
19'-4" x 26'
8' ceiling

Kitchen
13' x 10'

Morning Room
10' x 10'

Living Room
14' x 22'

Porch

Dining
11' x 13'-8"

Porch
16' x 6'

Width 68'
Depth 51'-8"

A Cozy Home Grows In Phases

Design GG9081-A

First Floor: 814 square feet

Optional Master Suite: 372 square feet

Second Floor: 520 square feet

Total: 1,706 square feet

Expandable Features: Master Suite, Family Room & Garage

● This design offers a home that can begin as an efficient two-bedroom cottage. With as little as 1,334 square feet, this plan possesses all the charm and integrity of design not often found in today's smaller homes. The optional master suite, family room and garage can be added as they are needed. With a living quarters above, the garage can even be built first, allowing the home to be completed later. The alternate plans indicate how the home can adapt to the changing needs of a growing family, while maintaining the exterior appeal. Plans include all the drawings for the alternates, enabling the home to be built in any of several variations.

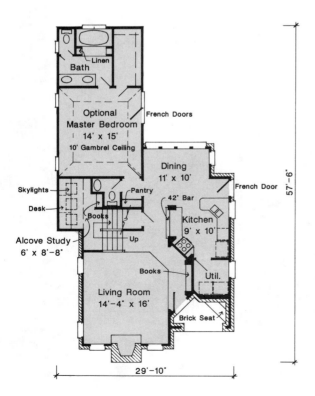

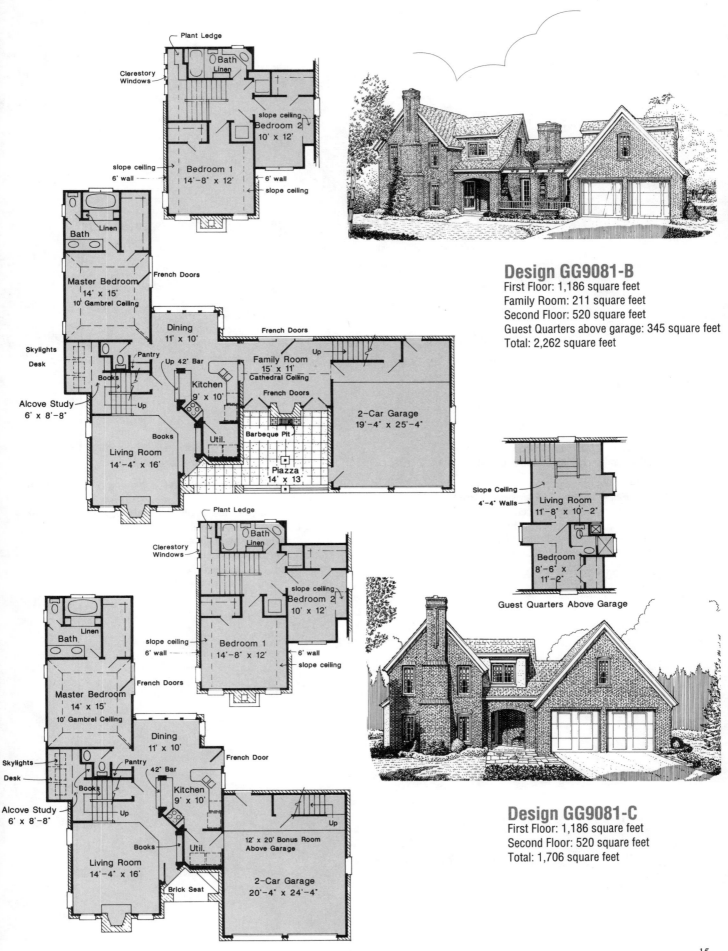

Plant Ledge

Bath
Linen

Clerestory Windows

slope ceiling
Bedroom 2
10' x 12'

slope ceiling
6' wall
Bedroom 1
14'-8" x 12'
6' wall
slope ceiling

Bath
Linen

Master Bedroom
14' x 15'
10' Gambrel Ceiling
French Doors

Dining
11' x 10'

French Doors

Skylights
Desk

Pantry
Up 42" Bar

Kitchen
9' x 10'

Family Room
15' x 11'
Cathedral Ceiling
French Doors

Up

Books
Alcove Study
6' x 8'-8"
Up

Books
Util.

Living Room
14'-4" x 16'

Barbeque Pit

2-Car Garage
19'-4" x 25'-4"

Piazza
14' x 13'

Design GG9081-B

First Floor: 1,186 square feet
Family Room: 211 square feet
Second Floor: 520 square feet
Guest Quarters above garage: 345 square feet
Total: 2,262 square feet

Slope Ceiling
4'-4" Walls
Living Room
11'-8" x 10'-2"

Bedroom
8'-6" x 11'-2"

Guest Quarters Above Garage

Plant Ledge

Bath
Linen

Clerestory Windows

slope ceiling
Bedroom 2
10' x 12'

slope ceiling
6' wall
Bedroom 1
14'-8" x 12'
6' wall
slope ceiling

Bath
Linen

Master Bedroom
14' x 15'
10' Gambrel Ceiling
French Doors

Dining
11' x 10'
French Door

Skylights
Desk

Pantry
42" Bar

Kitchen
9' x 10'

Up

Books
Alcove Study
6' x 8'-8"
Up

Books
Util.

12' x 20' Bonus Room
Above Garage

Up

Living Room
14'-4" x 16'

Brick Seat

2-Car Garage
20'-4" x 24'-4"

Design GG9081-C

First Floor: 1,186 square feet
Second Floor: 520 square feet
Total: 1,706 square feet

Traditional Style In Stages

Design GG9122

Square Footage (Basic Plan): 1,461
Expandable Features: Master Suite, Garage & Guest Quarters

● This unique plan represents a new dimension in home design. The basic plan allows for complete livability on a single level but can be enhanced with any or all of the additional phases as needs and budgets grow. The basic plan provides a spacious living area with a fireplace and a windowed gallery overlooking a covered porch. The formal dining room to the front of the plan complements the light-filled breakfast nook. Two bedrooms to the right of the plan share a full bath and feature large closets. With the Phase 2 garage addition comes a shop area, powder room and utility space. Phase 3 allows for a lovely master suite (adding 555 square feet) just off the living room gallery. It holds a walk-in closet and a pampering corner tub. An additional 271 square feet is available in the space above the garage to be developed into guest quarters, a mother-in-law suite or a handy studio.

Design by
Larry W.
Garnett &
Associates, Inc.

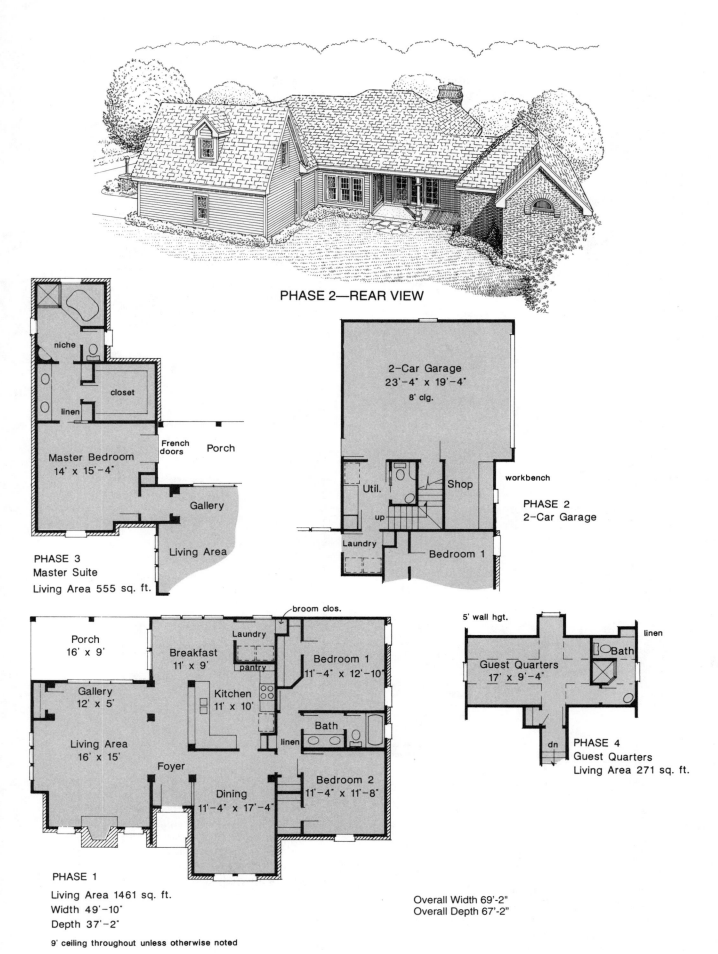

PHASE 2—REAR VIEW

niche

closet

linen

French doors   Porch

Master Bedroom
14' x 15'-4"

Gallery

Living Area

PHASE 3
Master Suite
Living Area 555 sq. ft.

2-Car Garage
23'-4" x 19'-4"
8' clg.

workbench

Util.   Shop

PHASE 2
2-Car Garage

up

Laundry   Bedroom 1

broom clos.

Porch
16' x 9'

Breakfast
11' x 9'

Laundry

pantry

Bedroom 1
11'-4" x 12'-10"

Gallery
12' x 5'

Kitchen
11' x 10'

Living Area
16' x 15'

Bath

linen

Foyer

Dining
11'-4" x 17'-4"

Bedroom 2
11'-4" x 11'-8"

5' wall hgt.   linen

Bath

Guest Quarters
17' x 9'-4"

dn   PHASE 4
Guest Quarters
Living Area 271 sq. ft.

PHASE 1

Living Area 1461 sq. ft.

Width 49'-10"

Depth 37'-2"

9' ceiling throughout unless otherwise noted

Overall Width 69'-2"
Overall Depth 67'-2"

Enlarging A Comfortable Cottage

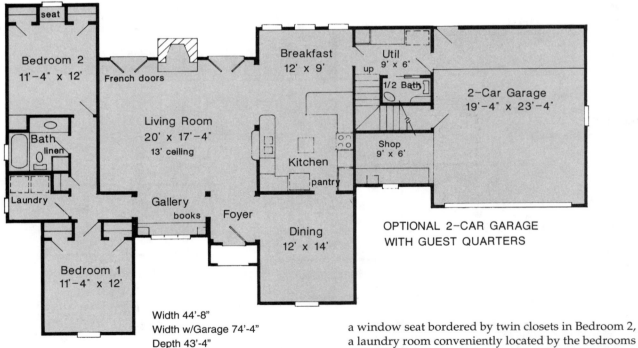

seat

Bedroom 2
11'-4" x 12'

French doors

Living Room
20' x 17'-4"
13' ceiling

Bath
linen

Laundry

Gallery
books

Foyer

Bedroom 1
11'-4" x 12'

Breakfast
12' x 9'

Util
9' x 6'
up

1/2 Bath

Kitchen
pantry

Shop
9' x 6'

2-Car Garage
19'-4" x 23'-4"

Dining
12' x 14'

OPTIONAL 2-CAR GARAGE
WITH GUEST QUARTERS

Width 44'-8"
Width w/Garage 74'-4"
Depth 43'-4"
Depth w/Master Suite 73'-8"

Design GG9187
Square Footage (Basic Plan): 1,462
Expandable Features: Master Suite, Guest Quarters & Garage

● Start small with this charming cottage and grow-as-you-go! The basic design offers amenities often found in homes twice the size. Special features include French doors flanking the warming fireplace in the living room, a window seat bordered by twin closets in Bedroom 2, a laundry room conveniently located by the bedrooms and bath and an efficient kitchen nestled between the formal dining room and breakfast nook. When you're ready, enlarging the plan is simple, and designed to finish in stages. A sumptuous master suite with a large walk-in closet and pampering bath may be added as the need for additional space arises. A two-car garage with a large shop area, a utility room and a half bath may be completed in the next phase. Completing the expansion of this terrific plan is the guest quarters located above the garage.

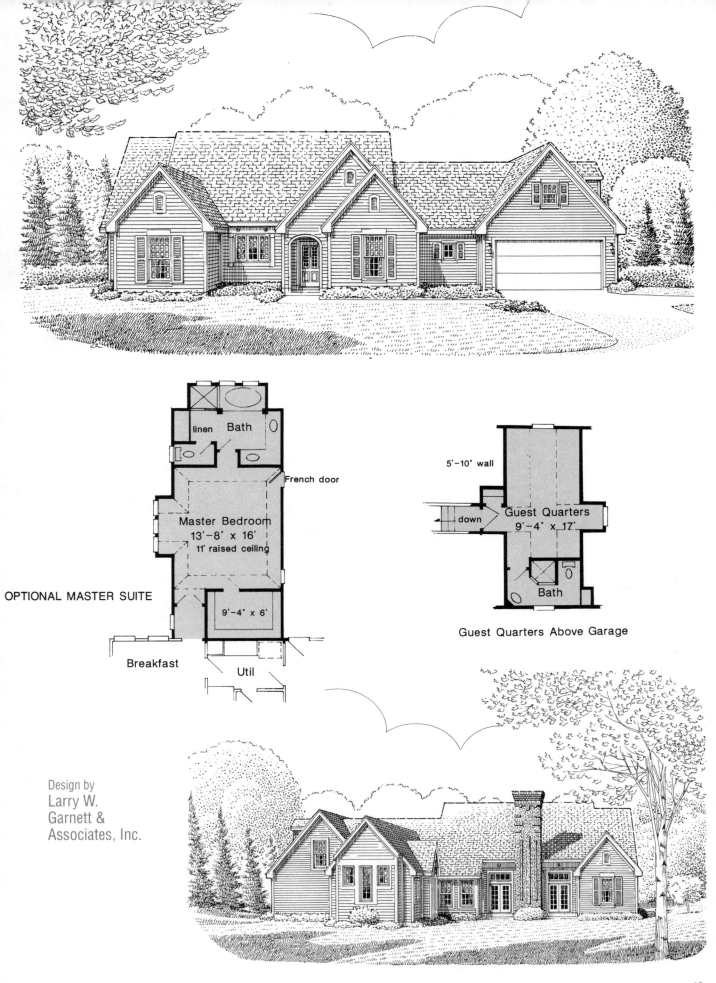

linen   Bath

French door

Master Bedroom
13'-8" x 16'
11' raised ceiling

OPTIONAL MASTER SUITE

9'-4" x 6'

Breakfast

Util

5'-10" wall

down   Guest Quarters
9'-4" x 17'

Bath

Guest Quarters Above Garage

Design by
Larry W.
Garnett &
Associates, Inc.

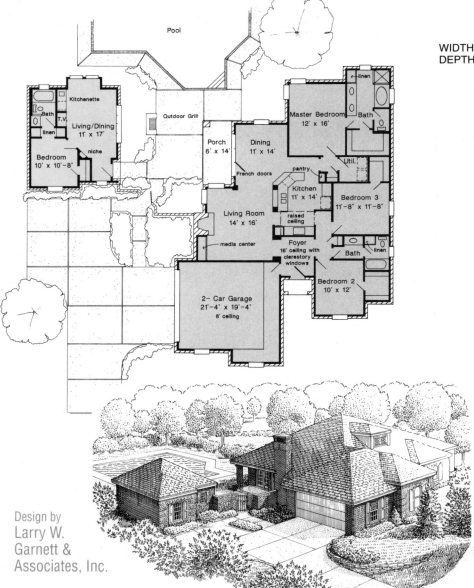

Pool

Outdoor Grill

Kitchenette

Bath

T.V.

linen

Living/Dining
11' x 17'

Bedroom
10' x 10'-8"

niche

Porch
6' x 14'

Dining
11' x 14'

French doors

pantry

Kitchen
11' x 14'

raised ceiling

Living Room
14' x 16'

media center

Foyer
16' ceiling with clerestory windows

2- Car Garage
21'-4" x 19'-4"
8' ceiling

Master Bedroom
12' x 16'

Bath

linen

Util.

Bedroom 3
11'-8" x 11'-8"

Bath

linen

Bedroom 2
10' x 12'

Design by
Larry W.
Garnett &
Associates, Inc.

WIDTH 46'
DEPTH 66'-8"

Design GG9159

Square Footage: 1,661
Guest Cottage: 456 square feet
Expandable Feature: Guest House

● If you're looking for a place to house guests, in-laws or college students, take a look at this plan. A one-bedroom, full-bath guest cottage sits off to the side of this very livable home. (Included with the plans for the main house are the plans for this guest cottage, Design GG9162.) The main house opens with a dramatic foyer lit by clerestory windows. The living room, to the left of the foyer, showcases a fireplace and a built-in media center. Open to both the living and dining rooms, the kitchen will make for delightful dining. For privacy, the three family bedrooms are well-segregated from the other rooms in the house. Also noteworthy is this plan's fabulous outdoor livability which just begins with a covered porch off the dining room.

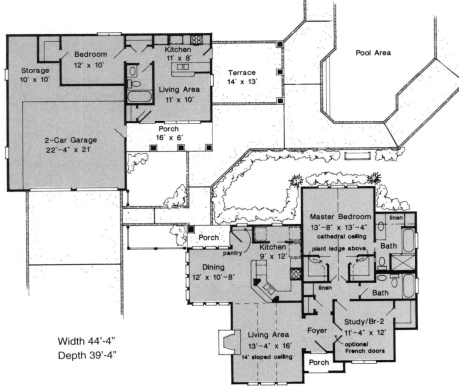

Storage
10' x 10'

Bedroom
12' x 10'

Kitchen
11' x 8'

Living Area
11' x 10'

Pool Area

Terrace
14' x 13'

2-Car Garage
22'-4" x 21'

Porch
16' x 6'

Width 44'-4"
Depth 39'-4"

Porch

pantry

Kitchen
9' x 12'

Dining
12' x 10'-8"

Master Bedroom
13'-8" x 13'-4"
cathedral ceiling
plant ledge above

linen

Bath

linen

Bath

Living Area
13'-4" x 16'
14' sloped ceiling

Foyer

Study/Br-2
11'-4" x 12'
optional French doors

Porch

Design by
Larry W.
Garnett &
Associates, Inc.

Design GG9096
Square Footage: 1,268
Guest Cottage: 468 square feet
Expandable Feature: Guest House

● The perfect plan for those with a live-in relative, long-term guest or a family member who works at home, this plan allows a separate cottage with complete livability. The main house features a living room with fireplace and sloped ceiling, a glass-enclosed dining room with porch, kitchen with plenty of counter space and two bedrooms with two baths (or make one a study). The separate cottage is attached to the garage and has its own living area, galley kitchen and bedroom with walk-in closet and full bath. It also features a front porch and private side terrace. It can work as complete living quarters or a private studio or office. A bright solution to today's living patterns.

COPYRIGHT LARRY E. BELK

Design GG8089

First Floor: 1,471 square feet
Second Floor: 1,040 square feet
Total: 2,511 square feet
Expandable Feature: 1 or 2 Full Baths on Second Floor

● Three arched windows dominate the entrance to this Southern original. The dining room and two-story great room are located at the rear of the home and are separated by a graceful arched opening flanked by columns. A roomy breakfast area opens off the kitchen and features a lovely bay window. The large work island in the kitchen has a 42" ledge—perfect for snacks and informal dining. The master suite includes a bath with a whirlpool tub, a shower, His and Hers vanities and a large walk-in closet. The upstairs offers two options: 3 bedrooms and 1½ baths; or 3 bedrooms and two baths. The game room opens to an expandable area perfect for that future office, weight room or hobby room. This plan is available with either a crawlspace or slab foundation. Please specify when ordering.

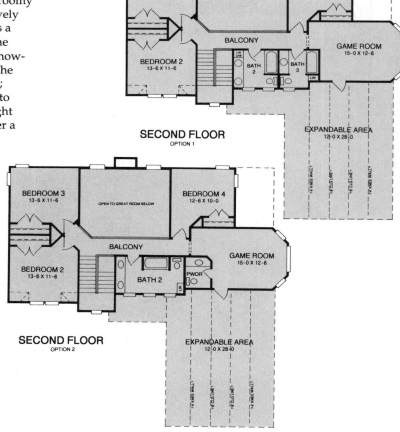

SECOND FLOOR
OPTION 1

WIDTH 56-10

FIRST FLOOR

Design by
Larry E. Belk
Designs

SECOND FLOOR
OPTION 2

Design GG9498 First Floor: 2,270 square feet
Second Floor: 788 square feet; Total: 3,058 square feet
Expandable Feature: 3 or 4 Bedroom Option

● Dramatic on the highest level, this spectacular plan offers a recessed entry, double rows of multi-paned windows and two dormers over the garage. On the inside, formal living and dining areas reside to the right of the foyer and are separated from it by columns. A private den is also accessed from the foyer through double doors. The family room with fireplace is to the rear. It adjoins the breakfast nook and attached island kitchen. The master suite is on the first floor to separate it from family bedrooms. They are found on the second floor—there are two with the option of another. There are also two full baths on this floor. Bonus space over the garage can be developed at a later time.

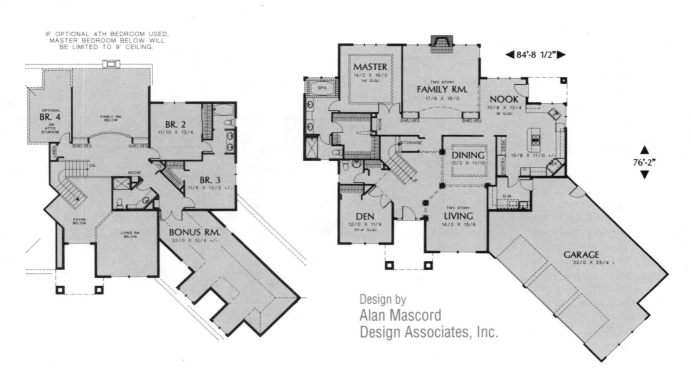

IF OPTIONAL 4TH BEDROOM USED,
MASTER BEDROOM BELOW WILL
BE LIMITED TO 9' CEILING.

OPTIONAL
BR. 4
OR
ATTIC
STORAGE

FAMILY RM.
BELOW

BR. 2
11/10 X 13/4

SHELVES

SHELVES

DN.

NICHE

BR. 3
11/6 X 13/0 +/-

FOYER
BELOW

LIVING RM.
BELOW

BONUS RM.
32/0 X 12/4 +/-

◀84'-8 1/2"▶

MASTER
14/2 X 16/0
(11' CLG.)

SPA

TWO STORY
FAMILY RM.
17/6 X 16/0

NOOK
10/8 X 13/4
(9' CLG.)

SHELVES

SHELVES

NICHE

STORAGE

DINING
12/2 X 11/10

PANTRY DESK

15/8 X 17/0 +/-

UP

DEN
12/0 X 11/4
(11'-4" CLG.)

TWO STORY
LIVING
14/0 X 15/6

D.W.

REF.

GARAGE
32/0 X 25/4

▲
76'-2"
▼

Design by
**Alan Mascord
Design Associates, Inc.**

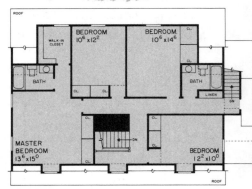

OPTIONAL SECOND FLOOR PLAN

Design GG2320

First Floor: 1,856 square feet
Second Floor: 1,171 square feet
Total: 3,027 square feet
Expandable Feature: 3 or 4 Bedroom Option

● This charming Colonial adaptation features an exterior with a Gambrel roof in front and a Saltbox rear. Casual living is easy with the large country kitchen and spacious family room with its warming fireplace, ideal for informal gatherings. For more formal pursuits, a living room with a welcoming fireplace and a dining room with a china cabinet are adjacent to the foyer. A study and convenient mud room/laundry area complete the first floor. Blueprints include details for both three- and four-bedroom options on the second floor.

Design by
Home Planners,
Inc.

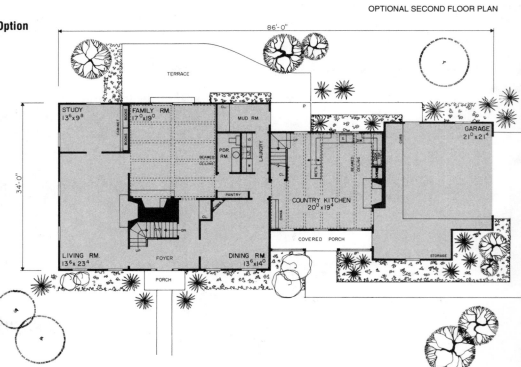

Design GG1956 First Floor: 990 square feet
Second Floor: 728 square feet; Total: 1,718 square feet
Expandable Feature: 3 or 4 Bedroom Option

D

Design by
Home Planners,
Inc.

● Simple, functional, and loaded with Colonial appeal, this versatile two-story plan features the finest in family floor plans. To the right of the entry foyer, a large formal living area connects to the dining room, allowing adequate space for entertaining in style. The U-shaped kitchen features a pass-through counter to the breakfast room. The sunken family room is enhanced by a beamed ceiling, raised-hearth fireplace, and built-in bookshelves. Upstairs are four bedrooms (or choose the three-bedroom option included in the blueprint package). Other highlights of the plan include a full-length rear terrace and storage space galore.

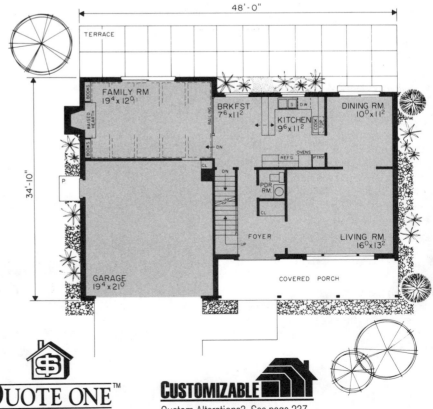

OPTIONAL 3-BEDROOM PLAN

Photo by Andrew D. Lautman

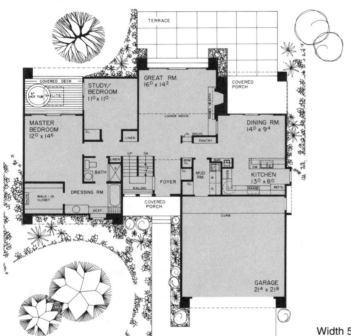

Width 54'-8"
Depth 54'

Design GG2822

First Floor: 1,363 square feet
Second Floor: 351 square feet
Total: 1,714 square feet
**Expandable Features:
Hobby Room or Guest Room**
L

● Here is a truly unique house whose interior was designed with the current decade's economies, life-styles and demographics in mind. While function-ing as a one-story home, the second floor provides an extra measure of livability when required. In addition, this two-story section adds to the dramatic appeal of both the exterior and the interior. Within only 1,363 square feet, this contemporary delivers refreshing and outstanding living patterns for those who are buying their first home, those who have raised their family and are looking for a smaller home and those in search of a retirement home.

ALTERNATE SECOND FLOOR

Design by
Home Planners,
Inc.

QUOTE ONE™

Cost to build? See page 232
to order complete cost estimate
to build this house in your area!

Design GG3330

First Floor: 1,394 square feet
Second Floor Lounge: 320 square feet
Total: 1,714 square feet
Expandable Features: Lounge or Master Bedroom

● Outdoor living and open floor planning are highlights of this moderately sized plan. Amenities include a private hot tub on a wooden deck that is accessible via sliding glass doors in both bedrooms, and a two-story gathering room. An optional second-floor plan allows for a full 503 square feet of space with a balcony.

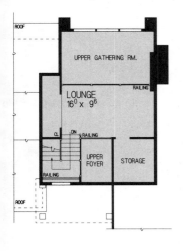

OPTIONAL FLOOR PLAN

Design by
Home Planners,
Inc.

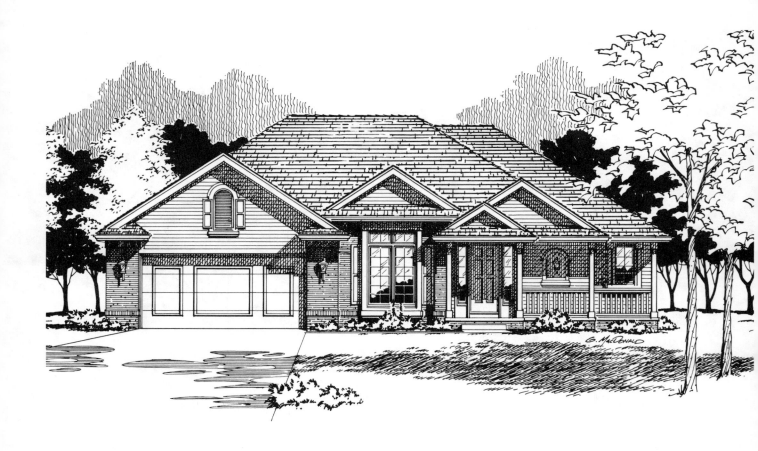

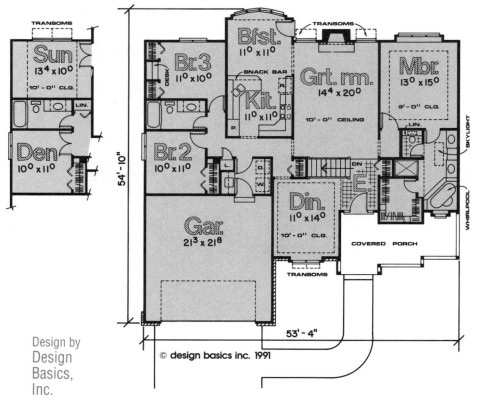

TRANSOMS

Sun
13⁴ x 10⁰
10' - 0" CLG.

LIN.

Den
10⁰ x 11⁰

Bfst.
11⁰ x 11⁰

TRANSOMS

Br. 3
11⁰ x 10⁰

DESK

SNACK BAR

Kit.
11⁰ x 11⁰

P.

Grt. rm.
14⁴ x 20⁰
10' - 0" CEILING

Mbr.
13⁰ x 15⁰
9' - 0" CLG.

LIN.

SKYLIGHT

Br. 2
10⁰ x 11⁰

L.

D

W

DN

WHIRLPOOL

54' - 10"

Gar.
21³ x 21⁸

Din.
11⁰ x 14⁰
10' - 0" CLG.

COVERED PORCH

TRANSOMS

53' - 4"

© design basics inc. 1991

Design by
Design
Basics,
Inc.

Design GG9321

Square Footage: 1,710
Expandable Feature: Sun Room & Den Optio

● Comfort awaits you in this
appealing ranch home. Notice the
repeating rooflines and the covered
porch before studying the inside
amenities. A formal dining room
features elegant ceiling details. In
the volume great room, designed
for daily family gatherings, pay
careful attention to a raised-hearth
fireplace flanked by sparkling
windows. Outdoor access and a
Lazy Susan are thoughtful details
designed into the kitchen and
bowed dinette. For added flexibility, two secondary bedrooms can
be easily converted to a sun room
with French doors and an optional
den. The secluded master suite is
enhanced by a boxed ceiling and
deluxe skylit dressing room.

2

1½ &
TWO-STORY DESIGNS

One-Size-Fits-All

Most of us are well acquainted with the One-Size-Fits-All label in garments, but what if that principle is applied to an efficiently designed home? The benefits are many. Take, for example, a single person or a couple beginning their adventure as home-owners. With an eye to the future, a well-designed home will meet their current needs and offer growth potential in preparation for life's events. Such wise planning results in a great investment and a wonderful place to call home as the years go by.

A first floor that can be utilized now with an upper floor to be finished later offers a perfect solution. The plans contained in this section provide fully functional, first-floor livability with second-floor bedrooms that significantly increase future possibilities. Many plans, such as Designs GG3437 and GG9325 (pages 31 and 46) feature a nearby media room or studio on the first floor that can easily become a nursery or office.

As the family grows and children mature, the second floor is ready to develop as a sleeping zone with comfortable space for everyone. Effective use of space is accomplished in Design GG3310 (page 35) which demonstrates that with a well-designed floor plan, privacy is easy to maintain. Two roomy bedrooms—each featuring its own walk-in closet, balcony and vanity—offer separate access to an adjoining bath.

If friends and family are frequent visitors, a plan such as Design GG3450 on page 41 provides a comfortable guest suite with an indulgent floor plan that includes a sitting area, a walk-in closet and an amenity-filled bath with a relaxing whirlpool tub. Who could ask for more?

The grand collection of plans that follow in this chapter represent the ingenious use of space designed to meet the changes in lifestyles as they occur. Exterior styles are attractive; thoughtfully arranged floor plans provide comfort and convenience for everyone.

Design GG3435

First Floor: 1,946 square feet
Second Floor: 986 square feet
Total: 2,932 square feet
Upper Level Feature: Additional Sleeping Quarters

L

● Here's a grand Spanish Mission home designed for family living. Enter at the angled foyer which contains a curved staircase to the second floor. Family bedrooms are here along with a spacious guest suite. The master bedroom is found on the first floor and has a private patio and whirlpool overlooking an enclosed garden area. Besides a living room and dining room connected by a through-fireplace, there is a family room with casual eating space. There is also a library with large closet. You'll appreciate the abundant built-ins and interesting shapes throughout this home.

CUSTOMIZABLE

Custom Alterations? See page 237 for customizing this plan to your specifications.

Design by
**Home Planners,
Inc.**

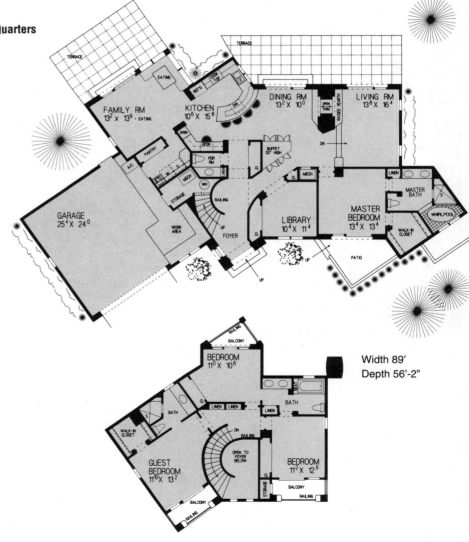

Width 89'
Depth 56'-2"

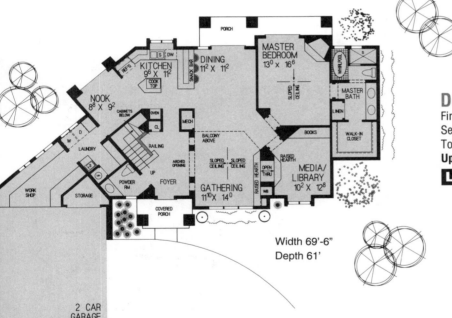

PORCH

KITCHEN
9⁶ X 11²

DINING
11² X 11²

MASTER
BEDROOM
13⁰ x 16⁶

NOOK
8⁸ X 9²

CABINETS
BELOW

OVEN

COOK
TOP

SNACK BAR

REF'G

S   DW

SLOPED CEILING

WHIRLPOOL

MASTER
BATH

LINEN

MECH

CL

BALCONY
ABOVE

BOOKS

WALK-IN
CLOSET

LAUNDRY

W   D

RAILING

ARCHED
OPENING

SLOPED
CEILING

SLOPED
CEILING

RAISED
HEARTH

OPEN
THRU

MEDIA/
LIBRARY
10² X 12⁸

POWDER
RM

UP

FOYER

GATHERING
11¹⁰ X 14⁰

RAISED HEARTH

WB

WORK
SHOP

STORAGE

COVERED
PORCH

2 CAR
GARAGE
19⁶ X 23⁸

CUSTOMIZABLE

Custom Alterations? See page 237
for customizing this plan to your
specifications.

Design GG3437

First Floor: 1,522 square feet
Second Floor: 800 square feet
Total: 2,322 square feet
Upper Level Feature: Additional Sleeping Quarters

QUOTE ONE™

Cost to build? See page 232
to order complete cost estimate
to build this house in your area!

Width 69'-6"
Depth 61'

● This two-story Spanish Mission-style home has character
inside and out. The first-floor master suite features a fireplace and gracious bath with walk-in closet, whirlpool,
shower, dual vanities, and linen storage. A second fireplace
serves both the gathering room and media room or library.
The kitchen with island cook top includes a snack bar and
an adjoining breakfast nook. Three bedrooms and two full
baths occupy the second floor.

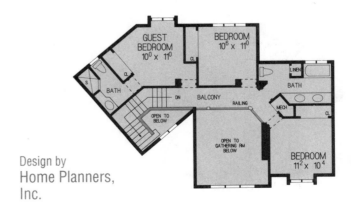

GUEST
BEDROOM
10⁰ X 11⁰

BEDROOM
10⁶ X 11⁰

S

BATH

CL

CL

LINEN

BATH

ON

BALCONY

RAILING

MECH

OPEN TO
BELOW

OPEN TO
GATHERING RM
BELOW

BEDROOM
11² X 10⁴

Design by
Home Planners,
Inc.

Design GG3323

First Floor: 1,923 square feet
Second Floor: 838 square feet
Total: 2,761 square feet
Upper Level Feature: Additional Sleeping Quarters

L

● This two-story southwestern home was designed to make living patterns as pleasant as they can be. Take a step down from the foyer and go where your mood takes you: a gathering room with fireplace and an alcove for reading or quiet conversations, a media room for enjoying the latest technology, or to the dining room with sliding glass doors to the terrace. The kitchen has an island range and eating space. Also on the first floor is a large master suite including a sitting area with terrace access, walk-in closet and whirlpool. An elegant spiral staircase leads to two family bedrooms sharing a full bath and a guest bedroom with private bath.

Width 53'
Depth 70'-4"

CUSTOMIZABLE
Custom Alterations? See page 237 for customizing this plan to your specifications.

Design by
Home Planners,
Inc.

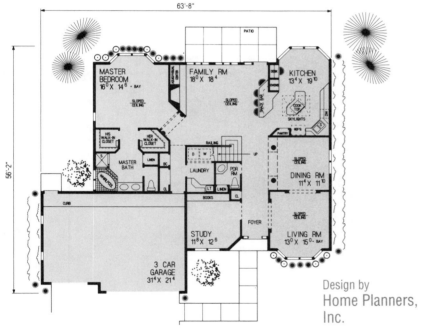

63'-8"

56'-2"

PATIO

MASTER BEDROOM
16⁰ X 14⁶ · BAY

FAMILY RM
18⁰ X 18⁴

KITCHEN
13⁴ X 19¹⁰

SLOPED CEILING

SLOPED CEILING

HIS WALK-IN CLOSET

HER WALK-IN CLOSET

MASTER BATH

LINEN

LAUNDRY

PDR RM

DINING RM
11⁴ X 11¹⁰

SLOPED CEILING

PANTRY

UP

CURB

BOOKS

FOYER

STUDY
11⁸ X 12⁶

LIVING RM
13⁰ X 15⁰ · BAY

SLOPED CEILING

3 CAR GARAGE
31⁴ X 21⁴

Design by
Home Planners,
Inc.

Design GG3441

First Floor: 2,022 square feet
Second Floor: 845 square feet
Total: 2,867 square feet
Upper Level Feature: Additional Sleeping Quarters

L

● Special details make the difference between a house and a home. A snack bar, audio/visual center and a fireplace make the family room livable. A desk, island cook top, bay, and skylights enhance the kitchen area. The dining room features two columns and a plant ledge. The first-floor master suite includes His and Hers walk-in closets, a spacious bath, and a bay window. On the second floor, one bedroom features a walk-in closet and private bath, while two additional bedrooms share a full bath.

CUSTOMIZABLE

Custom Alterations? See page 237 for customizing this plan to your specifications.

OPEN TO FAMILY RM BELOW

PLANT LEDGE

BATH

WALK-IN CLOSET

BEDROOM
13¹⁰ X 11⁰

DN

HALF WALL

LOFT
11⁶ X 6⁰

PLANT LEDGE

BATH

OPEN TO FOYER BELOW

BEDROOM
11⁰ X 11¹⁰

BEDROOM
10¹⁰ X 12¹⁰

QUOTE ONE™

Cost to build? See page 232 to order complete cost estimate to build this house in your area!

Design GG3455

First Floor: 1,408 square feet
Second Floor: 667 square feet
Total: 2,075 square feet

Upper Level Feature: Additional Sleeping Quarters

L **D**

● Whether you're just starting out or looking
to retire, this 1½-story, sun-country design will
make an excellent home. The focal point of the
first floor, the two-story living room utilizes a
central fireplace and columns for comfort and
elegance. Open to the living room, the dining
room complements this space with its influx of
natural light. The kitchen services this room
easily and also enjoys a cozy breakfast nook.
An island work counter in the kitchen guaran-
tees ease in food preparation. Note the service
entry to the garage; a full washer/dryer set-up
adds convenience to laundry chores. On the
second floor you'll find a skylit balcony—a
dramatic yet purposeful design feature—leading to two bedrooms.

QUOTE ONE™

Cost to build? See page 232
to order complete cost estimate
to build this house in your area!

Design by
**Home Planners,
Inc.**

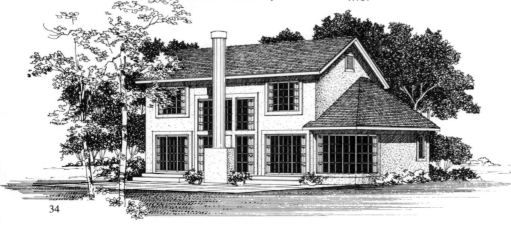

83' - 8"

59' - 8"

DECK

DECK

DECK

KITCHEN
17⁰ X 13⁶

DINING RM.
12⁶ X 15⁶

MASTER
BEDROOM
14² X 12²

FOYER
14⁰ X 11⁶

GREAT RM
16² X 20²

W.I.C.

MASTER
BATH

PDR.
RM.

GARAGE
22⁶ X 23⁸

BATH

LIN.

BALCONY

BALCONY

W.I.C.

W.I.C.

BEDROOM
12⁶ X 15⁶

BEDROOM
14² X 12²

DN

LOUNGE

OPEN BELOW

RAILING

SHELVES

UPPER
GREAT RM.
OPEN BELOW

Design GG3310
First Floor: 1,668 square feet
Second Floor: 905 square feet
Total: 2,573 square feet
**Upper Level Feature:
Additional Sleeping Quarters**

L **D**

● If you're looking for a different angle on a new home, try this enchanting transitional house. The open foyer creates a rich atmosphere. To the left you'll find a great room with raised-brick hearth and sliding glass doors that lead out onto a wraparound deck. The kitchen enhances the first floor with a snack bar and deck access. The master bedroom, with balcony and bath with whirlpool, is located on the first floor for privacy. Upstairs, two family bedrooms, both with balconies and walk-in closets, share a full bath. Don't overlook the lounge and elliptical window that give the second floor added charisma.

Quote One™

Cost to build? See page 232
to order complete cost estimate
to build this house in your area!

Design by
**Home Planners,
Inc.**

Design GG8679

First Floor: 2,531 square feet
Second Floor: 669 square feet
Total: 3,200 square feet

Upper Level Feature: Additional Sleeping Quarters

● This exquisite brick and stucco contemporary takes its cue from the tradition of Frank Lloyd Wright. The formal living and dining area combine to provide a spectacular view of the rear grounds. Unique best describes the private master suite, highlighted by a mitered bow window, a raised sitting area complete with a wet bar, oversized His and Hers walk-in closets and a lavish master bath complete with a relaxing corner tub, a separate shower and twin vanities. The family living area encompasses the left portion of the plan, featuring a spacious family room with a corner fireplace, access to the covered patio from the breakfast area and a step-saving kitchen. Bedroom 2 connects to a private bath. Upstairs, two bedrooms share a sitting room and full bath.

Design by
**Home Design
Services, Inc.**

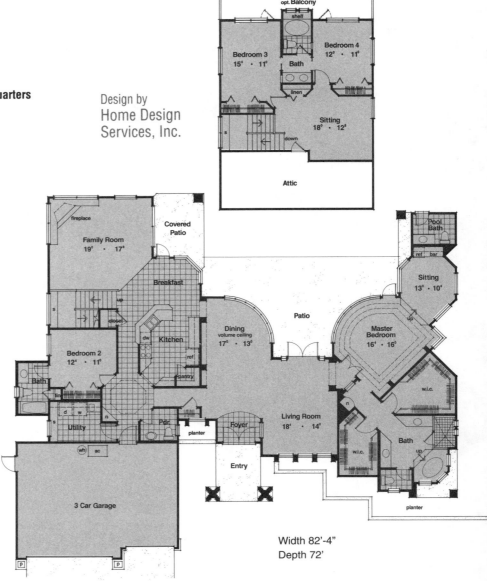

Width 82'-4"
Depth 72'

Cost to build? See page 232 to order complete cost estimate to build this house in your area!

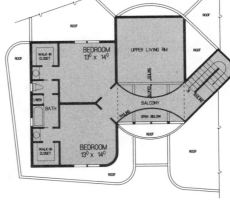

Design GG3403

First Floor: 2,240 square feet
Second Floor: 660 square feet
Total: 2,900 square feet

Upper Level Feature: Additional Sleeping Quarters

Design by
Home Planners,
Inc.

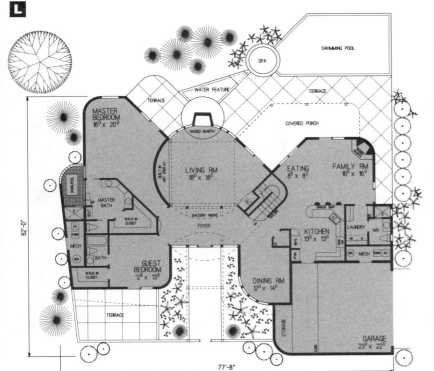

● There is no end to the distinctive features in this Southwestern contemporary. To the right of the plan, the kitchen and family room function well together as an informal living area. The optional guest bedroom or den and the master bedroom are located to the left of the plan. The second floor holds two bedrooms and a full bath.

California Engineered Plans and California Stock Plans are available for this home. Call 1-800-521-6797 for more information.

Design GG2488

First Floor: 1,113 square feet
Second Floor: 543 square feet
Total: 1,656 square feet
Upper Level Feature: Additional Sleeping Quarters

D

QUOTE ONE
Cost to build? See page 232
to order complete cost estimate
to build this house in your area!

Design by
Home Planners,
Inc.

CUSTOMIZABLE
Custom Alterations? See page 237
for customizing this plan to your
specifications.

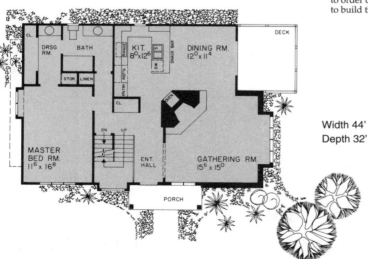

Width 44'
Depth 32'

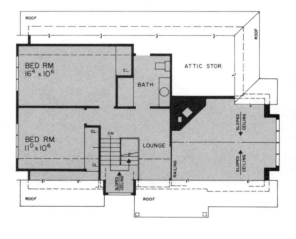

● A cozy cottage filled with versatility! Whether called upon to serve the young active family, or used as an empty-nester home, this charming design will perform well. The upstairs with its two sizable bedrooms, full bath and lounge area looking down into the gathering room below, will ideally accommodate the younger members of the household. If functioning as a retirement home, the second floor caters to visiting family members and friends. Other uses for the second floor may include an office, study, sewing room, music room or hobby room to name a few—the choices are many.

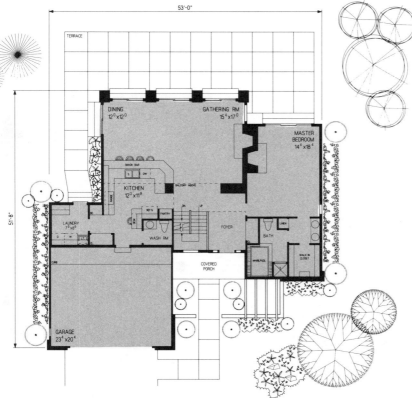

Design GG2490

First Floor: 1,414 square feet
Second Floor: 620 square feet
Total: 2,034 square feet
Upper Level Feature: Additional Sleeping Quarters

● Split-bedroom planning makes the most of this contemporary plan. The master suite pampers with a lavish bath and a fireplace. The living areas are open and have easy access to the rear terrace.

Design by
Home Planners, Inc.

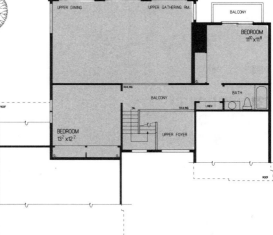

Design GG3347

First Floor: 1,915 square feet
Second Floor: 759 square feet
Total: 2,674 square feet
Upper Level Feature: Additional Sleeping Quarters

L

● Open living is the key to
the abundant livability of this
design. The gigantic gathering room/dining room area
shares a through-fireplace
with a unique sunken con-
versation area. An L-shaped
kitchen has a pass-through
snack bar to the breakfast
room. On the second floor,
two bedrooms are separated
by a lounge with a balcony
overlook.

Quote One™

Cost to build? See page 232
to order complete cost estimate
to build this house in your area!

Design by
**Home Planners,
Inc.**

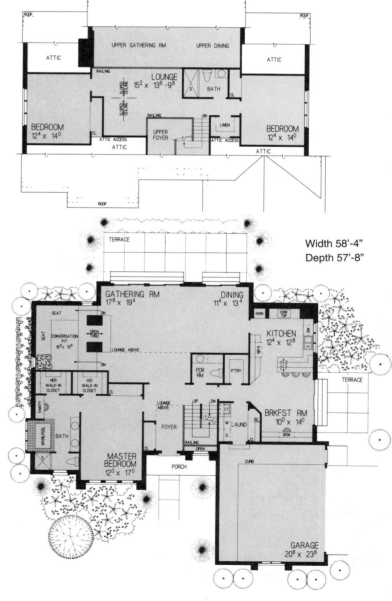

Width 58'-4"
Depth 57'-8"

Design GG3450

First Floor: 1,801 square feet
Second Floor: 1,086 square feet
Total: 2,887 square feet

Upper Level Feature: Additional Sleeping Quarters

L D

● A striking facade includes a covered front porch with four columns. To the left of the foyer is a large gathering room with a fireplace and bay window. The adjoining dining room leads to a covered side porch. The kitchen includes a snack bar, pantry, desk, and eating area. The first-floor master suite provides a spacious bath with walk-in closet, whirlpool and shower. Also on the first floor: a study and a garage workshop. Two bedrooms and a lavish guest suite share the second floor.

QUOTE ONE™

Cost to build? See page 232 to order complete cost estimate to build this house in your area!

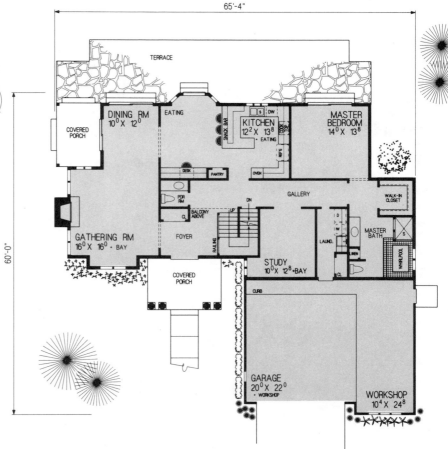

65'-4"

60'-0"

TERRACE

COVERED PORCH

DINING RM
10⁰ X 12⁰

EATING

KITCHEN
12² X 13⁸
• EATING

SNACK BAR

MASTER BEDROOM
14⁰ X 13⁸

DESK

PANTRY

OVEN

PDR RM

CL

BALCONY ABOVE

GALLERY

WALK-IN CLOSET

GATHERING RM
16⁰ X 16⁰ • BAY

FOYER

UP

DN

RAILING

LAUND.

MASTER BATH

WHIRLPOOL

LINEN

COVERED PORCH

STUDY
10⁰ X 12⁸ •BAY

CL

CURB

GARAGE
20⁰ X 22⁰
• WORKSHOP

WORKSHOP
10⁴ X 24⁸

BEDROOM
12⁰ X 13⁸

BEDROOM
11² X 13⁸

GUEST SUITE
11⁴ X 13⁸
• SITTING

CL

CL

BALCONY

RAILING

DN

OPEN TO FOYER BELOW

LINEN

SITTING

BATH

BATH

VANITY

WALK-IN CLOSET

WHIRLPOOL

S

LEDGE

CUSTOMIZABLE

Custom Alterations? See page 237 for customizing this plan to your specifications.

Design by
Home Planners,
Inc.

41

Design GG9489

First Floor: 1,574 square feet
Second Floor: 565 square feet
Total: 2,139 square feet
Upper Level Feature: Additional Sleeping Quarters

● This lovely brick two-story home contains all the livability your family will ever need. From the entry foyer radiate the formal and informal living areas of the home: living room with vaulted ceiling, dining room, kitchen with attached nook and vaulted family room. The master bedroom is also found on this floor and has a bath with spa tub. Upstairs are two secondary bedrooms that share a full bath. Separating the two bedrooms is a balcony area that overlooks the foyer on one side and the family room on the other. A rear terrace area is accessed from the breakfast nook.

Design by
Alan Mascord
Design Associates, Inc.

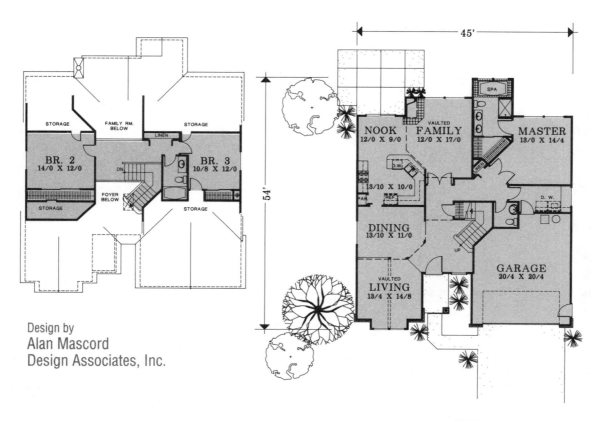

Design GG9540

First Floor: 1,230 square feet
Second Floor: 636 square feet
Total: 1,866 square feet
Upper Level Feature: Additional Sleeping Quarters

● An impressive entry leads the way to a spacious two-story great room warmed by a cheerful fireplace. The adjacent dining room supplies easy access to the rear grounds and is conveniently located to the efficient kitchen, making entertaining a breeze. A bay-windowed nook provides ideal space to linger over the morning paper or enjoy informal meals with the family. A large master suite sporting a vaulted ceiling offers a private, pampering retreat and completes the first floor. Three secondary bedrooms share a bath on the second floor.

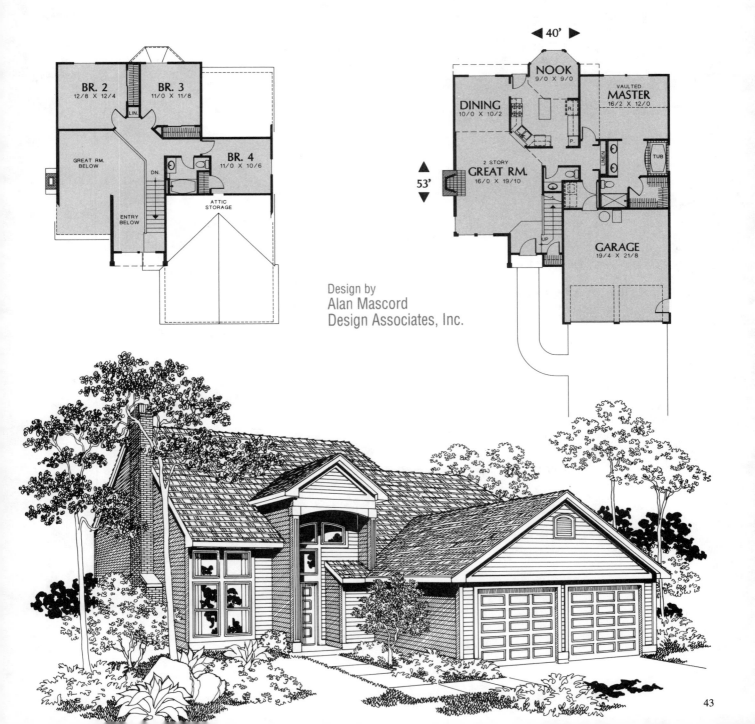

Design by
Alan Mascord
Design Associates, Inc.

43

Design GG9390

First Floor: 1,865 square feet
Second Floor: 774 square feet
Total: 2,639 square feet
Upper Level Feature: Additional Sleeping Quarters

Design by
Design
Basics,
Inc.

● A magnificent brick facade with a 3-car, side-load garage conceals a well-organized floor plan. A tiled foyer leads to the formal dining room, with wet bar and hutch space, on the left and a parlor on the right. Straight ahead is a spacious great room with arched windows flanking a fireplace. The kitchen offers a snack bar peninsula and adjoins a bayed breakfast area. The first-floor master bedroom includes a large walk-in closet and French doors leading to a master bath with angled whirlpool and shower with glass block. The second floor provides three bedrooms and two full baths. A reading seat flanked by two cabinets overlooks the volume entry.

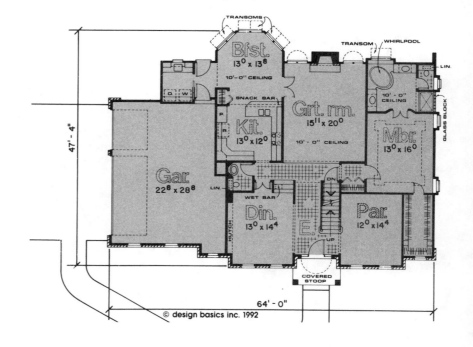

© design basics inc. 1992

44

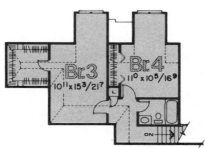

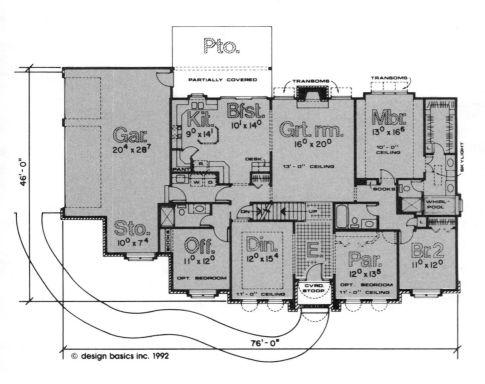

Design GG9394

First Floor: 2,172 square feet
Second Floor: 595 square feet
Total: 2,767 square feet
Upper Level Feature: Additional Sleeping Quarters

● A covered stoop leads to an entry which offers a terrific view of the spacious great room featuring a volume ceiling and transom windows flanking the fireplace. Two first-floor rooms provide unmatched versatility as bedrooms or an office and parlor. A handsome kitchen with a Lazy Susan and an extra-wide island is complemented by a large walk-in pantry and an airy dinette. Three extra-high windows bring natural light into the spacious master bedroom. A large, walk-in closet adjoins a master bath featuring dual lavatories, separate whirlpool and shower areas and an attractive plant shelf. Two extra-deep second-floor bedrooms are joined by a full bath.

Design by
Design Basics, Inc.

45

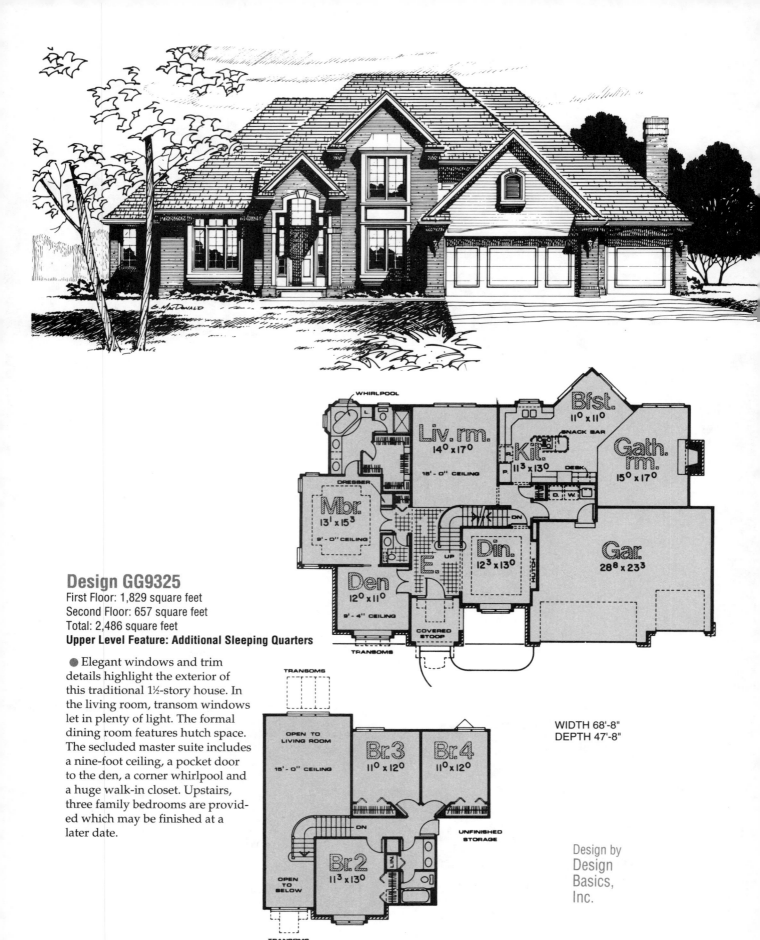

Design GG9325

First Floor: 1,829 square feet
Second Floor: 657 square feet
Total: 2,486 square feet
Upper Level Feature: Additional Sleeping Quarters

● Elegant windows and trim details highlight the exterior of this traditional 1½-story house. In the living room, transom windows let in plenty of light. The formal dining room features hutch space. The secluded master suite includes a nine-foot ceiling, a pocket door to the den, a corner whirlpool and a huge walk-in closet. Upstairs, three family bedrooms are provided which may be finished at a later date.

WIDTH 68'-8"
DEPTH 47'-8"

Design by
Design
Basics,
Inc.

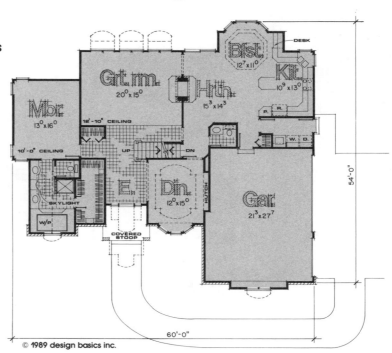

Design by
Design
Basics,
Inc.

Design GG9316

First Floor: 1,765 square feet
Second Floor: 743 square feet
Total: 2,508 square feet
Upper Level Feature: Additional Sleeping Quarters

● A dramatic volume entrance greets you from the street. Sharing the spotlight of the sunny bayed dinette graced by oak flooring is a gourmet island kitchen. A through fireplace warms the hearth room. Be sure to notice the convenient location of the mud/laundry room. Main floor living would not be complete without the secluded master bedroom and impressive skylit master bath with its unique double vanity. The upper bedrooms share a compartmented bath.

© 1989 design basics inc.

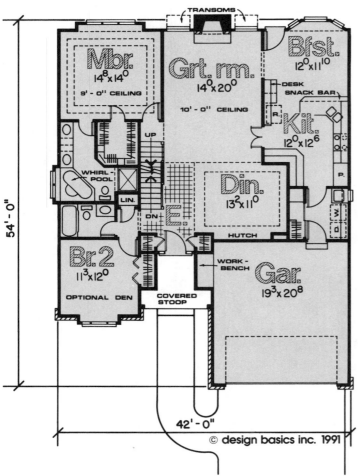

TRANSOMS

Mbr.
14⁸x14⁰
9'-0" CEILING

Grt. rm.
14⁰x20⁰
10'-0" CEILING

Bfst.
12⁰x11¹⁰

DESK
SNACK BAR

Kit.
12⁰x12⁶

UP

WHIRL-POOL

LIN.

DN

Din.
13²x11⁰

HUTCH

P.

D.W.

Br.2
11³x12⁰

OPTIONAL DEN

WORK-BENCH

Gar.
19³x20⁸

COVERED STOOP

54'-0"

42'-0"

© design basics inc. 1991

Design GG9339

First Floor: 1,517 square feet
Second Floor: 234 square feet
Total: 1,751 square feet

Upper Level Feature: Additional Sleeping Quarters

● Attractive brick and wood siding and a covered front porch make this a beautiful design—even for narrower lots. The entry gives way to a dining room with hutch space and then further opens to a bright, airy great room. The kitchen is highlighted by a French door entry, ample counters, and a roomy pantry. The first floor holds two bedrooms—a secondary bedroom with bath and the master suite with roomy walk-in closet, corner whirlpool, and dual lavs. On the second floor is a totally private third bedroom with its own bath.

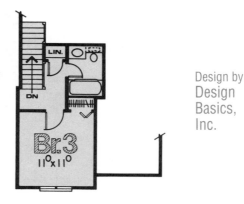

LIN.

DN

Br.3
11⁰x11⁰

Design by
Design
Basics,
Inc.

48

Design GG9265

First Floor: 1,297 square feet
Second Floor: 388 square feet
Total: 1,685 square feet
Upper Level Feature: Additional Sleeping Quarters

● A lovely covered porch welcomes family and guests to this delightful 1½-story home. From the entry, the formal dining room with boxed windows and the great room with fireplace are visible. A powder room for guests is located just beyond the dining room. An open kitchen/dinette features a pantry, planning desk and a snack-bar counter. The elegant master suite is appointed with formal ceiling detail and a window seat. The skylight above the whirlpool, the decorator plant shelf and the double lavatories all dress up the master bath. Secondary bedrooms on the second floor share a centrally located bath.

Design by
Design Basics, Inc.

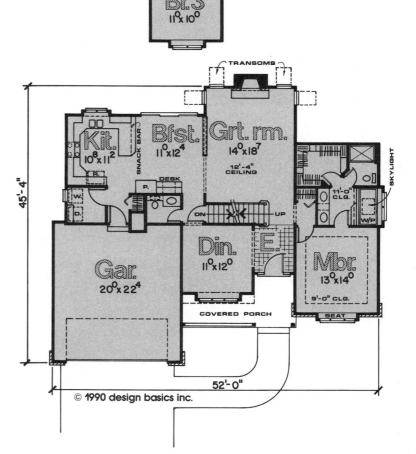

© 1990 design basics inc.

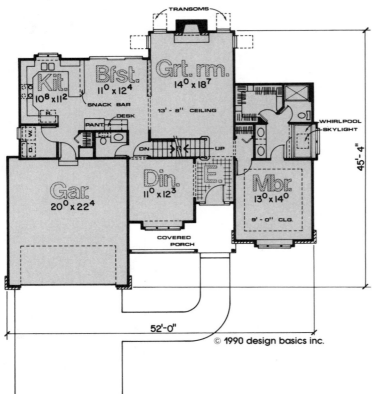

Design GG9247

First Floor: 1,297 square feet
Second Floor: 558 square feet
Total: 1,855 square feet
Upper Level Feature: Additional Sleeping Quarters

● Here's the perfect family plan with loads of livability. Go beyond the front covered porch and you'll find a thoughtful floor plan. A formal dining room with large boxed window is a complement to the great room with handsome fireplace and tall windows. A snack bar, pantry, two lazy Susans and planning desk grace the kitchen/breakfast room area. The master suite is conveniently located on the first floor and features a boxed window and well-appointed bath. Three family bedrooms upstairs share a full bath. Note the volume ceiling above the arched window in bedroom 4.

© 1990 design basics inc.

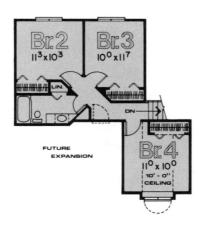

Design by
Design
Basics,
Inc.

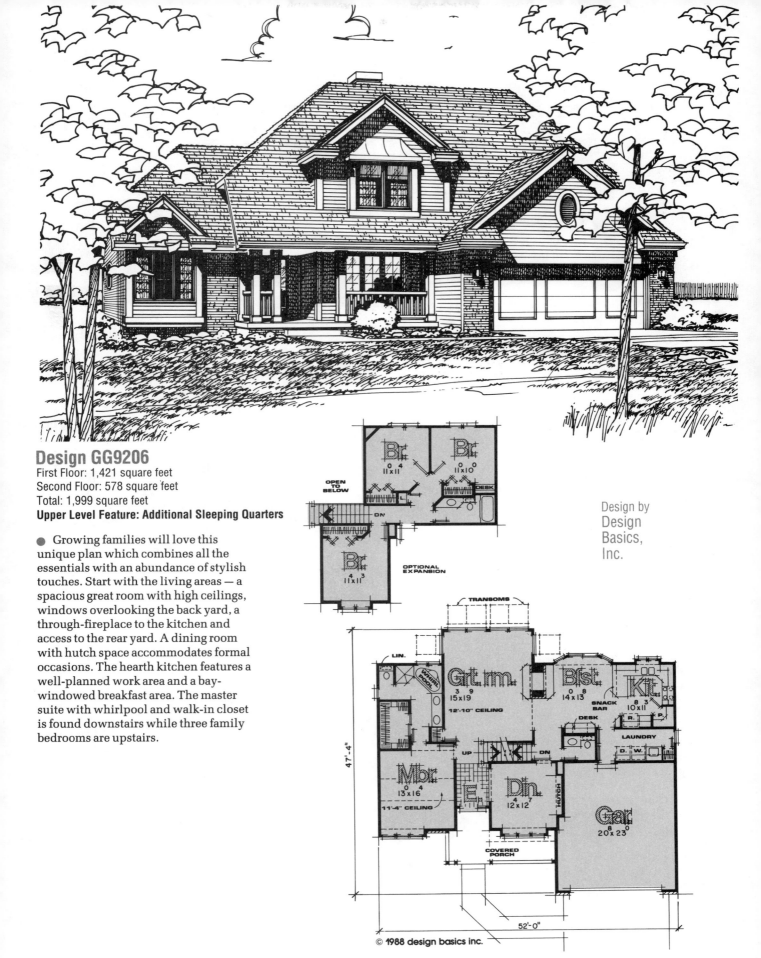

Design GG9206

First Floor: 1,421 square feet
Second Floor: 578 square feet
Total: 1,999 square feet
Upper Level Feature: Additional Sleeping Quarters

● Growing families will love this
unique plan which combines all the
essentials with an abundance of stylish
touches. Start with the living areas — a
spacious great room with high ceilings,
windows overlooking the back yard, a
through-fireplace to the kitchen and
access to the rear yard. A dining room
with hutch space accommodates formal
occasions. The hearth kitchen features a
well-planned work area and a bay-
windowed breakfast area. The master
suite with whirlpool and walk-in closet
is found downstairs while three family
bedrooms are upstairs.

Design by
Design
Basics,
Inc.

© 1988 design basics inc.

Design GG3458

First Floor: 1,617 square feet
Second Floor: 725 square feet
Total: 2,342 square feet

Upper Level Feature: Additional Sleeping Quarters

● With end gables, and five front gables, this design becomes an up dated "house of seven gables." Meanwhile, brick veneer, horizontal siding, radial head windows and an interesting roof add an extra measure of charm. The attached, side-opening, two-car garage is a delightfully integral part of the appearing exterior. Designed for a growing family with a modest building budget, the floor plan incorporates four bedrooms and both formal and informal living areas. The central foyer, with its open staircase to the second floor, looks up to the balcony. The spacious family room has a high ceiling and a dramatic view of the balcony. In the U-shaped kitchen, a snack bar caters to quick, on-the-run meals. A pantry facilitates stocking-up on foodstuffs. A basement allows for bonus space should development of recreational, hobby or storage space come into play.

Design by
**Home Planners,
Inc.**

QUOTE ONE™
Cost to build? See page 232
to order complete cost estimate
to build this house in your area!

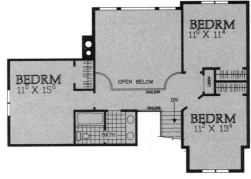

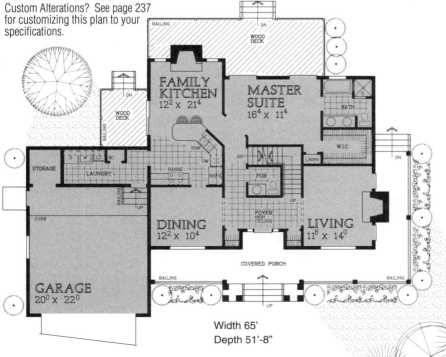

CUSTOMIZABLE

Custom Alterations? See page 237 for customizing this plan to your specifications.

BEDROOM
10⁴ x 14⁰
+ DORMER

DESK BOOKS DESK

HALL

RAILING

BEDROOM
11⁸ x 14⁰
+ DORMER

LINEN

DN

BATH

OPEN TO
FOYER BELOW

LEDGE   LEDGE

RAILING

DN

WOOD
DECK

FAMILY
KITCHEN
12² x 21⁴

MASTER
SUITE
16⁴ x 11⁴

BATH

DN

WOOD
DECK

RAILING

SINK

DW

W.I.C.

DN

STORAGE

D W L BC

LAUNDRY

RANGE

REF

DN

LINEN

RAILING

UP

PDR

UP

CURB

DINING
12² x 10⁴

FOYER
HIGH
CEILING

UP

LIVING
11⁸ x 14⁰

GARAGE
20⁰ x 22⁰

COVERED PORCH

RAILING

RAILING

UP

Width 65'
Depth 51'-8"

Design GG3467

First Floor: 1,276 square feet
Second Floor: 658 square feet
Total: 1,934 square feet
**Upper Level Feature: Additional
Sleeping Quarters**

L

● Bold and beautiful, this Neoclassic farmhouse will delight family and friends alike. Lap wood siding combined with a standing seam metal roof provides a wealth of visual appeal. Inside, living takes off with a great kitchen and family room combination. Or take in brunch on the wood deck located just off this area. For more formal occasions, a split dining room and living room—with a fireplace— will serve well. A covered wraparound porch is accessible from both rooms and makes outdoor living a pleasure. Located at the rear of the first floor, the master bedroom extends the finest accommodations including a private bath and a walk-in closet. Upstairs, two bedrooms with dormers may be finished at a later date.

Design by
**Home Planners,
Inc.**

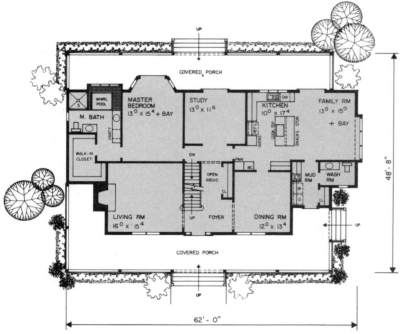

COVERED PORCH

MASTER
BEDROOM
13⁰ x 15⁴ + BAY

STUDY
13⁰ x 11⁶

KITCHEN
10⁰ x 17⁴

FAMILY RM
13⁰ x 15⁰
+ BAY

WHIRL
POOL

M. BATH

VANITY

WALK-IN
CLOSET

DN

OPEN
ABOVE

PAN

BC

CL

MUD
RM

WASH
RM

LIVING RM
16⁰ x 15⁴

UP

FOYER

DINING RM
12⁰ x 13⁴

UP

COVERED PORCH

UP

62' - 0"

48' - 8"

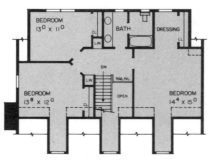

BEDROOM
13⁰ x 11⁰

BATH

DRESSING

CL

LIN

BEDROOM
13⁸ x 12⁰

DN

RAILING

LIN

OPEN

BEDROOM
14⁴ x 15⁰

Design by
Home Planners,
Inc.

Design GG3396

First Floor: 1,829 square feet
Second Floor: 947 square feet
Total: 2,776 square feet
Upper Level Feature: Additional Sleeping Quarters

L **D**

● Rustic charm abounds in this pleasant farm-house rendition. Covered porches to the front and rear enclose living potential for the whole family. Flanking the entrance foyer are the living and dining rooms. To the rear is the L-shaped kitchen with island cook top and snack bar. A small family room/breakfast nook is attached. A private study is tucked away on this floor next to the master suite. On the second floor are three bedrooms and a full bath. Two of the bedrooms have charming dormer windows.

QUOTE ONE™
Cost to build? See page 232
to order complete cost estimate
to build this house in your area!

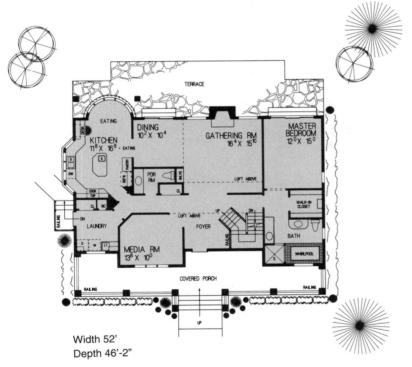

Width 52'
Depth 46'-2"

Design by
Home Planners,
Inc.

Design GG3321

First Floor: 1,636 square feet
Second Floor: 572 square feet
Total: 2,208 square feet
Upper Level Feature: Additional Sleeping Quarters

L **D**

● Cozy and completely functional, this 1½-story bungalow has many amenities not often found in homes its size. The covered porch at the front opens at the entry to a foyer with angled staircase. To the left is a media room, to the rear the gathering room with fireplace. Attached to the gathering room is a formal dining room with rear terrace access. The kitchen features a curved casual eating area and island work station. The right side of the first floor is dominated by the master suite. It has access to the rear terrace and a luxurious bath. Upstairs are two family bedrooms connected by a loft area overlooking the gathering room and foyer.

CUSTOMIZABLE
Custom Alterations? See page 237
for customizing this plan to your
specifications.

Design GG9516

First Floor: 1,396 square feet
Second Floor: 523 square feet
Total: 1,919 square feet
Upper Level Feature: Additional Sleeping Quarters

● A covered porch flanked with double columns provides special interest for this lovely traditional home. Separate entry through the den creates a perfect opportunity for use as an office or home-operated business. The foyer leads to all areas of the house, maximizing livability. The kitchen combines with the dining area and great room to make the most of this open space. The split bedrooms with the master suite on the first floor and two secondary bedrooms upstairs make this an ideal design for empty-nesters, young singles and families.

Design by
Alan Mascord
Design Associates, Inc.

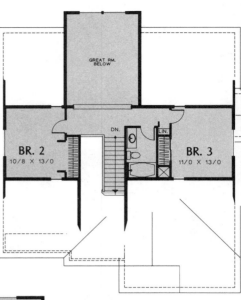

◀ 44' ▶

51'

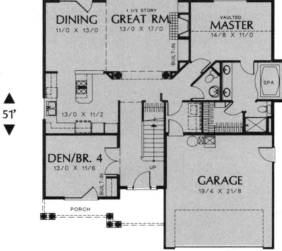

Design GG3462

First Floor: 1,395 square feet
Second Floor: 813 square feet
Total: 2,208 square feet
Upper Level Feature: Additional Sleeping Quarters

● Get off to a great start with this handsome family farmhouse. Covered porches front and rear assure comfortable outdoor living while varied roof planes add visual interest. Inside, distinct formal and informal living zones provide the best accommodations for any occasion. The columned foyer opens to both the dining and living rooms. The central kitchen services the large family room with an island work counter and snack bar. For everyday chores, a laundry room is conveniently located and also provides access to the garage. On the first floor you'll find the master bedroom suite. It enjoys complete privacy and luxury with its double closets and master bath with double-bowl vanity, whirlpool tub and separate shower. Upstairs, three family bedrooms extend fabulous livability.

RAILING

VERANDA

MASTER BEDROOM
11⁰ X 15⁰

WHIRLPOOL

GREAT RM
13⁸ X 15⁴

KITCHEN
9¹⁰ X 11⁸

SNACK BAR

D.W. SNK

REF.

BATH

DN

UP

PANTRY

POR

LAUNDRY

W. D.

CL

DINING ROOM
11⁰ X 11⁰

FOYER

LIVING ROOM
12⁰ X 13⁴

GARAGE
23⁰ X 24⁸

VERANDA

RAILING

Width 53'-8"
Depth 57'

Design by
Home Planners, Inc.

OPEN BELOW

STORAGE

BEDROOM
11⁰ X 13⁰

BATH

DN

LINEN

DESK

BEDROOM
12⁸ X 12⁰

BEDROOM
12⁰ X 14⁴

Design GG3461

First Floor: 1,391 square feet
Second Floor: 611 square feet
Total: 2,002 square feet
Upper Level Feature: Additional Sleeping Quarters

L

● A Palladian window set in a dormer provides a nice introduction to this 1½-story country home. The two-story foyer draws on natural light and a pair of columns to set a comfortable, yet elegant mood. The living room, to the left, presents a grand space for entertaining. From full-course dinners to family suppers, the dining room will serve its purpose well. The kitchen delights with an island work station and openness to the keeping room. Here, a raised-hearth fireplace provides added comfort. Sleeping accommodations are comprised of four bedrooms, one a first-floor master suite. With a luxurious private bath, including dual lavatories, this room will surely be a favorite retreat. Upstairs, three secondary bedrooms meet the needs of the growing family.

Design by
Home Planners,
Inc.

QUOTE ONE™

Cost to build? See page 232
to order complete cost estimate
to build this house in your area!

Design GG9074 First Floor: 1,288 square feet
Second Floor: 495 square feet; Total: 1,783 square feet
Upper Level Feature: Additional Sleeping Quarters

● With its brick-veneer exterior, dormer windows and wraparound porch, this home is a blend of the early 1900s farmhouse and the prairie style. Corner box windows provide a cozy sitting area next to the fireplace in the family room. The efficient kitchen overlooks the breakfast area with its full-length windows. A French door opens to a large covered porch. Double doors open to the master bedroom with a ten-foot gambrel ceiling. The bath features mirrored closet doors and double lavatories. Upstairs, there are two bedrooms, each with dormer window alcoves and sloping ceilings. Plans for a two-car detached garage are included.

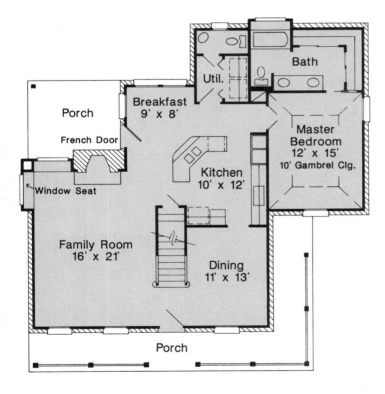

Width 44'
Depth 45'

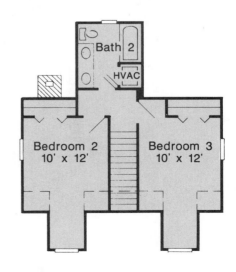

Design by
Larry W.
Garnett &
Associates, Inc.

Design GG9003

First Floor: 1,244 square feet
Second Floor: 551 square feet
Total: 1,795 square feet
Upper Level Feature: Additional Sleeping Quarters

● The timeless beauty and practicality of the wraparound veranda give this farmhouse a casual, yet distinctive appearance. The efficiently designed kitchen opens to a light-filled breakfast area with full-length windows and a French door that leads to the veranda. The master suite offers His and Hers lavatories and a large walk-in closet. Upstairs, optional skylights provide plenty of natural light to the balcony. Two bedrooms share a bath that has separate bathing and dressing areas. Plans for a two-car detached garage are included.

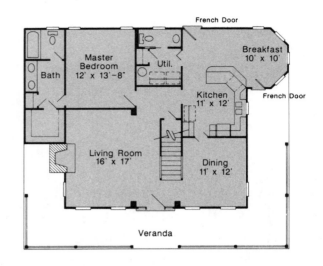

Width 46'
Depth 38' - 8"

Design by
Larry W.
Garnett &
Associates, Inc.

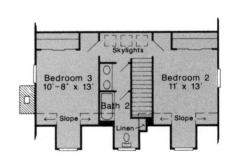

60

Design by
**Larry W.
Garnett &
Associates, Inc.**

Width 69'
Depth 78'-1"

Design GG9120

First Floor: 2,109 square feet
Second Floor: 950 square feet
Total: 3,059 square feet
Upper Level Feature: Additional Sleeping Quarters

● This distinctive Greek Revival Style home works well in a 1½-story plan. The 10'-deep covered porch of this home opens to an entry foyer that connects the dining room and living room and contains the stairway to the second floor. Stairs at the breakfast room provide access to a 12' x 26' future room. The master bedroom is complemented by a bath with many amenities. Tucked away to the right of the plan is a bedroom that works well as guest quarters or could hold a home office or study. For additional sleeping space, there are two bedrooms with dormer windows and walk-in closets, plus a full bath on the second floor.

Design GG2500

First Floor: 1,851 square feet
Second Floor: 762 square feet
Total: 2,613 square feet
Upper Level Feature: Additional Sleeping Quarters

L **D**

● The large family will enjoy
the wonderful living patterns of
this charming home. Don't miss
the covered rear porch and the
many features of the family
room. The master suite, conveniently separated from the family
bedrooms on the second floor,
has its own bath and a huge
walk-in closet. Two more giant-
sized storage areas—one a linen
closet—are found upstairs.

Design by
Home Planners,
Inc.

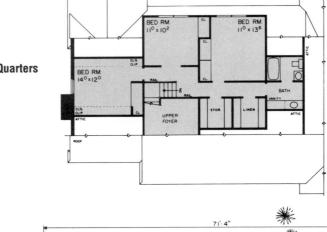

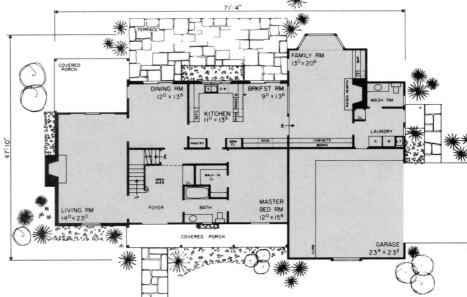

Design GG2699

First Floor: 2,188 square feet
Second Floor: 858 square feet
Total: 3,046 square feet
Upper Level Feature: Additional Sleeping Quarters

L

● This handsome Cape Cod offers lots of room for the family to grow. To the left of the foyer, a spacious master suite invites relaxation with its pampering master bath and an adjacent study which could easily convert into a nursery. A large living room with access to the rear terrace is warmed in the winter by a cheerful fireplace. The right side of the plan is comprised of a media room, a dining room and a country kitchen that is a cook's delight. A conveniently located mud room and laundry room complete the first floor. The second floor—which may be finished for future use—contains two secondary bedrooms, two baths and a lounge.

Design by
Home Planners,
Inc.

Design GG1964

First Floor: 2,150 square feet

Second Floor: 680 square feet

Total: 2,830 square feet

Upper Level Feature: Additional Sleeping Quarters

● Symmetrical balance is provided by the two-car garage and sleeping zone of this fine traditional home. The entry leads to an open, well-designed floor plan. Formal occasions will be enjoyed in the living room with its welcoming fireplace which flows easily into the dining room. The family room with its raised-hearth fireplace, the nearby kitchen and the breakfast area provide access to the rear terrace, and are perfect for informal family gatherings. The master suite and two secondary bedrooms sharing a bath complete the first floor. Upstairs, two additional bedrooms and a full bath may be finished later to accommodate family growth.

Design by
Home Planners,
Inc.

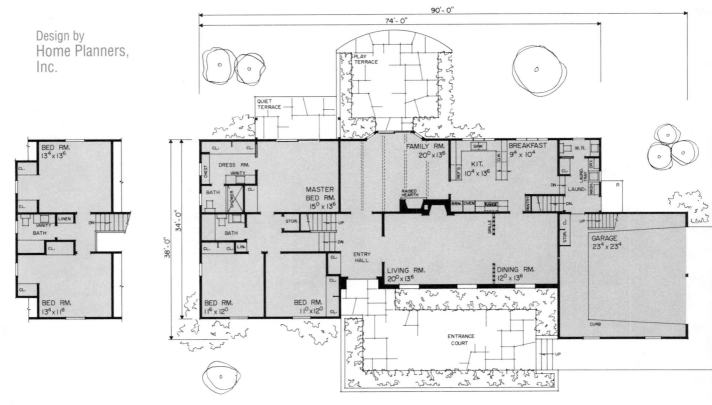

Design GG1967

First Floor: 1,804 square feet
Second Floor: 496 square feet
Total: 2,300 square feet
Upper Level Feature: Additional Sleeping Quarters

● This inviting home is sure to make a lasting impression with its horizontal siding, interesting roof lines and welcoming front porch. To the left of the entry is the winning combination of the breakfast room, kitchen and beamed-ceilinged family room warmed by a cheerful fireplace. For more formal occasions, the adjacent dining room leads to the living room, sharing views of the rear grounds. The master bedroom and two secondary bedrooms complete the first floor. Two bedrooms and a full bath are contained on the second floor for future use.

Design by
**Home Planners,
Inc.**

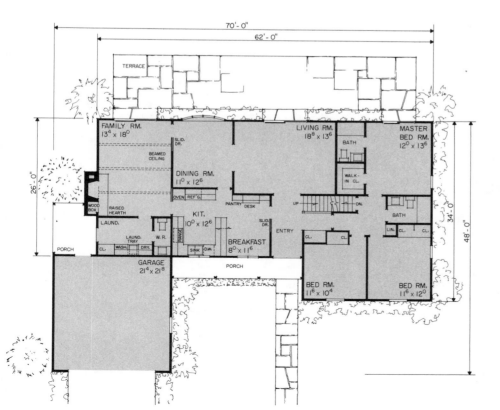

● For spacious living, this good-looking house will make a fine home-building candidate. The entry gives way to double closets—more than just a coat closet for your storage needs. This area also dons an open staircase. Directly in back of the foyer is the gathering room with its through-fireplace to a quaint seating area—perfect for intimate conversations. The dining room remains open to these living spaces and enjoys direct terrace access through a set of sliding glass doors. The large, gourmet kitchen features a wall of cooking amenities and also makes use of a snack-bar pass-through to the breakfast nook. Three bedrooms grace this plan and include a first-floor master suite and two secondary bedrooms off a second-floor lounge.

Design GG2718

First Floor: 1,941 square feet
Second Floor: 791 square feet
Total: 2,732 square feet
Upper Level Feature: Additional Sleeping Quarters

D

Design by
Home Planners,
Inc.

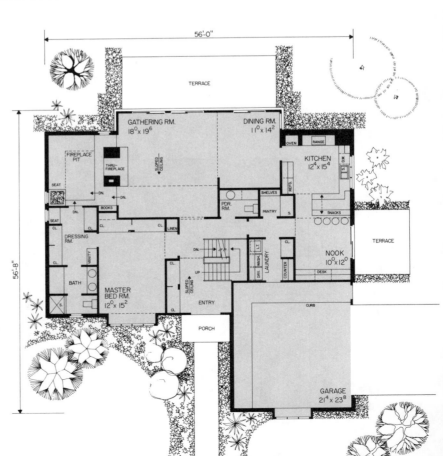

Design GG2510 First Floor: 1,191 square feet
Second Floor: 533 square feet; Total: 1,724 square feet
Upper Level Feature: Additional Sleeping Quarters

L **D**

● The exterior of this charming traditional home features stone accents. A pleasant in-line kitchen is flanked by a separate dining room and a family room with a bay window. The formal living room features a central fireplace and sliding glass doors to a rear terrace. The master bedroom is located on the first floor, while two more bedrooms are located upstairs. The washer and dryer are conveniently placed on the first floor. The garage offers plenty of storage space.

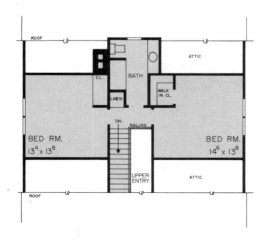

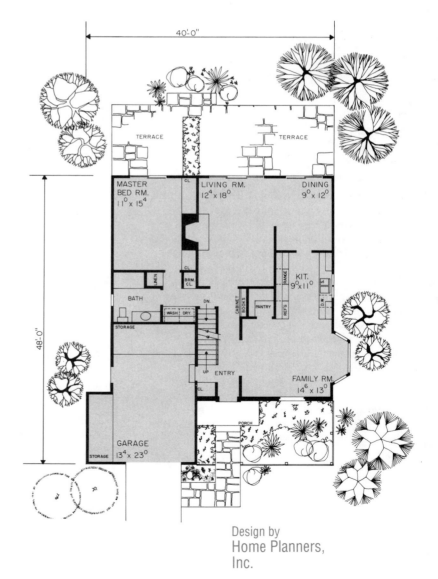

Design by
Home Planners,
Inc.

COPYRIGHT 1992 LARRY E. BELK

Design GG8017

First Floor: 1,824 square feet
Second Floor: 893 square feet
Total: 2,717 square feet

Upper Level Feature: Additional Sleeping Quarters

● Stucco accents add a touch of sophistication to this impressive brick, four-bedroom home. A grand foyer leads directly to the living room, framed by columns positioned on half walls. To the right of the foyer is the formal dining room, defined by columns on two sides and continuing the feeling of grace and elegance. A see-through fireplace warms both the living room and family room. Informal gatherings will be welcome in the efficiently designed kitchen, breakfast room and family room. A spacious master suite offers a private retreat and features His and Hers walk-in closets, a double-bowl vanity, and a corner whirlpool tub. Upstairs, three bedrooms and a full bath complete the home. This plan is available with either a slab or crawlspace foundation. Please specify when ordering.

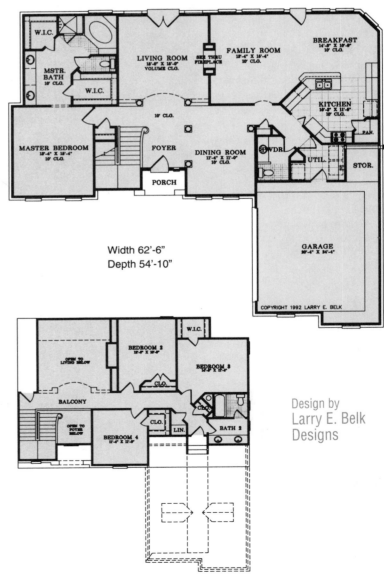

Width 62'-6"
Depth 54'-10"

Design by
Larry E. Belk
Designs

THREE-STORY DESIGNS

A Room With a View

It's easy to picture yourself on the third-floor balcony of Design GG8025 (page 71) or climbing the ladder to the widow's walk on Design GG2690 (page 79). Homes with a third story offer a real bonus and provide a very special space. Children and adults alike will find it a favorite getaway spot. Of course, additional benefits are realized in the enhanced exteriors of these homes and immediate savings are realized since the third story may be left unfinished and converted later.

With great views and lots of natural light, this area is well-suited for use as an artist's studio, hobby room or sewing room. Designs GG3383 and GG2659 (pages 77 and 83) provide an ideal place to pursue those creative talents.

Perhaps the remote location and the promise of peace and quiet are motivating factors for selecting this space for an office. Design GG3510 on page 85 has a wonderful space designed with cabinets and an adjacent bonus room for taking a breather and enjoying more relaxing or recreational pursuits such as reading or exercise.

Not to be overlooked is the practical use of this area for additional sleeping quarters. Whether offering the eldest child a sense of independence or providing space for visitors, ample room and amenities ensure comfort for all. Design GG3382 (page 76) provides a bedroom with a private bath, while Design GG3386 (page 78) furnishes extra space with multiple bedrooms. No matter which option you prefer, the third story will quickly become the most sought-after space in the house.

Developing the third floor grants true privacy and will result in up-to-date floor plans that transport a person worlds away from daily routines. The plans in this chapter—from studios to sleeping quarters—are designed for more than just practical, expandable space. Special consideration has been given to the child in all of us that longs for their own place to dream in.

COPYRIGHT LARRY E. BELK

Design GG8095

First Floor: 2,194 square feet
Second Floor: 870 square feet
Total: 3,064 square feet
Third Story Feature: Bedroom (251 sq. ft.)

● With equally appealing front and side entrances, a charming Victorian facade beckons one to enter this stunning home. The foyer showcases the characteristic winding staircase and opens to the large great room with a masonry fireplace. An enormous kitchen features a cooktop island and a breakfast bar large enough to seat four. A lovely bay window distinguishes the nearby dining room. The master suite with a masonry fireplace is located on the first floor. The amenity-filled master bath features double vanities, a whirlpool tub, a separate shower and a gigantic His and Hers walk-in closet with an additional cedar closet. The second floor contains two bedrooms—one with access to the outdoor balcony on the side of the home. The third floor is completely expandable. This plan is available with either a crawlspace or slab foundation. Please specify when ordering.

Design by
Larry E. Belk
Designs

Width 50'-11"
Depth 91'-2"

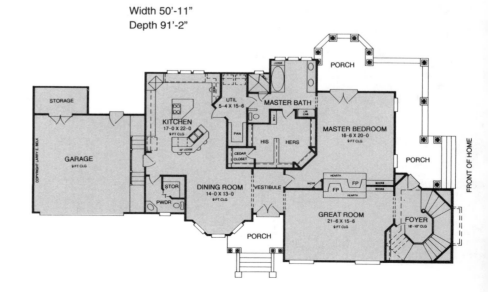

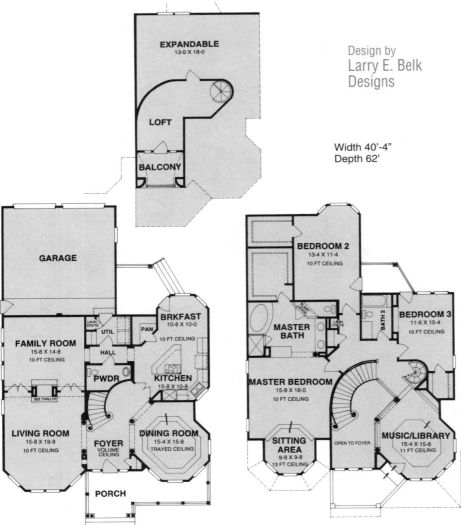

EXPANDABLE
13-0 X 18-0

LOFT

BALCONY

Design by
Larry E. Belk
Designs

Width 40'-4"
Depth 62'

GARAGE

FAMILY ROOM
15-8 X 14-8
10 FT CEILING

BRKFAST
10-8 X 10-0
10 FT CEILING

LAUN CHUTE   UTIL   PAN

HALL

PWDR

KITCHEN
15-8 X 10-8

SEE THRU FP

LIVING ROOM
15-8 X 19-8
10 FT CEILING

FOYER
VOLUME
CEILING

DINING ROOM
15-4 X 15-8
TRAYED CEILING

PORCH

BEDROOM 2
13-4 X 11-4
10 FT CEILING

MASTER BATH

LAUN CHUTE

BATH 2

BEDROOM 3
11-6 X 15-4
10 FT CEILING

MASTER BEDROOM
15-8 X 16-0
10 FT CEILING

SITTING AREA
9-8 X 9-8
13 FT CEILING

OPEN TO FOYER

MUSIC/LIBRARY
15-4 X 15-8
11 FT CEILING

Design GG8025

First Floor: 1,329 square feet
Second Floor: 1,917 square feet
Total: 3,246 square feet
Third Story Feature: Loft (234 sq. ft.)

● This stunning Victorian captures the mood of an era still celebrated today. While speaking clearly of the past with the turret and fish-scale shingles, the inside of this home coincides with the open, flowing interiors of the nineties. Whether dining in the elegant dining room with a tray ceiling or moving through the double French doors between the formal living room and informal family room, one senses the livability of this charming home. The kitchen boasts a large pantry and corner sink with a window. An island cooktop and eating bar complete this area. The lovely master suite is located upstairs. A see-through fireplace between the bedroom and bath makes this suite a haven. The raised sitting area off the master bedroom provides the owner with a mini-retreat for reading and relaxing. The second floor also includes two large bedrooms and a library/music room.

71

Design GG3389 First Floor: 1,161 square feet
Second Floor: 1,090 square feet; Total: 2,251 square feet
Third Story Feature: Guest Suite (488 sq. ft.)

L **D**

● A Victorian turret accents the facade of this compact three-story plan. Downstairs rooms include the grand-sized living room/dining room combination that handles both formal and informal gatherings. The U-shaped kitchen has a snack-bar pass-through to the dining room. Just to the left of the entry foyer is a private study. On the second floor are three bedrooms and two full baths. The master bedroom has a whirlpool spa and a large walk closet. The third floor is a perfect loca tion for a guest bedroom with a priva bath.

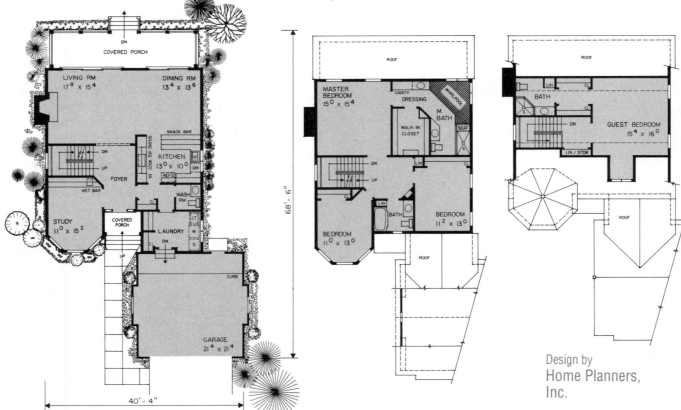

Design by
Home Planners,
Inc.

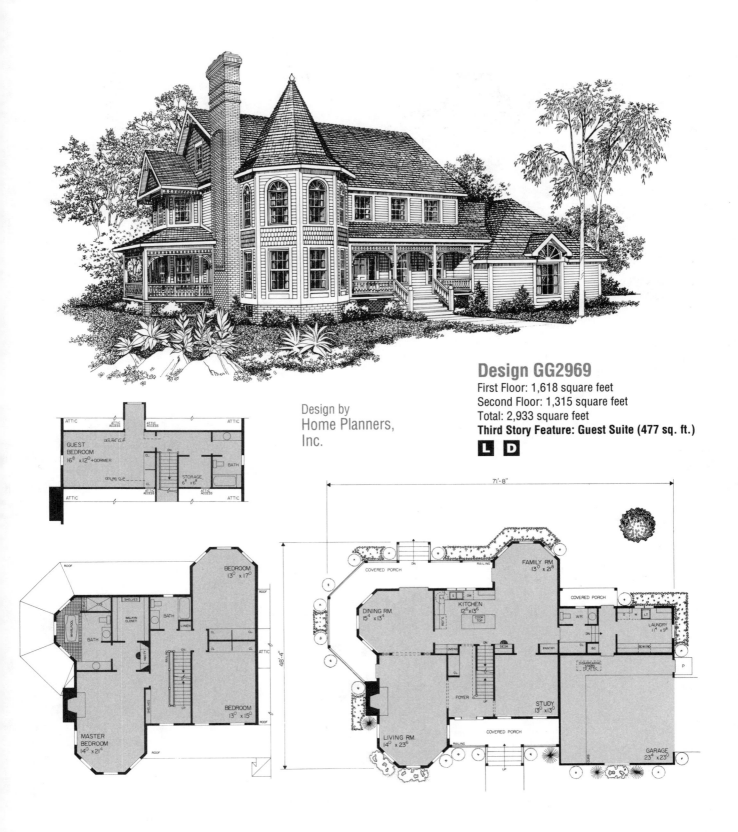

Design by
Home Planners,
Inc.

Design GG2969

First Floor: 1,618 square feet
Second Floor: 1,315 square feet
Total: 2,933 square feet
Third Story Feature: Guest Suite (477 sq. ft.)

L **D**

● What could beat the charm of a turreted Victorian with covered porches to the front, side and rear? This delicately detailed exterior houses an outstanding family oriented floor plan. Projecting bays make their contribution to the exterior styling. In addition, they provide an extra measure of livability

to the living, dining and family rooms, plus two of the bedrooms. The efficient kitchen, with its island cooking station, functions well with the dining and family rooms. A study provides a quiet first floor haven for the family's less active pursuits. Upstairs there are three big bedrooms and a fine master bath.

The third floor provides a guest suite and huge bulk storage area (make it a cedar closet if you wish). This house has a basement for the development of further recreational and storage facilities. Don't miss the two fireplaces, large laundry and attached two-car garage. A great investment.

Design GG2970 First Floor: 1,538 square feet
Second Floor: 1,526 square feet; Total: 3,064 square feet
Third Story Feature: 2 Bedrooms-Opt. Study (658 sq. ft.)

L

● This charming Victorian features a covered outdoor living area on all four sides! It even ends at a screened porch which features a sun deck above. This interesting plan offers three floors of livability. And what liability it is! Plenty of formal and informal living facilities to go along with the potential of five bedrooms. The master suite is just that. It is adjacent to an interesting sitting room. It has a sun deck and excellent bath/personal care facilities. The third floor will make a wonderful haven for the family's student members.

Design by
Home Planners, Inc.

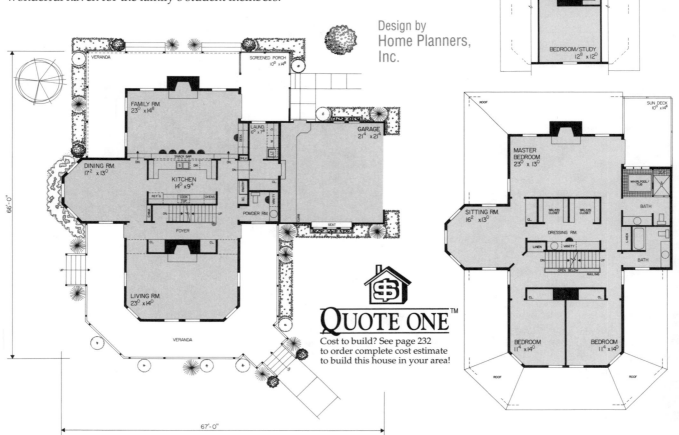

QUOTE ONE™

Cost to build? See page 232 to order complete cost estimate to build this house in your area!

Photo by Bob Greenspan

Design GG2974 First Floor: 911 square feet
Second Floor: 861 square feet; Total: 1,772 square feet
Third Story Feature: Attic conversion (1,131 sq. ft.)

L

● Victorian houses are well known for their orientation on narrow building sites. From the front covered porch, the foyer directs traffic all the way to the back of the house with its open living and dining rooms. The U-shaped kitchen conveniently services both the dining room and the front breakfast room. Well worth mentioning is the veranda and the screened porch which both highlight the

QUOTE ONE™

Cost to build? See page 232
to order complete cost estimate
to build this house in your area!

outdoor livability presented in this design. Three bedrooms are contained on the second floor, while recreational, hobby and storage space is offered by the basement and the attic.

California Engineered Plans and California Stock Plans are available for this home. Call 1-800-521-6797 for more information.

Design by
Home Planners,
Inc.

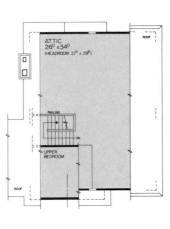

Design GG3382

First Floor: 1,366 square feet
Second Floor: 837 square feet
Total: 2,203 square feet
Third Story Feature: Guest Suite (363 sq. ft.)

L **D**

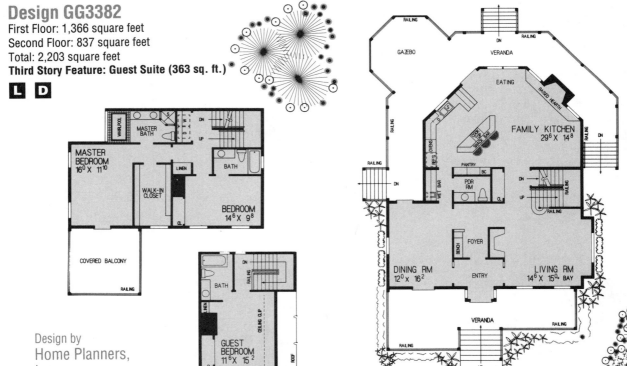

Design by
Home Planners,
Inc.

Width 48'-2"
Depth 69'

● A simple but charming Queen Anne Victorian, this enchanting three-story home boasts delicately turned rails and decorated columns on its covered front porch. Inside is a floor plan that includes a living room with fireplace and dining room that connects to the kitchen via a wet bar. The adjoining family room contains another fireplace. The second floor holds two bedrooms, one a master suite with grand bath. A tucked-away guest suite on the third floor has a private bath.

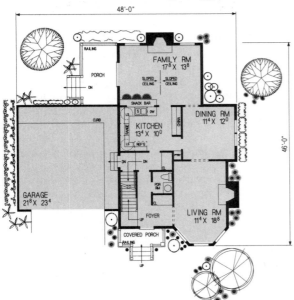

Design GG3383 First Floor: 995 square feet
Second Floor: 1,064 square feet; Total: 2,059 square feet
Third Story Feature: Studio (425 sq. ft.)

L **D**

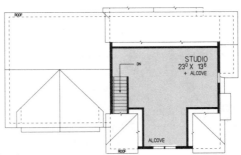

Design by
Home Planners,
Inc.

● This delightful Victorian cottage features three floors of living potential and exterior details that perfectly complement the convenient plan inside. Note the central placement of the kitchen, near to the dining room and the family room. A lovely side porch is the ideal location for weekend relaxing. Two fireplaces keep things warm and cozy. Three second-floor bedrooms include a master suite with bay window and two family bedrooms, one with an alcove and walk-in closet. Use the third-floor studio as a study, office or playroom for the children.

Design GG3386 First Floor: 1,683 square feet
Second Floor: 1,388 square feet; Total: 3,071 square feet
Third Story Features: 2 Bedrooms & 1 bath (808 sq. ft.)

L D

● This beautiful Folk Victorian has all the properties of others in its class. Living areas include a formal Victorian parlor, a private study and large gathering room. The formal dining room has its more casual counterpart in a bay-windowed breakfast room. Both are near the well-appointed kitchen. Five bedrooms serve family and guest needs handily. Three bedrooms on the second floor include a luxurious master suite. For outdoor entertaining, there is a covered rear porch leading to a terrace.

Design by
Home Planners,
Inc.

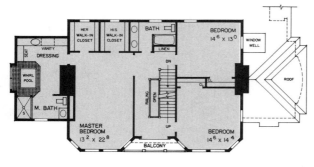

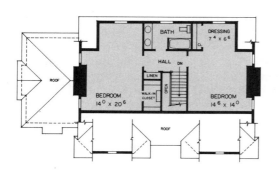

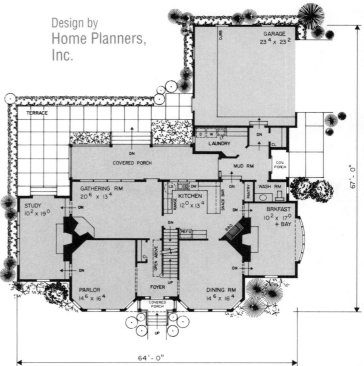

Design GG2690

First Floor: 1,559 square feet
Second Floor: 1,344 square feet
Total: 2,903 square feet
Third Story Feature: Studio (176 sq. ft.)

Design by
Home Planners,
Inc.

● This Cape Cod Georgian recalls the Julia Wood House built approximately 1790 in Falmouth, Mass. Such homes generally featured a balustraded roof deck or "widow's walk" where wives of captains looked to sea for signs of returning ships. Our updated floor plans include four bedrooms including master suite on the second floor and country kitchen, study, dining room, and living room on the first floor. A third floor makes a fine 15 x 10 studio, with ladder leading up to the widow's walk.

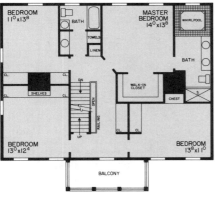

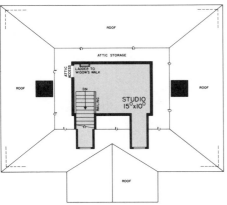

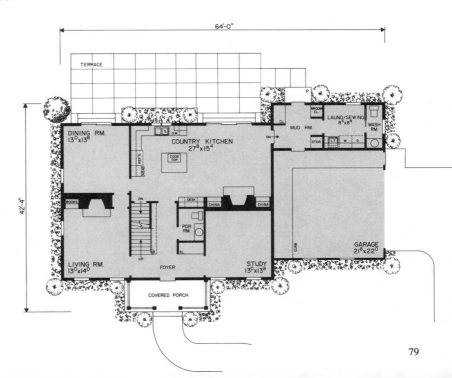

Design GG3503

First Floor: 1,748 square feet
Second Floor: 1,748 square feet
Total: 3,496 square feet
**Third Story Features: Bedroom,
Bath & Library/Playroom (1,100 sq. ft.)**

L **D**

● A brick exterior serves as a
nice introduction to this charming home. Enter the eleven-foot-
high foyer and take a seat in the
warm living room with its welcoming, warming fireplace.
Built-in shelves grace the hallway as well as the living and
dining rooms. The handy
kitchen, with its island and
snack bar, opens up into a
conversation room with a sun-
filled bay and a fireplace. The
service entrance leads to both
the laundry and the garage. This
house features four bedrooms:
the spacious master suite with a
fireplace, a bay-windowed sitting area, a walk-in closet and a
whirlpool; two family bedrooms
that share a full bath with a
double-bowl vanity; and a guest
bedroom that shares the third
floor with the library. This
design would work well on a
narrow lot.

Design by
Home Planners,
Inc.

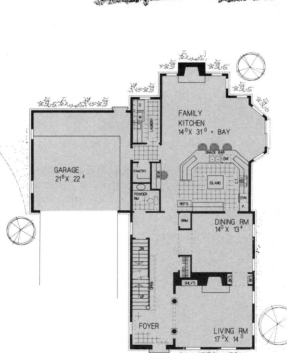

Width 50'
Depth 63'

Design GG2192

First Floor: 1,884 square feet
Second Floor: 1,521 square feet
Total: 3,405 square feet
Third Story Features: Studio, Bath & Study (808 sq. ft.)

L **D**

● This is surely a fine adaptation from the 18th Century, when formality and elegance were bywords. The authentic detailing of this design centers around the fine proportions, the dentils, the window symmetry, the massive chimneys and the masonry work. Inside, the formal living room features a corner fireplace. A second fireplace is found in the sunken family room. Built-in amenities include a wall of bookshelves and cabinets in the library, corner china cabinets in the formal dining room, cabinets in both passages to the family room and a china cabinet in the breakfast room.

Design by
Home Planners,
Inc.

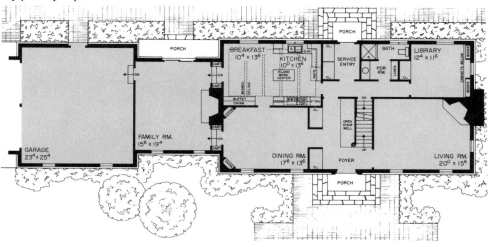

Width 99'
Depth 29'-6"

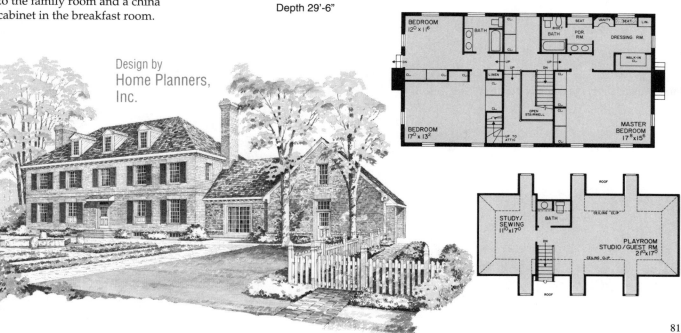

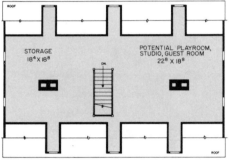

STORAGE
18⁴ X 18⁸

POTENTIAL PLAYROOM,
STUDIO, GUEST ROOM
22⁸ X 18⁸

DN.

ROOF

ROOF

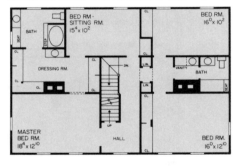

BED RM -
SITTING RM.
15⁸ x 10²

BED RM.
16⁰ x 10²

BATH

SEAT

CL

CL

DRESSING RM.

LIN

VANITY BATH

MASTER
BED RM.
18⁴ x 12¹⁰

HALL

BED RM.
16⁰ x 12¹⁰

UP

CL

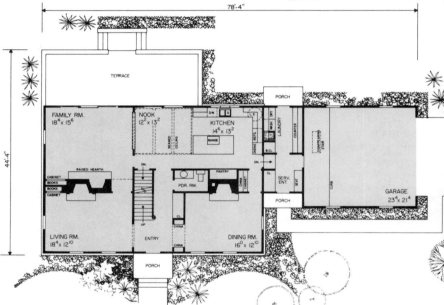

78'-4"

44'-4"

TERRACE

PORCH

FAMILY RM.
18⁴ x 15⁶

NOOK
12² x 13²

KITCHEN
14⁶ x 13²

LAUNDRY

COUNTER

RAISED HEARTH

CABINET
BOOKS
BOOKS
CABINET

RANGE

DN.

PANTRY

PDR. RM.

CHINA

SERV.
ENT.

SEAT

GARAGE
23⁴ x 21⁴

LIVING RM.
18⁴ x 12¹⁰

UP

ENTRY

CHINA

DINING RM.
16⁰ x 12¹⁰

CHINA

PORCH

PORCH

Design GG2556

First Floor: 1,675 square feet
Second Floor: 1,472 square feet
Total: 3,147 square feet
Third Story Feature: Playroom or Studio (176 sq. ft.)

D

Design by
Home Planners,
Inc.

Design GG2659

First Floor: 1,023 square feet
Second Floor: 1,008 square feet
Total: 2,031 square feet
Third Story Features: Study & Studio/Sewing (476 sq. ft.)

L D

● The facade of this three-storied, pitch-roofed house has a symmetrical placement of windows and a restrained but elegant central entrance. The central hall, or foyer, expands midway through the house to a family kitchen. Off the foyer are two rooms, a living room with fireplace and a study. The windowed third floor attic can be used as a study and studio. Three bedrooms are housed on the second floor.

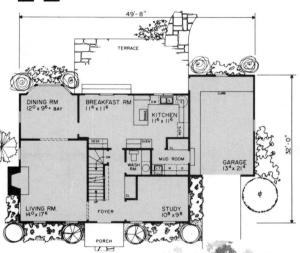

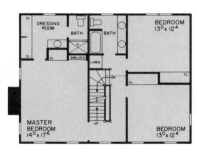

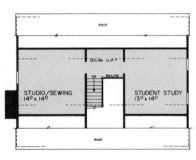

Design by
Home Planners,
Inc.

Design GG2633

First Floor: 1,338 square feet
Second Floor: 1,200 square feet
Total: 2,538 square feet
Third Story Features: Study & Studio/Sewing (506 sq. ft.)

● This is certainly a pleasing Georgian. Its facade features a front porch with a roof supported by 12" diameter wooden columns. The garage wing has a sheltered service entry and brick facing which complements the design. Sliding glass doors link the terrace and family room, providing an indoor/outdoor area for entertaining as pictured in the rear elevation. The floor plan has been designed to serve the family efficiently. The stairway in the foyer leads to four second-floor bedrooms. The third floor is windowed and can be used as a studio and study.

Design by
Home Planners,
Inc.

Design GG3510

First Floor: 1,120 square feet
Second Floor: 1,083 square feet
Total: 2,203 square feet
Third Story Features: Bonus Room & Office (597 sq. ft.)

● From the front and back covered porches to the open foyer with dining and living rooms on each side, this Colonial home offers a glimpse of the Old South. The large kitchen features an island cooktop, a breakfast nook and a convenient planning desk. The master bedroom exudes Southern flair with a spacious bathroom and a separate make-up table. An additional third-floor bonus room is also available. Fireplaces in the dining room, the living room and the family room complete the warmth and vitality of this fine home. All in all, it will serve your family well for generations to come.

Design by
Home Planners, Inc.

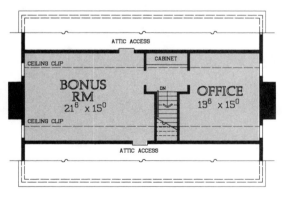

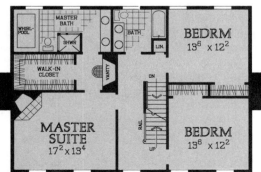

Design GG2988

First Floor: 1,458 square feet
Second Floor: 1,075 square feet
Total: 2,533 square feet

Third Story Features: Exercise Room & Study/Sewing (462 sq. ft.)

L D

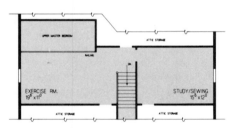

Design by
Home Planners,
Inc.

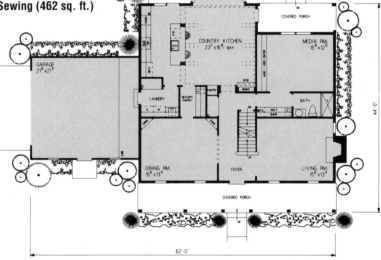

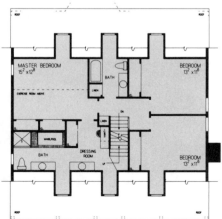

● The Joseph Guyon farmhouse, built in 1740, served as inspiration for this beautiful modern version. Three floors of living space encompass a country kitchen, living room, media room and dining room on the first floor; three bedrooms and two baths on the second floor; and an exercise room and study or sewing room on the third floor. Don't miss the covered porches front and rear, full guest bath near the media room and built-in wet bar.

4

BONUS ROOM DESIGNS

Ready When You Are

A bonus room that offers finish-later space is like finding forgotten treasure—one that displays a wealth of livability. Uses for a bonus room are numerous and may take the form of bedrooms, offices, playrooms or a study, just to name a few.

In many instances this space may be initially planned when the home is built and left as-is until it is needed. A practical and popular area for the location of a bonus room rests over the garage. Once developed, this space offers a private getaway for a variety of pursuits and is practical as well as ornamental, enhancing exterior elevations as represented by Designs GG9738 (page 89), GG9702 (page 99) and GG8981 (page 130).

Bonus room space may bring two-story livability to a one-story home as illustrated in Design GG9734 (page 91). Or, if second-story sleeping quarters exist, utilizing adjacent bonus room space, as shown on pages 93 and 104 (Designs GG9736 and GG9420), will provide an additional bedroom to meet future needs. Conversion of this space translates into a cost-saving expansion.

Stand-alone space, such as that found in the attic of Design GG2774 on page 103, paves the way smoothly for the development of a playroom or media room. Design GG9410 on page 119 takes the idea in a different direction, providing direct access to the bonus room on the second floor via a staircase leading from the family room on the first floor.

The plans in this chapter illustrate exceptional designs for these ideas and more. As you can see, the opportunities for developing this space are endless. If future requirements do not include transforming the bonus room into livable floor space, it will be appreciated for something that everyone needs—more storage.

Design GG9750

Square Footage: 1,575
Bonus Room: 276 square feet

● A covered porch and dormers combine to create the inviting exterior on this three-bedroom country home. The foyer leads through columns to an expansive great room with a cozy fireplace, built-in bookshelves and access to the rear covered porch. To the right, an open kitchen is conveniently situated to easily serve the bay-windowed breakfast area and the formal dining room. Sleeping quarters are located on the left, where the master suite enjoys access to the covered porch, a walk-in closet and a relaxing master bath complete with double-bowl vanities, a whirlpool tub and a separate shower. A utility room, two secondary bedrooms and a full bath complete the plan. A bonus room over the garage provides room for future growth.

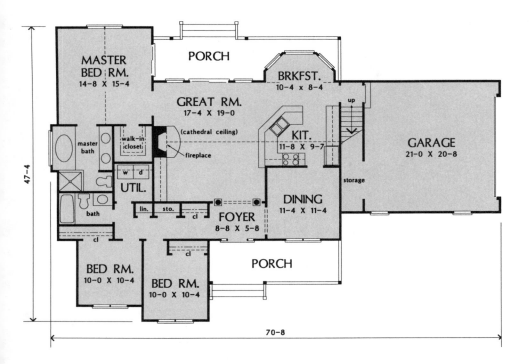

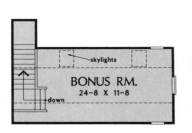

Design by
Donald A.
Gardner,
Architects, Inc.

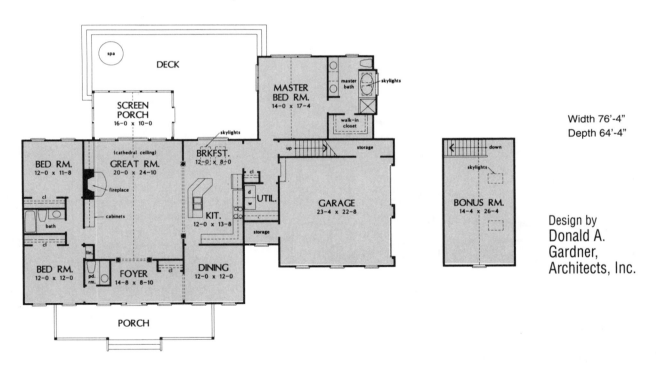

DECK

spa

SCREEN
PORCH
16-0 x 10-0

MASTER
BED RM.
14-0 x 17-4

master
bath

skylights

walk-in
closet

up

storage

Width 76'-4"
Depth 64'-4"

skylights

BRKFST.
12-0 x 8-0

BED RM.
12-0 x 11-8

(cathedral ceiling)

GREAT RM.
20-0 x 24-10

fireplace

cabinets

cl

d
w

UTIL.

KIT.
12-0 x 13-8

storage

GARAGE
23-4 x 22-8

BONUS RM.
14-4 x 26-4

down

skylights

Design by
Donald A.
Gardner,
Architects, Inc.

bath

cl

lin.

pd.
rm.

FOYER
14-8 x 8-10

cl

DINING
12-0 x 12-0

BED RM.
12-0 x 12-0

PORCH

Design GG9738
Square Footage: 2,136
Bonus Room: 405 square feet

● This exciting three-bedroom country home overflows with amenities. Traditional details such as columns, cathedral ceilings and open living areas combine to create the ideal floor plan for today's active family lifestyle. The spacious great room features built-in cabinets and a fireplace and a cathedral ceiling which continues into the adjoining screened porch. An efficient kitchen with a food preparation island is conveniently grouped with the great room, the dining room and the skylit breakfast area for the cook who enjoys visiting while preparing meals. A private master bedroom features a cathedral ceiling, a large walk-in closet and a relaxing master bath with a skylit whirlpool tub and a separate shower. Two secondary bedrooms share a full bath at the opposite end of the home.

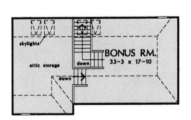

BONUS RM.
33-3 x 17-10

skylights

attic storage

down

down

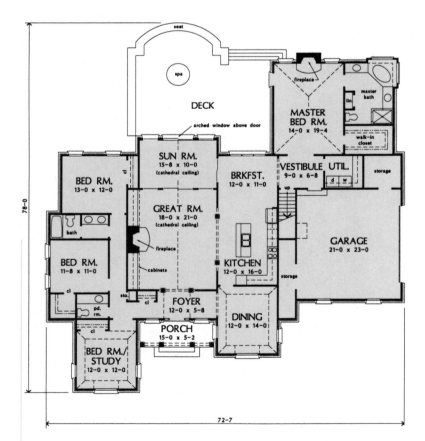

seat

spa

DECK

arched window above door

SUN RM.
15-8 x 10-0
(cathedral ceiling)

BRKFST.
12-0 x 11-0

fireplace

MASTER
BED RM.
14-0 x 19-4

master
bath

lin

walk-in
closet

BED RM.
13-0 x 12-0

GREAT RM.
18-0 x 21-0
(cathedral ceiling)

VESTIBULE UTIL.
9-0 x 6-8

storage

d w

up

bath

fireplace

cabinets

KITCHEN
12-0 x 16-0

GARAGE
21-0 x 23-0

BED RM.
11-8 x 11-0

cl

sto.

cl

FOYER
12-0 x 5-8

storage

pd.
rm.

DINING
12-0 x 14-0

cl

PORCH
15-0 x 5-2

BED RM./
STUDY
12-0 x 12-0

78-0

72-7

Design GG9709
Square Footage: 2,663
Bonus Room: 653 square feet

● This stately one-story home
displays large arched windows,
round columns, a covered
porch, and brick veneer siding.
The arched window in the
clerestory above the entrance
provides natural light to the
interior. The great room boasts a
cathedral ceiling, a fireplace,
built-in cabinets, and bookshelves. Sliding glass doors
lead to the sun room. The
L-shaped kitchen services the
dining room, the breakfast area
and the great room. The master
bedroom suite, with a fireplace,
uses private passage to the deck
and its spa. Three additional
bedrooms—one could serve as a
study—are at the other end of
the house for privacy. This plan
is available with a crawl-space
foundation.

Design by
Donald A.
Gardner,
Architects, Inc.

Design GG9734

Square Footage: 1,977
Bonus Room: 430 square feet

● A two-story foyer with a Palladian window above sets the tone for this sunlit home. Columns mark the passage from the foyer to the great room, where a centered fireplace and built-in cabinets are found. A screened porch with four skylights above and a wet bar provides a pleasant place to start the day or wind down after work. The kitchen is flanked by the formal dining room and the breakfast room with sliding glass doors to the large, rear deck. Hidden quietly in the rear, the master suite includes a bath with dual vanities and skylights. Two family bedrooms (one an optional study) share a bath with twin sinks.

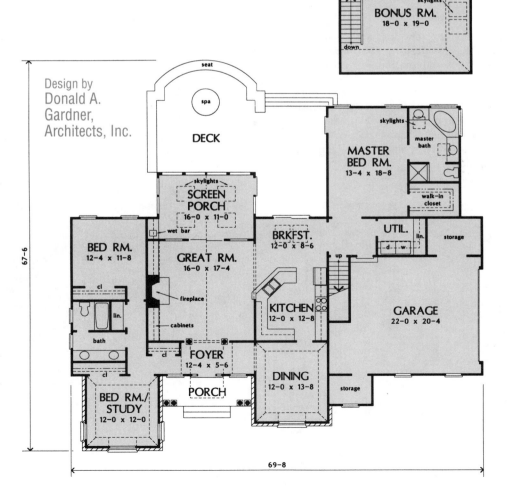

Design by Donald A. Gardner, Architects, Inc.

BONUS RM.
18-0 x 19-0

attic storage
skylights
down

DECK
seat
spa

SCREEN PORCH
16-0 x 11-0
skylights
wet bar

GREAT RM.
16-0 x 17-4
fireplace
cabinets

BED RM.
12-4 x 11-8
cl
bath
lin.
cl

BRKFST.
12-0 x 8-6

KITCHEN
12-0 x 12-8

MASTER BED RM.
13-4 x 18-8
master bath
skylights
walk-in closet

UTIL.
d   w
lin.

storage

GARAGE
22-0 x 20-4

FOYER
12-4 x 5-6

DINING
12-0 x 13-8

PORCH

BED RM./STUDY
12-0 x 12-0

storage
up

67-6
69-8

B. NATHAN.

Design GG9661

First Floor: 1,416 square feet
Second Floor: 445 square feet
Total: 1,861 square feet
Bonus Room: 284 square feet

● An arched entrance and windows provide a touch of class to the exterior of this plan. The foyer leads to all areas of the house minimizing corridor space. The dining room displays round columns at the entrance while the great room boasts a cathedral ceiling, fireplace and arched window over exterior doors to the deck. In the master suite is a walk-in closet and lavish bath. On the second level are two bedrooms and a full bath. Bonus space over the garage can be developed later. The plan is available with a crawl-space foundation.

DECK

seat

spa

arched window above door

GREAT RM.
15-4 × 18-0
(cathedral ceiling)

fireplace

KIT./BRKFST.
16-8 × 16-0

master bath

walk-in closet

walk-in closet

up

sto.

pd. rm.

cl

MASTER BED RM.
13-0 × 13-6

FOYER
7-8 × 9-0

DINING
12-4 × 12-4

UTILITY
10-0 × 6-4

w
d

up

storage

PORCH

GARAGE
20-0 × 20-0

58-3

68-9

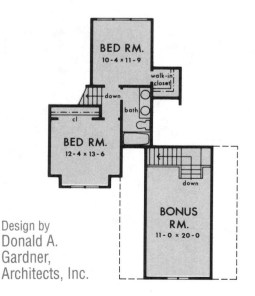

BED RM.
10-4 × 11-9

walk-in closet

down

bath

cl

BED RM.
12-4 × 13-6

down

BONUS RM.
11-0 × 20-0

Design by
Donald A.
Gardner,
Architects, Inc.

Design by
Donald A.
Gardner,
Architects, Inc.

Design GG9736

First Floor: 1,839 square feet
Second Floor: 527 square feet
Total: 2,366 square feet
Bonus Room: 344 square feet

● An arched entrance and windows combine with round columns to develop a touch of class on the exterior of this four-bedroom plan. The plan layout allows no wasted space. The foyer leads to all areas of the house, minimizing corridor space. The large, open kitchen with an island cooktop is convenient to the breakfast and dining rooms. The master bedroom suite has plenty of walk-in closet space and a well-planned master bath. A nearby bedroom would make an excellent guest room or study, with an adjacent full bath. An expansive rear deck boasts a location for a spa tub and generous space for outdoor living. The second level offers two bedrooms, with sloped ceilings and walk-in closets, and a full bath. A bonus room is available over the garage. This plan includes a crawlspace foundation.

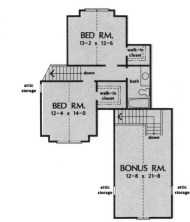

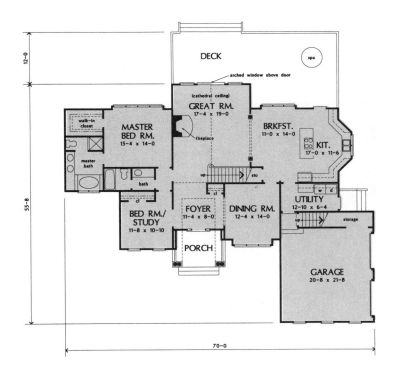

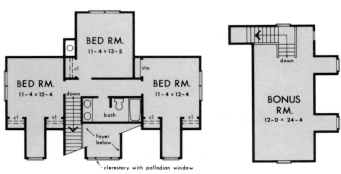

BED RM.
11-4 x 13-5

BED RM.
11-4 x 12-4

BED RM.
11-4 x 12-4

down

cl

cl

cl

cl

cl

sto.

bath

foyer below

clerestory with palladian window

down

BONUS RM.
12-0 x 24-4

Design GG9706

First Floor: 1,585 square feet
Second Floor: 731 square feet
Total: 2,316 square feet
Bonus Room: 401 square feet

● This complete farmhouse projects an exciting and comfortable feeling with its wraparound porch, arched windows and dormers. A Palladian window in the clerestory above the entrance foyer allows an abundance of natural light. The large kitchen, with carefully planned layout incorporating a cooking island, easily services the breakfast area and dining room. The generous great room with fireplace is accessible to the spacious screened porch for mosquito-free outside living. The master bedroom suite, located on the first level for privacy and convenience, has a luxurious master bath. The second level allows for three bedrooms and a full bath. Don't miss the garage with bonus room—both meet the main house via a covered breezeway. The plan is available with a crawl-space foundation.

Design by
Donald A.
Gardner,
Architects, Inc.

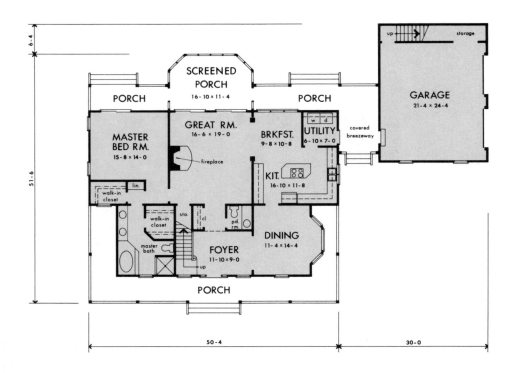

up

storage

GARAGE
21-4 x 24-4

6-4

51-6

SCREENED PORCH
16-10 x 11-4

PORCH

PORCH

covered breezeway

MASTER BED RM.
15-8 x 14-0

GREAT RM.
16-6 x 19-0

BRKFST.
9-8 x 10-8

UTILITY
6-10 x 7-0

w

d

fireplace

walk-in closet

lin.

KIT.
16-10 x 11-8

walk-in closet

sto.

cl

pd. rm.

master bath

up

FOYER
11-10 x 9-0

DINING
11-4 x 14-4

PORCH

50-4

30-0

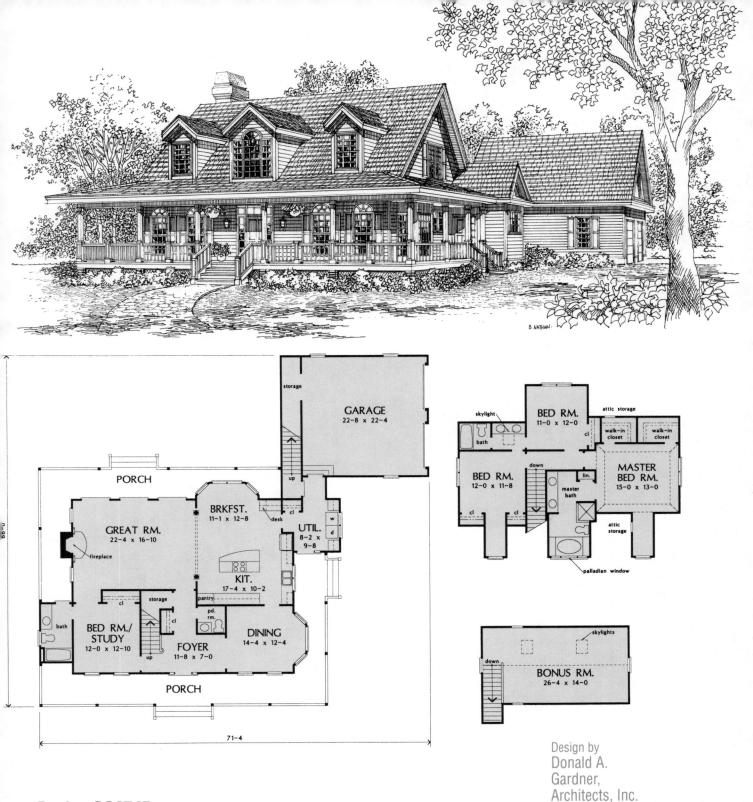

B. NATHAN.

storage

GARAGE
22-8 x 22-4

PORCH

BRKFST.
11-1 x 12-8

desk

UTIL.
8-2 x
9-8

w
d

up

cl

GREAT RM.
22-4 x 16-10

fireplace

KIT.
17-4 x 10-2

pantry

storage

cl

pd.
rm.

BED RM./
STUDY
12-0 x 12-10

bath

cl

FOYER
11-8 x 7-0

DINING
14-4 x 12-4

up

PORCH

71-4

skylight

bath

BED RM.
11-0 x 12-0

attic storage

cl

walk-in
closet

walk-in
closet

BED RM.
12-0 x 11-8

down

lin.

cl

cl

master
bath

MASTER
BED RM.
15-0 x 13-0

attic
storage

palladian window

down

skylights

BONUS RM.
26-4 x 14-0

Design by
Donald A.
Gardner,
Architects, Inc.

Design GG9745

First Floor: 1,576 square feet; Second Floor: 947 square feet
Total: 2,523 square feet; **Bonus Room: 405 square feet**

● Enjoy balmy breezes as you relax on the wraparound porch of this delightful country farmhouse. The foyer introduces a dining room to the right and a bedroom or study to the left. The expansive great room—with its cozy fireplace—has direct access to the rear porch. Columns define the kitchen and breakfast area. The house gourmet will enjoy preparing meals at the island cooktop which also allows for additional eating space. A built-in pantry and a desk are additional popular features in this well-planned combo. A powder room and a utility room are located nearby. The master bedroom features a tray ceiling along with a luxurious bath. Two additional bedrooms share a skylit bath.

Design by
Donald A.
Gardner,
Architects, Inc.

Design GG9644

First Floor: 943 square feet
Second Floor: 840 square feet
Total: 1,783 square feet
Bonus Room: 323 square feet

● Roundtop windows and an inviting covered porch offer an irresistible appeal for this three-bedroom plan. A two-story foyer provides a spacious feeling to this well-organized open layout. Round columns between the great room and kitchen add to the impressive quality of the plan. An expansive deck promotes casual outdoor living to its fullest. The master suite with walk-in closet and complete master bath is on the second floor along with two additional bedrooms and a full bath. The bonus room over the garage offers room for expansion.

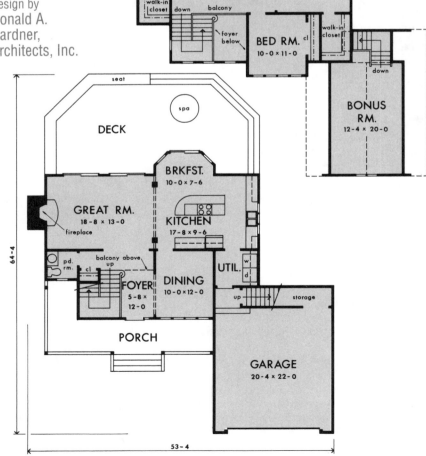

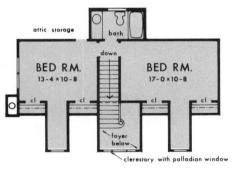

attic storage

bath

BED RM.
13-4 × 10-8

down

BED RM.
17-0 × 10-8

cl   cl   cl   cl

foyer below

clerestory with palladian window

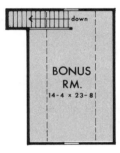

down

BONUS RM.
14-4 × 23-8

Design by
Donald A.
Gardner,
Architects, Inc.

Design GG9606

First Floor: 1,289 square feet
Second Floor: 542 square feet
Total: 1,831 square feet
Bonus Room: 393 square feet

● This cozy country cottage is perfect for the growing family—offering both an unfinished basement option and a bonus room. Enter through the two-story foyer with a Palladian window in a clerestory dormer above. The master suite is on the first floor for privacy and accessibility. Its accompanying bath boasts a whirlpool tub with a skylight above and a double-bowl vanity. The second floor contains two bedrooms, a full bath and plenty of storage. Note that all first-floor rooms except the kitchen and utility room boast nine foot ceilings. This plan is available with either a basement or crawlspace foundation. Please specify when ordering.

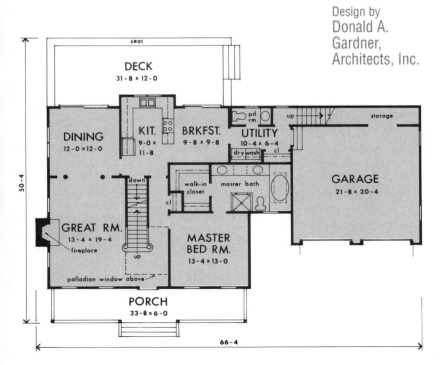

seat

DECK
31-8 × 12-0

DINING
12-0 × 12-0

KIT.
9-0 × 11-8

BRKFST.
9-8 × 9-8

pd. rm.

UTILITY
10-4 × 6-4

up

storage

dry wash   cl

GARAGE
21-8 × 20-4

down

walk-in closet

master bath

cl

50-4

GREAT RM.
13-4 × 19-4
fireplace

up

MASTER
BED RM.
13-4 × 13-0

palladian window above

PORCH
33-8 × 6-0

66-4

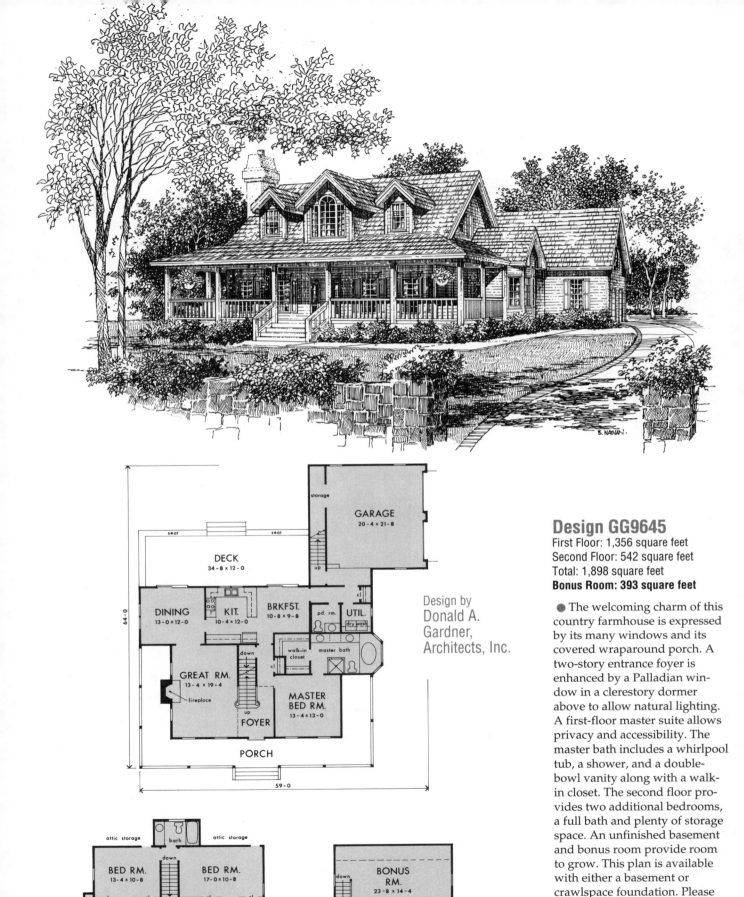

DECK
34-8 x 12-0

GARAGE
20-4 x 21-8

storage

up

seat   seat

DINING
13-0 x 12-0

KIT.
10-4 x 12-0

BRKFST.
10-8 x 9-8

pd. rm.

UTIL.

dry wash

cl

Design by
Donald A.
Gardner,
Architects, Inc.

walk-in
closet

master bath

cl

down

GREAT RM.
13-4 x 19-4

fireplace

up

MASTER
BED RM.
13-4 x 13-0

FOYER

64-0

59-0

PORCH

attic storage   attic storage

bath

BED RM.
13-4 x 10-8

down

BED RM.
17-0 x 10-8

cl   cl   cl   cl

foyer
below

clerestory with palladian window

BONUS
RM.
23-8 x 14-4

down

Design GG9645

First Floor: 1,356 square feet
Second Floor: 542 square feet
Total: 1,898 square feet
Bonus Room: 393 square feet

● The welcoming charm of this country farmhouse is expressed by its many windows and its covered wraparound porch. A two-story entrance foyer is enhanced by a Palladian window in a clerestory dormer above to allow natural lighting. A first-floor master suite allows privacy and accessibility. The master bath includes a whirlpool tub, a shower, and a double-bowl vanity along with a walk-in closet. The second floor provides two additional bedrooms, a full bath and plenty of storage space. An unfinished basement and bonus room provide room to grow. This plan is available with either a basement or crawlspace foundation. Please specify when ordering.

B. NATHAN.

B. NATHAN

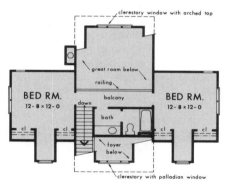

clerestory window with arched top

great room below.

railing

BED RM.
12-8 x 12-0

balcony

BED RM.
12-8 x 12-0

cl

cl

down

bath

cl

cl

foyer
below

clerestory with palladian window

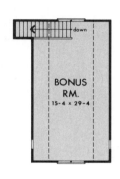

down

BONUS
RM.
15-4 x 29-4

Design GG9702

First Floor: 1,618 square feet
Second Floor: 570 square feet
Total: 2,188 square feet
Bonus Room: 495 square feet

● A wraparound covered porch, an open deck with a spa and seating, arched windows and dormers enhance the already impressive character of this three-bedroom farmhouse. The spacious great room boasts a fireplace, cabinets and bookshelves. The kitchen, with a cooking island, is conveniently located between a dining room and a breakfast room with an open view of the great room. A generous master bedroom has plenty of closet space as well as an expansive master bath. Bonus space over the garage allows for room to grow. The plan includes a crawlspace foundation.

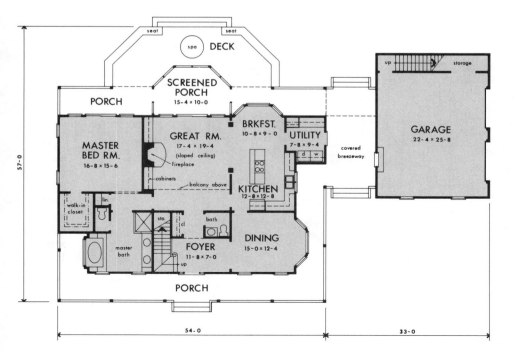

seat

spa

seat

DECK

SCREENED
PORCH
15-4 x 10-0

PORCH

up

storage

BRKFST.
10-8 x 9-0

GREAT RM.
17-4 x 19-4
(sloped ceiling)

fireplace

UTILITY
7-8 x 9-4

d w

GARAGE
22-4 x 25-8

MASTER
BED RM.
16-8 x 15-6

cabinets

balcony above

covered
breezeway

KITCHEN
12-8 x 12-8

walk-in
closet

lin.

sto.

cl

bath

57-0

master
bath

FOYER
11-8 x 7-0

DINING
15-0 x 12-4

up

PORCH

54-0

33-0

Design by
Donald A.
Gardner,
Architects, Inc.

Design GG9625

First Floor: 1,436 square feet
Second Floor: 549 square feet
Total: 1,945 square feet
Sun Room: 145 square feet
Bonus Room: 334 square feet

● Great flexibility is available in this plan—the great room/dining room can be reworked into one large great room with the dining room relocated to the family room. A sun room with a cathedral ceiling and a sliding glass door to the deck is accessible from both the breakfast and dining rooms. A large kitchen boasts a convenient cooking island. The master bedroom has a fireplace, a walk-in closet and a spacious master bath. Two second-level bedrooms are equal in size and share a full bath with a double-bowl vanity. Both bedrooms have a dormer window and a walk-in closet. A large bonus room over the garage is accessible from the utility room below. This plan is available with either a basement or crawlspace foundation. Please specify when ordering.

Design by
Donald A.
Gardner,
Architects, Inc.

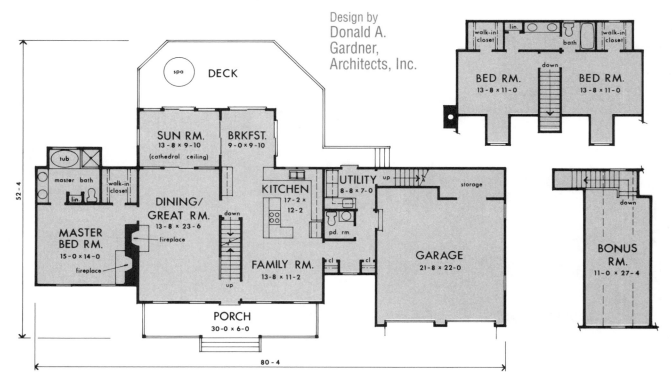

Design GG9626

First Floor (crawlspace foundation): 1,057 square feet
First Floor (basement foundation): 1,110 square feet
Second Floor (crawlspace or basement foundation): 500 square feet
Total (crawlspace foundation): 1,557 square feet
Total (basement foundation): 1,610 square feet
Bonus Room: 342 square feet

● This compact, two-story, cozy country cottage is perfect for the economically conscious family. Its entrance foyer is highlighted by a clerestory dormer above for natural light. The master suite is conveniently located on the first level for privacy and accessibility. Its attached master bath boasts a whirlpool tub with a skylight above, a separate shower and a double-bowl vanity. Second-level bedrooms share a full bath and there's a wealth of storage on this level. An added advantage to this house is the bonus room above the garage. This plan is available with either a basement or crawlspace foundation. Please specify when ordering.

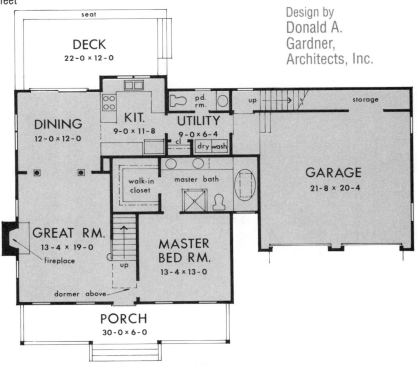

Design by
Donald A.
Gardner,
Architects, Inc.

Width 59'-4"
Depth 50'

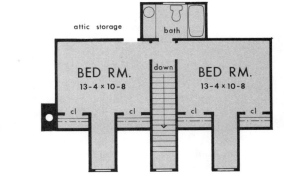

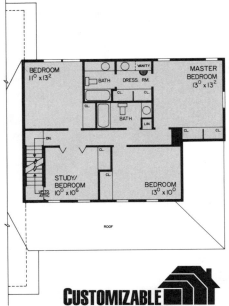

ATTIC 29⁴ x 26⁴
(HEADROOM 29⁴ x 10⁴)

ROOF

BEDROOM
11⁰ x 13²

MASTER
BEDROOM
13⁰ x 13²

VANITY
BATH   DRESS. RM.

BATH

STUDY/
BEDROOM
10⁰ x 10⁶

BEDROOM
13⁰ x 10⁰

ROOF

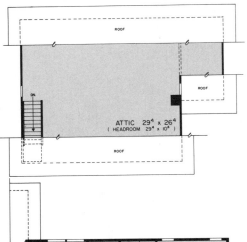

CUSTOMIZABLE

Custom Alterations? See page 237
for customizing this plan to your
specifications.

Design by
Home Planners,
Inc.

Design GG2945

First Floor: 1,644 square feet
Second Floor: 971 square feet
Total: 2,615 square feet
Bonus Room: 971 square feet

FAMILY RM.
21⁰ x 18⁰
SLOPED ← CEILING

RAISED HEARTH

TERRACE

BAR   W.R.

LIVING RM.
24⁰ x 13⁶

DINING RM.
13⁰ x 13⁶

LAUNDRY RM.
10⁰ x 7⁶

MUD RM.

GAME
STOR.

FOYER

KITCHEN
12⁰ x 13⁶

COOK
TOP

BRKFST.
9⁰ x 13⁶

DESK

PANTRY

GARAGE
21⁴ x 21⁸

CURB

COVERED PORCH

Width 59'-8"
Depth 56'

● Here is a new floor plan designed to go with the almost identical exterior of one of Home Planners' most popular houses. A masterfully affordable design, this plan manages to include all the basics - and then adds a little more. Note the wraparound covered porch, large family room with raised-hearth fireplace and wet bar, spacious kitchen with island cook top, formal dining room, rear terrace, and extra storage on the first floor. Upstairs, the plan's as flexible as they come: three or four bedrooms (the fourth could easily be a study or playroom) and lots of unfinished attic just waiting for you to transform it into living space. This could make a fine studio, sewing room, home office, or just a place for the safe, dry storage of the family's paraphernalia, Christmas decorations, etc.

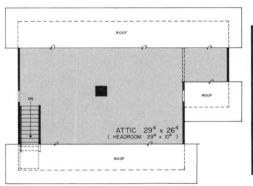

ATTIC 29⁴ x 26⁴
(HEADROOM 29⁴ x 10⁴)

Width 59'-6"
Depth 46'

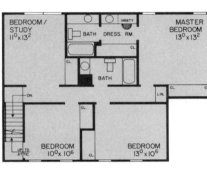

BEDROOM / STUDY 11⁰ x 13²
MASTER BEDROOM 13⁰ x 13²
BATH DRESS. RM.
BATH
BEDROOM 10⁰ x 10⁶
BEDROOM 13⁰ x 10⁶

Design by
Home Planners, Inc.

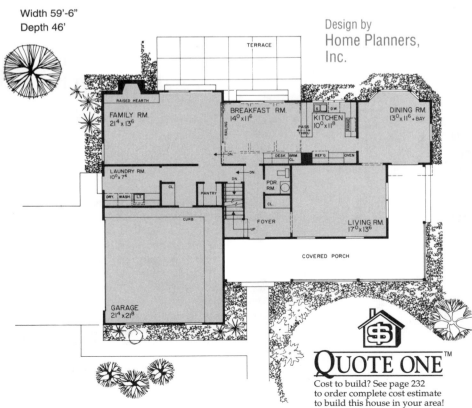

TERRACE

RAISED HEARTH

FAMILY RM. 21⁴ x 13⁶
BREAKFAST RM. 14⁰ x 11⁶
KITCHEN 10⁰ x 11⁸
DINING RM. 13⁰ x 11⁶ + BAY

LAUNDRY RM. 10⁰ x 7⁶

DRY. WASH. PANTRY
CURB

PDR. RM.

FOYER

LIVING RM. 17⁰ x 13⁶

GARAGE 21⁴ x 21⁸

COVERED PORCH

Design GG2774

First Floor: 1,366 square feet
Second Floor: 969 square feet
Total: 2,335 square feet
Bonus Room: 969 square feet

L **D**

● Beginning with the formal areas, this design offers pleasures for the entire family. There is the quiet corner living room which has an opening to the sizable dining room. This room will enjoy plenty of natural light from the delightful bay window overlooking the rear yard. The kitchen features many built-ins with a pass-through to the beam-ceilinged breakfast room. Sliding glass doors to the terrace are fine attractions in both the sunken family room and breakfast room. Recreational activities and hobbies can be pursued in the basement area. Four bedrooms and two baths are upstairs. The attic provides added livability for the future.

California Engineered Plans and California Stock Plans are available for this home. Call 1-800-521-6797 for more information.

Design GG9420

First Floor: 1,587 square feet
Second Floor: 716 square feet
Total: 2,303 square feet
Bonus Room: 427 square feet

Design by
Alan Mascord
Design Associates, Inc.

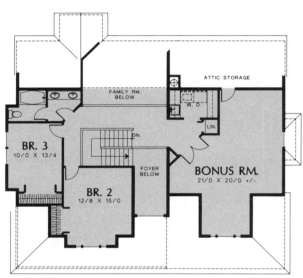

● This compact Victorian home has its fully featured master bedroom on the main floor. A wraparound porch with a pair of French doors leading from the dining room complements the facade. The upper hallway overlooks the vaulted family room on one side and the two-story foyer on the other. A bonus room over the garage allows some expansion space to either add another bedroom or a game room.

Design GG8002 First Floor: 1,530 square feet
Second Floor: 968 square feet; Total: 2,498 square feet
Bonus Room: 326 square feet

● The timeless influence of the French Quarter is exemplified in this home designed for river-front living. The double French door entry opens into a large living room/dining room area separated by a double archway. The living room ceiling opens up through two stories to the cupola above. A railed balcony with a loft on the second floor overlooks the living room. A pass-through between the kitchen and dining room also provides seating at a bar for informal dining. The spacious master bedroom at the rear includes a sitting area and a roomy master bath with a large walk-in closet. Two additional bedrooms, a bath and a bonus area for an office or game room are located upstairs. With ten-foot ceilings downstairs and nine-foot ceilings upstairs, there is a feeling of spaciousness. The inclusion of fabulous decks on the front and back of the second story makes this home perfect for entertaining.

Design by
Larry E. Belk
Designs

COPYRIGHT 1993 LARRY E. BELK

Width 40'
Depth 66'

Design GG9486

First Floor: 1,368 square feet
Second Floor: 972 square feet
Total: 2,340 square feet
Bonus Room: 344 square feet

Design by
**Alan Mascord
Design Associates, Inc.**

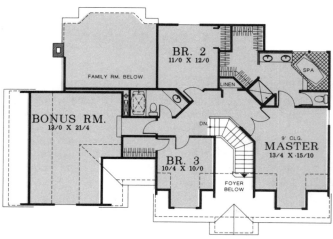

BR. 2
11/0 X 12/0

FAMILY RM. BELOW

SPA

LINEN

BONUS RM.
13/0 X 21/4

DN.

9' CLG.
MASTER
13/4 X -15/10

BR. 3
10/4 X 10/0

FOYER
BELOW

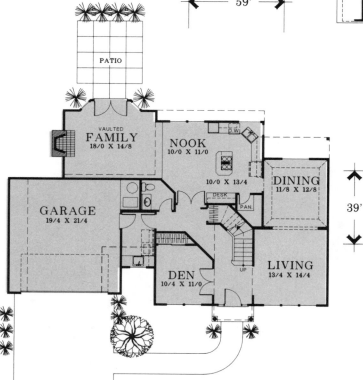

59'

39'

PATIO

VAULTED
FAMILY
18/0 X 14/8

NOOK
10/0 X 11/0

D.W.

10/0 X 13/4

DINING
11/8 X 12/8

GARAGE
19/4 X 21/4

DESK

PAN.

DEN
10/4 X 11/0

UP

LIVING
13/4 X 14/4

● Special details such as the two dormer windows and double-columned front entry add so much to this well-designed home. Inside, it features formal living and dining rooms, tucked-away den and large family room with vaulted ceiling and fireplace. The island kitchen is adjacent to a breakfast nook and has a wonderful walk-in pantry. Upstairs, there are three bedrooms including a lovely master suite with whirlpool spa. Bonus room over the garage can be developed later into a fourth bedroom, office space or a play room for children.

Design GG2622

First Floor: 624 square feet
Second Floor: 624 square feet
Total: 1,248 square feet
Bonus Room: 247 square feet

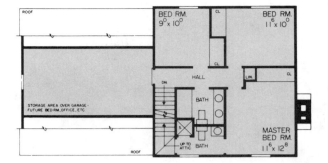

● This Colonial adaptation
provides a functional design
that allows for expansion in
the future. A cozy fireplace
in the living room adds
warmth to this space as well
as to the adjacent dining area.
The roomy L-shaped kitchen
features a breakfast nook and
an over-the-sink window.
Upstairs, two secondary
bedrooms share a full bath
with double vanity. The master
bedroom is on this floor as
well. Its private bath contains
access to attic storage. An additional storage area over the
garage can become a bedroom,
office or study in the future.

Custom Alterations? See page 237
for customizing this plan to your
specifications.

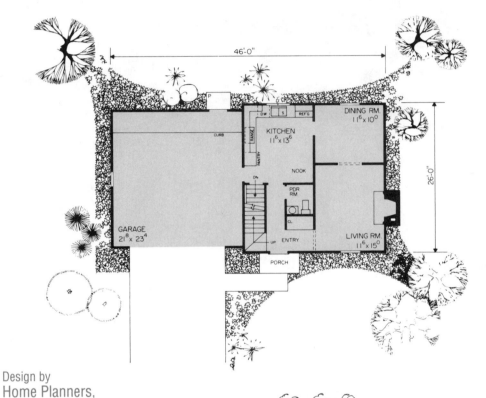

Design by
Home Planners,
Inc.

COPYRIGHT LARRY E. BELK

FP

MASTER BATH
8 FT CLG

K.S.

PWDR

LIN

SEAT

GREAT ROOM
19-0 X 17-0
VOLUME CLG

← SLOPE

PORCH

BRKFST ROOM
11-6 X 10-0
9 FT CLG

KITCHEN
16-6 X 15-4

9 FT CLG

MASTER BEDRM
13-0 X 15-6
9 FT CLG

FOYER
9 FT CLG

COATS

DINING ROOM
12-6 X 13-6
9 FT CLG

PAN

UTIL
9-6 X 5-8"

STORAGE

PORCH

GARAGE

COPYRIGHT LARRY E BELK

BEDROOM 2
14-0 X 13-8

BATH 2

OPEN TO BELOW

ATTIC

LINEN

EXPANDABLE AREA 1
12-6 X 17-0

BEDROOM 3
12-6 X 10-6

EXPANDABLE AREA 2
12-0 X 25-0

4" KNEE WALL   8" CLG LINE   8" CLG LINE   4" KNEE WALL

Width 49'-6"
Depth 37'-9"

Design by
Larry E. Belk
Designs

Design GG8090
First Floor: 1,635 square feet
Second Floor: 624 square feet
Total: 2,259 square feet
Bonus Room: 550 square feet

● A large front porch provides a perfect retreat for those lazy summer evenings and adds charm to this traditional Southern facade. A compact floor plan awaits inside with the kitchen, breakfast room and great room conveniently grouped. The master suite is located downstairs and features His and Hers vanities with a seating area, a corner whirlpool tub and a separate shower with a seat. An oversized walk-in closet is also noteworthy. The second floor is comprised of two secondary bedrooms and a bath. The bonus area contains two expandable spaces: Area 1 is designed for Bedroom 4, Area 2 is great for use as a recreation room or office. This plan is available with either a crawlspace or slab foundation. Please specify when ordering.

COPYRIGHT 1993

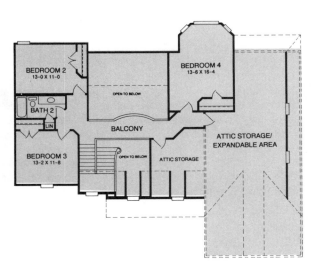

BEDROOM 2
13-0 X 11-0

BATH 2

LIN

BEDROOM 3
13-2 X 11-8

OPEN TO BELOW

BALCONY

OPEN TO BELOW

BEDROOM 4
13-6 X 16-4

ATTIC STORAGE/
EXPANDABLE AREA

ATTIC STORAGE

Design GG8050

First Floor: 1,844 square feet
Second Floor: 841 square feet
Total: 2,685 square feet
Bonus Room: 455 square feet

● Two shed dormers and a front porch perfect for evening relaxation evoke the charm of the country farmhouse in a home designed for the constraints of a suburban lot. Inside, impact is created at the front door with a dining room defined by columns and connecting arched openings. The conveniently designed kitchen features a work island and eating bar. The family room with corner fireplace has access to a rear covered porch. Three bedrooms and a bath are located on the second floor. A large area perfect for a game room or craft room is located over the garage and makes this plan a great pick for the growing family.

Design by
Larry E. Belk
Designs

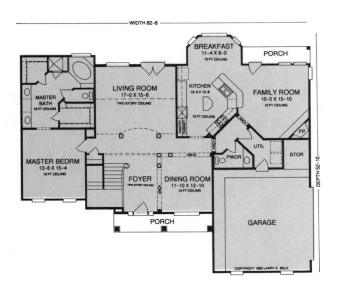

WIDTH 62-6

BREAKFAST
11-4 X 8-0
10 FT CEILING

PORCH

MASTER
BATH
10 FT CEILING

LIVING ROOM
17-0 X 15-6
TWO STORY CEILING

KITCHEN
13-0 X 13-6

FAMILY ROOM
15-0 X 15-10
10 FT CEILING

10 FT CEILING

PANTRY
CABINET

FP

MASTER BEDRM
13-6 X 15-4
10 FT CEILING

UTIL

STOR

DEPTH 52-10

FOYER
TWO STORY CEILING

ARCH

PWDR

DINING ROOM
11-10 X 12-10
10 FT CEILING

PORCH

GARAGE

COPYRIGHT 1993 LARRY E. BELK

Copyright 1992 Stephen S. Fuller, Inc.

Design GG9870 First Floor: 2,155 square feet
Second Floor: 1,020 square feet; Total: 3,175 square feet
Bonus Room: 262 square feet

● To highlight the exterior of this home, wood siding and paneled shutters have been artfully combined with arched transoms, gables and a sweeping roof line. The open foyer reveals the large living and dining rooms and a classic great room with a coffered ceiling and hearth. Double doors open to the master bedroom with a unique tray ceiling and a fireplace. The master bath includes double vanities and a shower, a corner garden tub and His and Hers closets. The exercise room can be accessed from either the master bedroom or great room and opens onto the porch at the rear of the home. The corner breakfast area also opens to the porch. The large kitchen with a cook-top island, the pantry and the laundry room complete the main level. The gallery features built-in bookshelves and a computer/study nook with easy access from all three bedrooms on the upper level. A bonus room offers room for expansion. This home is designed with a basement foundation.

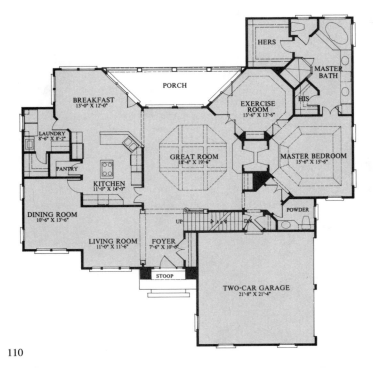

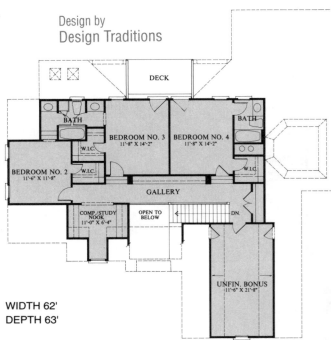

Design by
Design Traditions

WIDTH 62'
DEPTH 63'

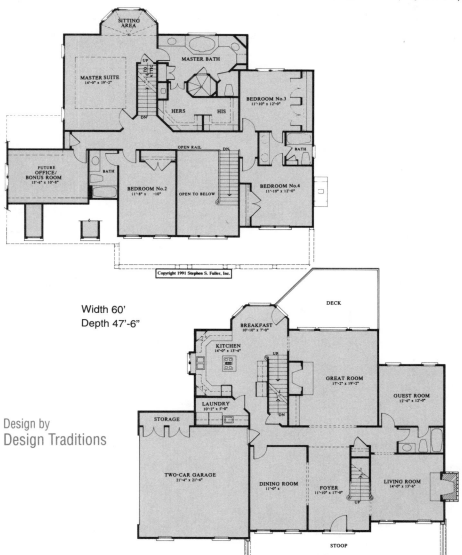

Width 60'
Depth 47'-6"

Design by
Design Traditions

Design GG9909

First Floor: 1,700 square feet
Second Floor: 1,585 square feet
Total: 3,285 square feet
Bonus Room: 176 square feet

● The covered front stoop of this two-story, traditionally styled home gives way to the foyer and formal areas inside. A cozy living room with a fireplace sits on the right and an elongated dining room—perfect for an elegant table—is on the left. For fine family living, a great room—also with a fireplace—and a kitchen/breakfast area account for the rear of the first-floor plan. Notice the deck off the breakfast room. A guest room with a nearby full bath finishes off the accommodations. Upstairs, four bedrooms include a master suite fit for a king. In it are a bayed sitting area and a private bath with His and Hers closets, dual lavatories, a spa tub, an octagonal shower stall and a compartmented toilet. A bonus room rests near Bedroom 3 and would make a great office or additional bedroom. This home is designed with a basement foundation.

Design GG9804

First Floor: 2,199 square feet
Second Floor: 1,235 square feet
Total: 3,434 square feet
Bonus Room: 150 square feet

● The covered front porch of this home warmly welcomes family and visitors. To the right of the foyer is a versatile option room. On the other side is the formal dining room, located just across from the open great room—which also opens into the breakfast room. The kitchen includes a cooking island/breakfast bar. Adjacent to the breakfast room is the sun room. At the rear of the main level is the master suite, which features a lavish bath loaded with features. Just off the bedroom is a private deck. On the second level, three additional bedrooms and two baths are found. This home is designed with a basement foundation.

Width 62'-6"
Depth 54'-3"

Design by
Design Traditions

Design GG9823
First Floor: 1,960 square feet
Second Floor: 905 square feet
Total: 2,865 square feet
Bonus Room: 297 square feet

● The classical styling of this Colonial home will be appreciated by traditionalists. The foyer opens to both a banquet-sized dining room and a formal living room with a fireplace. Just beyond is the two-story great room. The entire right side of the main level is taken up by the master suite. The other side of the main level includes a large kitchen and a breakfast room. Upstairs, each bedroom features ample closet space and direct access to bathrooms. The detached garage features a bonus room on its second level. This home is designed with a basement foundation.

Width 69'-6"
Depth 74'-6"

Design by
Design Traditions

113

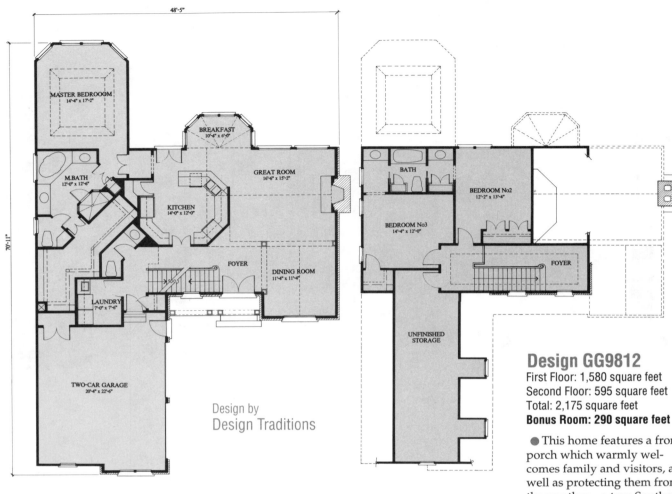

48'-5"

70'-11"

MASTER BEDRROOM
14'-4" x 17'-2"

BREAKFAST
10'-4" x 6'-0"

GREAT ROOM
16'-6" x 15'-2"

M.BATH
12'-0" x 12'-6"

KITCHEN
14'-0" x 12'-0"

FOYER

DINING ROOM
11'-4" x 11'-4"

LAUNDRY
7'-0" x 7'-6"

TWO-CAR GARAGE
20'-4" x 22'-6"

Design by
Design Traditions

BATH

BEDROOM No2
12'-2" x 13'-4"

BEDROOM No3
14'-4" x 12'-0"

FOYER

UNFINISHED
STORAGE

Design GG9812
First Floor: 1,580 square feet
Second Floor: 595 square feet
Total: 2,175 square feet
Bonus Room: 290 square feet

● This home features a front
porch which warmly wel-
comes family and visitors, as
well as protecting them from
the weather—a true Southern
Original. Inside, the spacious
foyer leads directly to a large
vaulted great room with a
massive fireplace. The dining
room also receives the vaulted ceiling treatment. The
grand kitchen offers both
storage and large work areas
opening up to the breakfast
room. In the privacy and
quiet of the rear of the home
is the master suite with its
garden bath, His and Hers
vanities and oversized closet.
The second floor provides
two additional bedrooms
with a shared bath along
with a balcony overlook
to the foyer below. Ample
amounts of storage space or
an additional bedroom can
be created in space over
the garage. This home is
designed with a basement
foundation.

Floor Plan Labels

First Floor:
- DECK
- BREAKFAST 10'-10" x 7'-0"
- KITCHEN 14'-0" x 13'-4"
- GREAT ROOM 17'-2" x 19'-2"
- GUEST ROOM 12'-6" x 12'-0"
- LAUNDRY 10'-2" x 5'-8"
- STORAGE
- TWO-CAR GARAGE 21'-4" x 21'-4"
- DINING ROOM 11'-0" x 15'-0"
- FOYER 11'-10" x 17'-0"
- LIVING ROOM 14'-0" x 13'-6"
- STOOP
- 60'-0"
- 48'-0"

Second Floor:
- SITTING AREA
- MASTER BATH
- MASTER SUITE 14'-0" x 19'-2"
- HERS
- HIS
- BEDROOM No.3 11'-10" x 12'-0"
- FUTURE OFFICE/ BONUS ROOM 15'-6" x 10'-8"
- BATH
- OPEN RAIL
- DN
- BEDROOM No.2 11'-8" x 12'-10"
- OPEN TO BELOW
- BEDROOM No.4 11'-10" x 12'-0"

Design GG9833

First Floor: 1,683 square feet
Second Floor: 1,544 square feet
Total: 3,227 square feet
Bonus Room: 176 square feet

● Handsomely arranged, this country cottage possesses an inviting quality. The stucco exterior, mixed with stone and shingles creates a warmth that is accented with a fan-light transom and a pendant door frame. The formal two-story foyer opens onto all the drama of the staircase and then flows easily into the dining room, living room and great room. The great room features a fireplace and bookcases on the side wall and opens to a well-lit breakfast and kitchen area. To complete the main level of this home, a guest room or office is planned, offering visitors the utmost in privacy. Provided upstairs are three additional bedrooms and space for a bonus or play room. The master suite features a tray ceiling and an adjoining sitting area with special ceiling treatment. The master bath offers a large garden tub with separate vanities, His and Hers closets and an octagonal glass shower. This home is designed with a basement foundation.

Design by
Design Traditions

Design GG9842

First Floor: 1,053 square feet
Second Floor: 1,053 square feet
Total: 2,106 square feet
Bonus Room: 212 square feet

● Brick takes a bold stand in grand traditional style in this treasured design. The front study has a nearby full bath, making it a handy guest bedroom. The family room with fireplace opens to a cozy breakfast area. For more formal entertaining there's a dining room just off the entry. The kitchen features a prep island and huge pantry. Upstairs, the master bedroom has its own sitting room and a giant-sized closet. Two family bedrooms share a full bath. This home is designed with a basement foundation.

Design by
Design Traditions

WIDTH 52'
DEPTH 34'

Copyright 1992 Stephen S. Fuller, Inc.

Design by
Design Traditions

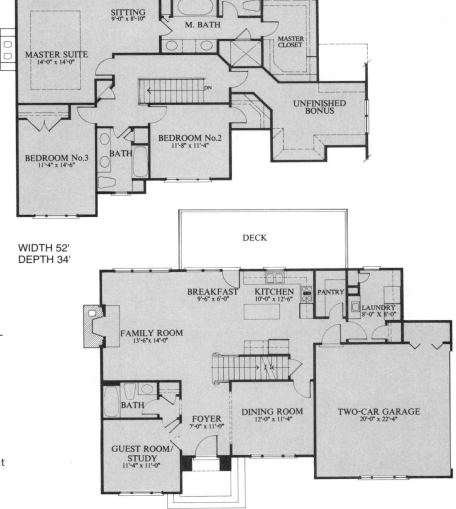

SITTING
9'-0" x 8'-10"

M. BATH

MASTER CLOSET

MASTER SUITE
14'-0" x 14'-0"

DN

UNFINISHED BONUS

BEDROOM No.3
11'-4" x 14'-6"

BATH

BEDROOM No.2
11'-8" x 11'-4"

DECK

WIDTH 52'
DEPTH 34'

BREAKFAST
9'-6" x 6'-0"

KITCHEN
10'-0" x 12'-6"

PANTRY

LAUNDRY
8'-0" X 8'-0"

FAMILY ROOM
13'-6" x 14'-0"

BATH

FOYER
7'-0" x 11'-0"

DINING ROOM
12'-0" x 11'-4"

TWO-CAR GARAGE
20'-0" x 22'-4"

GUEST ROOM/STUDY
11'-4" x 11'-0"

Design GG9900

First Floor: 1,103 square feet
Second Floor: 1,103 square feet
Total: 2,206 square feet
Bonus Room: 212 square feet

● A stucco exterior provides a European appeal for this family home. An expansive family room provides space for entertaining. The formal dining room is just off the foyer. Upstairs, the master suite includes a sitting area and an enormous bath with a dual vanity, a whirlpool tub, a separate shower and a walk-in closet. Two family bedrooms share a full bath with a dual vanity. The bonus room makes a great home office. This home is designed with a basement foundation.

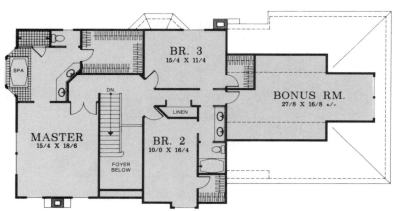

Width 72'
Depth 39'-6"

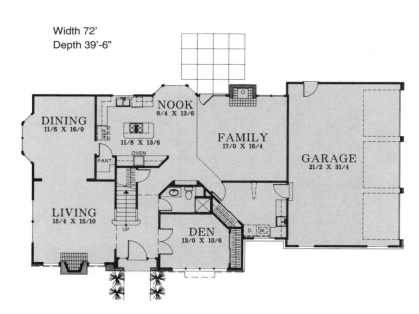

Design GG9438

First Floor: 1,595 square feet
Second Floor: 1,294 square feet
Total: 2,889 square feet
Bonus Room: 378 square feet

● Here's a great-looking Tudor with a splash of elegant brickwork. Its appealing style and functional design make it a very popular plan. The main floor den is arranged to work well as an office right off the entry with a pair of French doors. An open family room adjacent to the nook and kitchen heralds casual living. To the left are the formal living and dining areas. All the bedrooms are generously sized, especially the master which features all the amenities plus a huge walk-in closet. A large bonus room allows space for a fourth bedroom or a game room. The side-entry, three-car garage makes this a convenient plan for corner lots.

Design by
Alan Mascord
Design Associates, Inc.

118

Design GG9410

First Floor: 1,484 square feet
Second Floor: 1,402 square feet
Total: 2,886 square feet
Bonus Room: 430 square feet

● This impressive Tudor is designed for lots that slope up slightly from the street — the garage is five feet below the main floor. Just to the right of the entry, the den is arranged to work well as an office. Formal living areas include a living room with fireplace and an elegant dining room. The family room also has a fireplace and is close to the bumped-out nook — a great casual dining area. All the bedrooms are generously sized, especially the master which features all the amenities plus a huge walk-in closet. A large vaulted bonus room is provided with convenient access both from the family room and the upper hallway.

Design by
Alan Mascord
Design Associates, Inc.

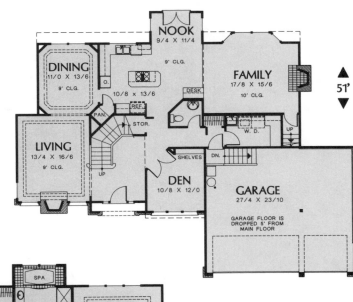

Design GG9440

First Floor: 1,758 square feet
Second Floor: 1,109 square feet
Total: 2,867 square feet
Bonus Room: 623 square feet

● Representing expansive elegance in a timeless design, this home offers as its focal point a graciously curved staircase in its two-story foyer. A second stairway leads to bonus space over the garage. Besides spacious living areas on the first floor, there is a powder room with shower which allows the den to serve as a guest room when needed. The family room features a fireplace and built-ins. To the rear of the second floor is the master suite containing a bay window overlooking the rear yard and a deluxe bath with spa tub. Two family bedrooms share a compartmented bath. An oversized three-car garage provides enough room for a workshop or additional storage space.

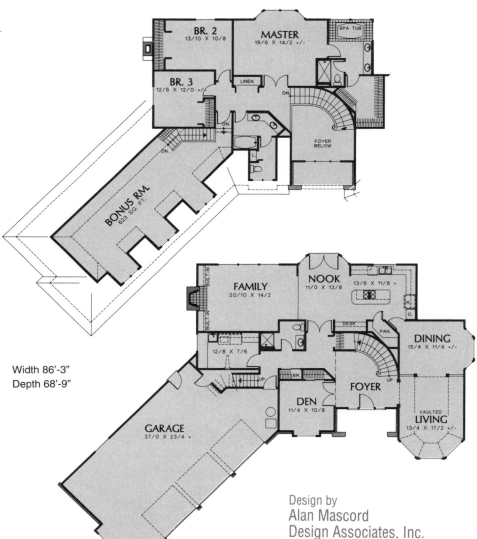

Width 86'-3"
Depth 68'-9"

Design by
Alan Mascord
Design Associates, Inc.

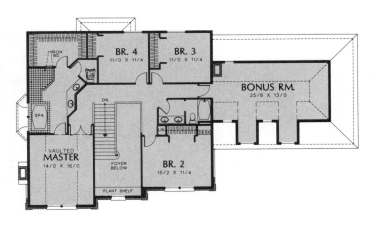

◄ 74' ►

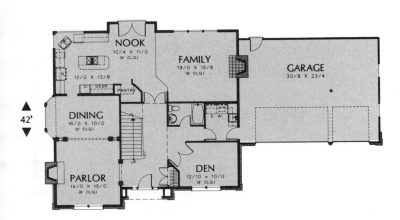

▲
42'
▼

Design GG9511

First Floor: 1,575 square feet
Second Floor: 1,329 square feet
Total: 2,904 square feet
Bonus Room: 424 square feet

● This elegant four-bedroom home easily accommodates the large family. A stately brick facade with twin chimneys greets visitors. A covered entryway leads to a two-story foyer with coat closet and plant shelf. A formal parlor with a fireplace is to the left, adjacent to the formal dining room with bay window. The kitchen provides an island cooktop, planning desk, pantry and breakfast nook. A second fireplace is located in the family room. With a full bath located on the first floor, the den can alternate as a guest room. The second floor offers four bedrooms and a large bonus room. The master bedroom with vaulted ceiling includes a luxurious bath with spa tub, dual vanities and a walk-in closet with a built-in ironing board.

Design by
Alan Mascord
Design Associates, Inc.

121

Design GG9541

First Floor: 1,214 square feet
Second Floor: 995 square feet
Total: 2,209 square feet
Bonus Room: 261 square feet

● A combined hip and gable roof, keystones and horizontal wood siding lend this lovely traditional home an air of distinction. The floor plan flows easily with the dining room to the left of the foyer and the living room to the right. The combined space at the rear portion of the house contains a family room with a fireplace, a bay-windowed breakfast nook with a door leading to the back yard and a step-saving kitchen. Upstairs, a master suite with a pampering master bath invites relaxation. Bedrooms 2 and 3 share a full bath, while the bonus space makes room for Bedroom 4. This plan includes an alternate side-load garage.

Design by
**Alan Mascord
Design Associates, Inc.**

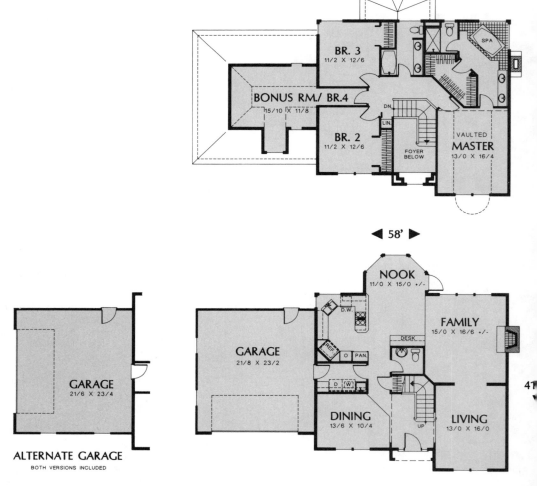

122

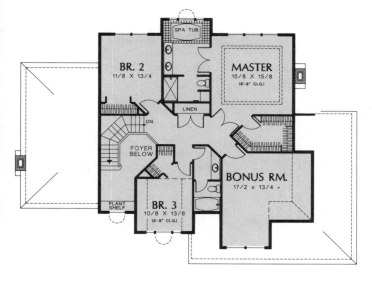

BR. 2
11/8 X 13/4

SPA TUB

MASTER
15/8 X 15/8
(9'-9" CLG.)

LINEN

DN.

FOYER
BELOW

BONUS RM.
17/2 x 13/4

PLANT
SHELF

BR. 3
10/8 X 13/6
(9'-9" CLG.)

◄ 63' ►

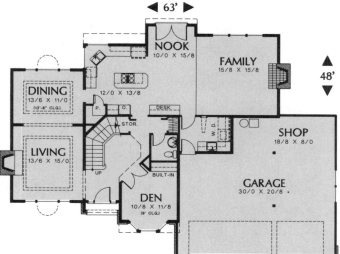

NOOK
10/0 X 15/8

FAMILY
15/8 X 15/8

48'

DINING
13/6 X 11/0
(13'-8" CLG.)

12/0 X 13/8

P.

O.

DESK

STOR.

W.D.

SHOP
18/8 X 8/0

LIVING
13/6 X 15/0

UP

BUILT-IN

DEN
10/8 X 11/8
(9' CLG.)

GARAGE
30/0 X 20/8

Design GG9542

First Floor: 1,465 square feet
Second Floor: 1,103 square feet
Total: 2,568 square feet
Bonus Room: 303 square feet

● Here's traditional style at its
best! The bay-windowed den
with built-in bookshelves is conveniently located to the front of
the plan, making it ideal for use
as an office or home-based business. To the left, the formal area
contains a living and dining
room, both with a tray ceiling.
Cooks will find the kitchen a
delight, with its sunlit corner
sink, cooktop island, large
pantry and built-in planning
desk. A bumped-out eating nook
opens to the rear yard through
double doors. Completing the
first floor is a spacious family
room with a fireplace. The second floor contains the sleeping
zone. A master suite with a
relaxing spa tub, a separate
shower and a huge walk-in closet is sure to please. Bedrooms 2
and 3 share a full bath. The
three-car garage provides ample
space for a workshop.

Design by
**Alan Mascord
Design Associates, Inc.**

Width 60'
Depth 76'-8"

fireplace

Family Room
vaulted ceiling
18⁰ · 16⁰

Breakfast
volume ceiling

Covered Patio

dw

Master
Bedroom
volume ceiling
16⁰ · 19⁰

Bedroom 2
volume ceiling
11⁰ · 10⁰

Kitchen

ref

pantry

Living Room
volume ceiling
14⁸ · 12⁰

Bath

n

up

w.i.c.

w.i.c.

Bedroom 3
11⁰ · 10⁸

storage

Dining
volume ceiling
10⁴ · 15⁰

Foyer

Den Study
volume ceiling
10⁰ · 10⁸

Bath

up

stor

Entry

Utility

d

ac

w

wh

Double Garage

down

Bonus Room
15⁸ · 23⁴

Design GG8681
Square Footage: 2,322
Bonus Room: 370 square feet

● Grand Palladian windows
create a classic look for this sensa-
tional stucco home. A magnificent
view from the living room provides
unlimited vistas of the rear grounds
through a wall of glass, with the
nearby dining room completing the
formal area. The kitchen, breakfast
nook and family room comprise the
family wing, coming together to
create the perfect place for casual
gatherings. Two secondary bedrooms share a bath and provide
complete privacy to the master suite
located on the opposite side of the
plan. The master bedroom sets the
mood for relaxation and the lavish
master bath pampers with a sumptuous soaking tub flanked by a step-
down shower and a compartmented
toilet. Bonus space may be completed at a later date to accommodate
additional space requirements.

Design by
Home Design
Services, Inc.

J.N. HANSEN P.T.L.

Design GG8682
Square Footage: 2,551
Bonus Room: 287 square feet

● Shutters and multi-pane windows dress up the exterior of this lovely stucco home. Formal and informal areas flow easily, beginning with the dining room sized to accommodate large parties and function with the adjacent living room. This area is joined to the family room by an archway, thus allowing easy circulation during large gatherings. A gourmet kitchen is complete with a walk-in pantry and is a step away from the breakfast nook. Double doors lead to the spacious master suite. The lavish master bath features His and Hers walk-in closets, a tub framed by a column archway and an over-sized shower. Off the angular hallway are two bedrooms that share a pullman-style bath and a study desk. A bonus room over the garage provides additional space.

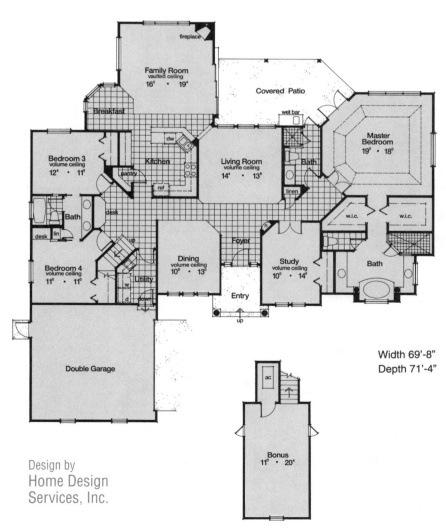

Width 69'-8"
Depth 71'-4"

Design by
Home Design
Services, Inc.

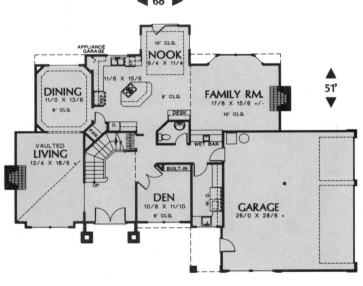

◀ 68' ▶

APPLIANCE
GARAGE

NOOK
9/4 X 11/4
10' CLG.

11/8 X 15/6

DINING
11/0 X 13/6
9' CLG.

FAMILY RM.
17/8 X 15/6 +/-
10' CLG.

9' CLG.

DESK

▲
51'
▼

VAULTED
LIVING
13/4 X 18/6

WET BAR

BUILT-IN

UP

DEN
10/8 X 11/10
9' CLG.

W.O.

GARAGE
26/0 X 28/6

Design GG9400

First Floor: 1,618 square feet
Second Floor: 1,212 square feet
Total: 2,830 square feet
Bonus Room: 376 square feet

● This attractive European-styled plan
has a stucco finish and arched windows
complementing the facade. Nine-foot
ceilings are standard throughout both
levels with some areas, such as the
nook, family room and master bedroom,
having ten-foot ceilings. From the two-
story foyer with its angled stair, look to
the dramatically vaulted living room on
one side and den with French doors on
the other. Upstairs a sumptuous master
suite includes spa tub, shower and large
walk-in closet. Over the garage is a
vaulted bonus room, perfect as a game
or hobby room.

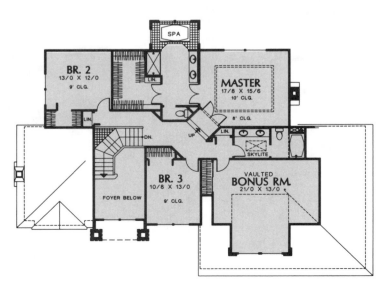

SPA

BR. 2
13/0 X 12/0
9' CLG.

LIN.

MASTER
17/8 X 15/6
10' CLG.

LIN.

8' CLG.

DN.

UP

LIN.

SKYLITE

BR. 3
10/8 X 13/0
9' CLG.

FOYER BELOW

VAULTED
BONUS RM.
21/0 X 13/0

Design by
Alan Mascord
Design Associates, Inc.

◄ 63' ►

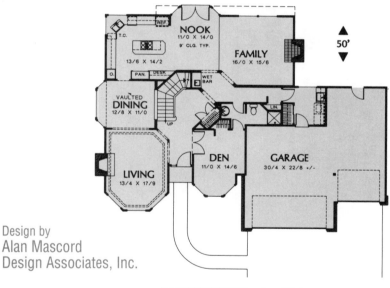

Design by
Alan Mascord
Design Associates, Inc.

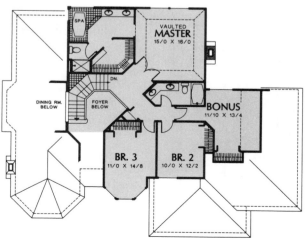

Design GG9478

First Floor: 1,586 square feet
Second Floor: 960 square feet
Total: 2,546 square feet
Bonus Room: 194 square feet

● This exquisite plan features two tower structures that enhance its dramatic facade. Inside, it contains a beautifully functioning room arrangement that caters to family lifestyles. The living areas radiate around the central hallway which also contains the stairway to the second floor. The areas are large, open and convenient for both casual and formal occasions. Three bedrooms upstairs include two family bedrooms and a grand master suite with a bath fit for a king. An oversized walk-in closet and vaulted ceiling are found here. Bonus space over the garage can be developed at a later time to suit changing needs.

Design GG3351

First Floor: 1,794 square feet

Second Floor: 887 square feet

Total: 2,681 square feet

Bonus Room: 720 square feet

L **D**

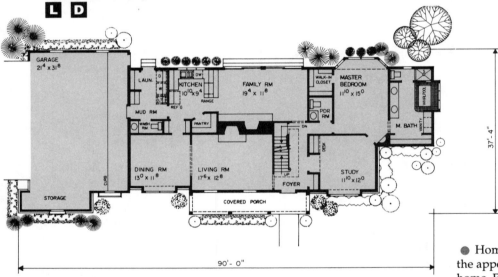

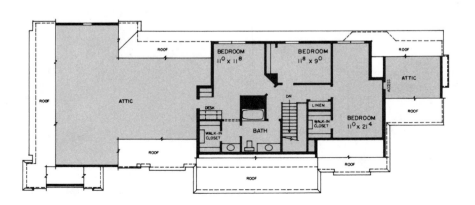

● Home-grown comfort is the key to the appeal of this traditionally styled home. From the kitchen with attached family room to the living room with fireplace and attached formal dining room, this plan has it all. Notice the first-floor master bedroom with whirlpool tub and adjacent study. A nearby powder room turns the study into a convenient guest room. On the second floor are three more bedrooms with ample closet space and a full bath. The two-car garage has a large storage area.

Design by
Home Planners,
Inc.

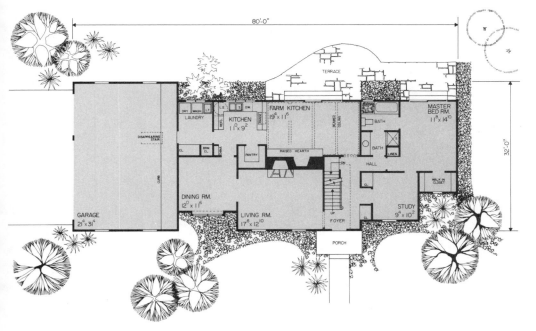

80'-0"

32'-0"

GARAGE 21⁴ x 31⁴

DISAPPEARING STAIR

LAUNDRY

DRY WASH

KITCHEN 11⁰ x 9²

FARM KITCHEN 19⁴ x 11⁶

BATH

BATH

MASTER BED RM. 11⁸ x 14¹⁰

TERRACE

PANTRY

RAISED HEARTH

HALL

LINEN

WALK IN CLOSET

DINING RM. 12⁰ x 11⁶

LIVING RM. 17⁸ x 12¹⁰

FOYER

UP

DN

STUDY 9⁴ x 10²

PORCH

BED RM. 11⁶ x 11⁴

SITTING RM. 9⁴ x 9⁰

BED RM. 11⁰ x 17⁸

STORAGE OVER GARAGE

ROOF

ATTIC

HALL

DN

WALK IN CLOSET

STOR.

BATH

SHELVES

ACCESS

ATTIC

ATTIC

ACCESS

ROOF

Design GG2563

First Floor: 1,500 square feet
Second Floor: 690 square feet
Total: 2,190 square feet
Bonus Room: 1990 square feet

L D

● This charming Cape Cod definitely will capture your heart with its warm appeal. This home offers you and your family a lot of livability. Upon entering this home, to your left, is a nice-sized living room with fireplace. Adjacent is a dining room. An efficient kitchen and a large, farm kitchen eating area with fireplace will be enjoyed by all. A unique feature on this floor is the master bedroom with a full bath and walk-in closet. Also take notice of the first-floor laundry, the pantry and a study for all of your favorite books. Note the sliding glass doors in the farm kitchen and master bedroom. Upstairs you'll find two bedrooms, one with a walk-in closet. Also here, a sitting room and a full bath are available. Lastly, this design accommodates a three-car garage.

QUOTE ONE™

Cost to build? See page 232 to order complete cost estimate to build this house in your area!

CUSTOMIZABLE

Custom Alterations? See page 237 for customizing this plan to your specifications.

Design by
Home Planners,
Inc.

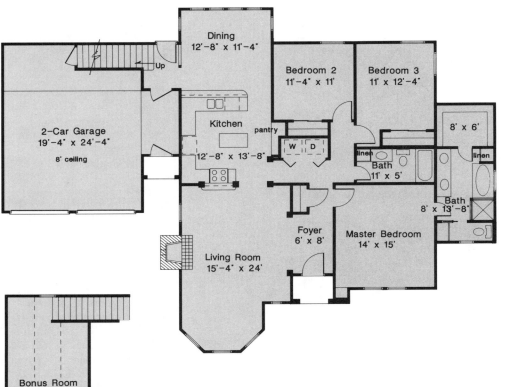

Dining
12'-8" x 11'-4"

Up

Bedroom 2
11'-4" x 11'

Bedroom 3
11' x 12'-4"

2-Car Garage
19'-4" x 24'-4"
8' ceiling

Kitchen
12'-8" x 13'-8"

pantry

W   D

8' x 6'

linen

Bath
11' x 5'

linen

Bath
8' x 13'-8"

Design by
Larry W.
Garnett &
Associates, Inc.

Width 69'-8"
Depth 50'-6"

Foyer
6' x 8'

Master Bedroom
14' x 15'

Living Room
15'-4" x 24'

Bonus Room
11'-4" x 20'-8"+
8' ceiling

4' high wall

Design GG8981
Square Footage: 1,703
Bonus Room: 280 square feet

● This quaint cottage features a shingled exterior reminiscent of the homes often found in coastal areas. A living room is located to the left of the foyer, creating special interest with a bay window and a warmly welcoming fireplace. The efficient U-shaped kitchen and dining room combine to makes meal preparation a breeze. On the right side of the plan rests the sleeping wing. The pleasant master suite sports double-bowl vanities, a separate tub and shower and a large walk-in closet. Two additional bedrooms share a full bath. For future use, a bonus room is conveniently located over the garage.

5

DAYLIGHT BASEMENT DESIGNS

Building a Strong Foundation for Family Living

A basement that has been thoughtfully planned provides a hub for family activities and enhances indoor/outdoor living relationships with the easy access it provides to the rear or side yards. Besides providing casual living space enjoyed by the entire family, many basement plans offer sleeping quarters that accommodate those family members seeking an extra measure of privacy.

Many one-story homes double their square footage through the use of a basement. Utilization of this space can result in floor plans large enough to lodge any size family. Design GG9831 on page 132 provides space for gatherings by developing the family and recreation rooms as well as an additional bedroom and bath. Another example is shown on page 134 (Design GG9844). It offers room for family activities as well as a guest suite, media room and a workshop to house individual endeavors.

If a swimming pool plays a role in your leisure time, Design GG7222 (page 138) presents a fine basement option. It includes a separate entry that leads to the lower level dressing area and bath facility, and continues into the family room complete with a snack bar, two bedrooms and a bath to round out livability.

An interesting variation of the traditional basement is the island basement, which is also represented in this section. This type of basement is often found in flood regions and used for island-style or tidewater area homes that are elevated on pilings to conform to building requirements. The lower area provides finish-later space for a media or game room, workshop, home office or exercise facility, with additional space to park vehicles. Designs GG6621, GG6615 and GG6616 (see pages 145, 147 and 148) provide fine examples of this unique style.

Not to be forgotten is the use of lower-level living during the summer months to beat the heat. Any cook faced with meal preparation on a hot afternoon will appreciate the cool summer kitchen that Design GG2847 (page 162) employs. Rounding out the remaining portion of this basement is a family room, a bedroom which doubles as a study, and easy access to the back yard where you may enjoy a relaxing swim or sooth away tension in a hot tub or sauna.

These alternatives are intended to give you ideas for integrating basement design with daily activities. The following pages contain a great collection of plans with skillfully designed basements that offer an abundance of possibilities sure to suit your needs.

WIDTH 64'
DEPTH 64'-4"

Design by
Design Traditions

Design GG9831
Square Footage: 2,150
Basement Features: Bedroom, Family & Recreation Room (2,150 sq. ft.)

● This home draws its inspiration from both French and English country homes. From the foyer and across the spacious great room, French doors give a generous view of the covered rear porch. The adjoining dining room is subtly defined by the use of columns and a large triple window. The kitchen, with its generous work-island, adjoins the breakfast area and keeping room with a fireplace, a vaulted ceiling and an abundant use of windows. A bedroom to the front of the first floor may act as guest quarters. Another bedroom shares a bath with this one. The home is completed by a quiet master suite located at the rear. It contains a bay window, a garden tub and His and Hers vanities. Space on the lower level can be developed later.

Design GG9843 Square Footage: 2,120
Basement Features: Bedroom, Media & Recreation Room (1,191 sq. ft.)

● As quaint as the European countryside, this charming cottage boasts a unique interior. Living patterns revolve around the central family room—notice the placement of the formal dining room, the kitchen with an attached breakfast nook and the sun room. Family bedrooms are tucked quietly away to the rear, while the master suite maintains privacy at the opposite end of the plan. A den with a fireplace attaches to the master bedroom or can be accessed from the entry foyer. Bonus space in the basement can be developed later.

Width 62'
Depth 62'-6"

133

Design GG9844

Square Footage: 2,090

Basement Features: Workshop, Game, Media & Family Rooms, Bedroom (2,090 sq. ft.)

Design by
Design Traditions

● Grace and elegance in one-story living abound in this traditional English country home. It contains all the necessary elements of a convenient floor plan as well: great room with fireplace, formal dining room, kitchen with attached breakfast nook, guest room/office and three bedrooms including a master suite. A large, unfinished basement area allows a variety of options for future expansion.

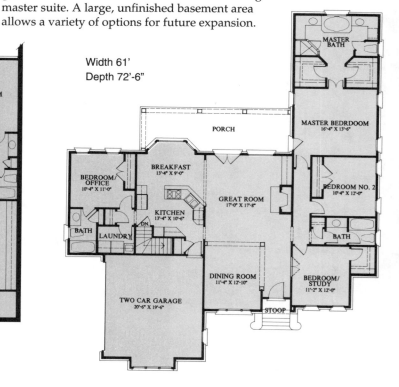

Width 61'
Depth 72'-6"

Design GG9846

Square Footage: 2,295

**Basement Features: Recreation & Game Rooms, Bedroom & Bath
(2,295 sq. ft.)**

● The abundance of details in this plan make it the finest in one-story living. The great room and formal dining room are loosely defined by a simple column at the entry foyer, allowing for an open, dramatic sense of space. The kitchen with prep island shares the right side of the plan with a bayed breakfast area and keeping room with fireplace. Sleeping accommodations to the left of the plan include a master suite with sitting area, double closet and separate tub and shower. Two family bedrooms share a full bath. Additional living and sleeping space can be developed in the unfinished basement.

Design by
Design Traditions

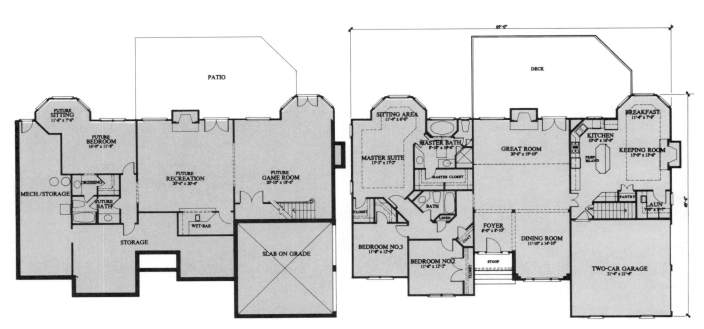

Design by
Design Traditions

Design GG9839 Square Footage: 1,800
Basement Features: Family Room, Guest Room & Bath (981 sq. ft.)

● This European-inspired cottage contains one of the most efficient floor plans available. From the formal dining room at the front of the plan to the commodious great room at the rear, it accommodates various lifestyles in less than 2,000 square feet. An opulent master suite with deck access and grand bath dominates the right wing of the house. Two family bedrooms and a full bath are found to the left. There's even a powder room for guests. The gourmet-style kitchen has an attached breakfast area with glassed bay for sunny brunches. Bonus space in the basement allows for future development.

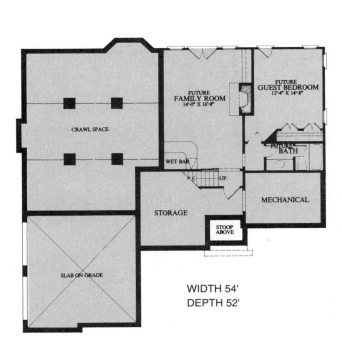

WIDTH 54'
DEPTH 52'

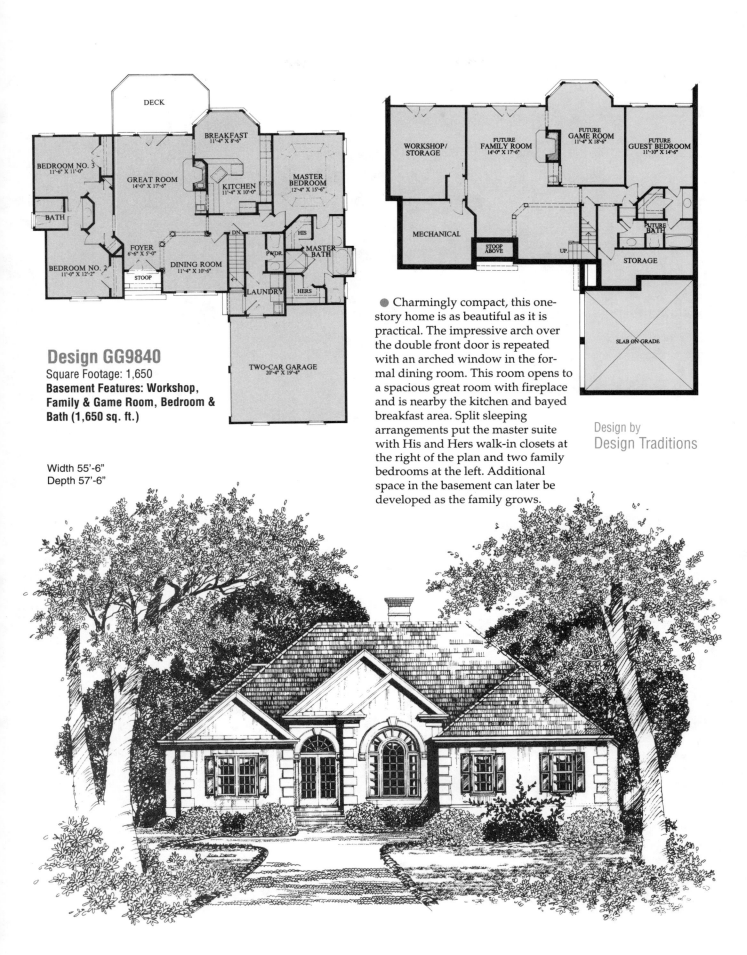

DECK

BREAKFAST
11'-4" X 8'-6"

BEDROOM NO. 3
11'-6" X 11'-0"

GREAT ROOM
14'-0" X 17'-6"

KITCHEN
11'-4" X 10'-0"

MASTER
BEDROOM
12'-4" X 15'-6"

BATH

DN

HIS

FOYER
6'-6" X 5'-0"

BEDROOM NO. 2
11'-0" X 12'-2"

DINING ROOM
11'-4" X 10'-6"

PWDR.

MASTER
BATH

STOOP

LAUNDRY

HERS

Design GG9840
Square Footage: 1,650
**Basement Features: Workshop,
Family & Game Room, Bedroom &
Bath (1,650 sq. ft.)**

TWO-CAR GARAGE
20'-4" X 19'-4"

Width 55'-6"
Depth 57'-6"

WORKSHOP/
STORAGE

FUTURE
FAMILY ROOM
14'-0" X 17'-6"

FUTURE
GAME ROOM
11'-4" X 18'-6"

FUTURE
GUEST BEDROOM
11'-10" X 14'-6"

MECHANICAL

STOOP
ABOVE

UP

FUTURE
BATH

STORAGE

SLAB ON GRADE

● Charmingly compact, this one-story home is as beautiful as it is practical. The impressive arch over the double front door is repeated with an arched window in the formal dining room. This room opens to a spacious great room with fireplace and is nearby the kitchen and bayed breakfast area. Split sleeping arrangements put the master suite with His and Hers walk-in closets at the right of the plan and two family bedrooms at the left. Additional space in the basement can later be developed as the family grows.

Design by
Design Traditions

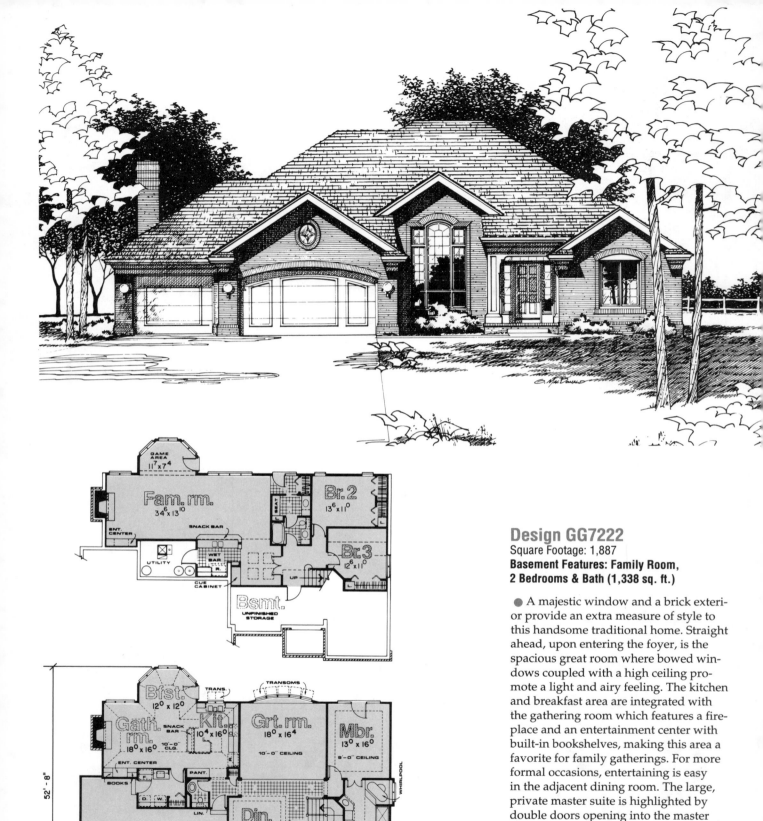

Design GG7222

Square Footage: 1,887
**Basement Features: Family Room,
2 Bedrooms & Bath (1,338 sq. ft.)**

● A majestic window and a brick exterior provide an extra measure of style to this handsome traditional home. Straight ahead, upon entering the foyer, is the spacious great room where bowed windows coupled with a high ceiling promote a light and airy feeling. The kitchen and breakfast area are integrated with the gathering room which features a fireplace and an entertainment center with built-in bookshelves, making this area a favorite for family gatherings. For more formal occasions, entertaining is easy in the adjacent dining room. The large, private master suite is highlighted by double doors opening into the master dressing area which features angled lavs and a huge walk-in closet complete with a cedar chest. The basement is designed for finishing as space is needed.

Design by
Design
Basics,
Inc.

Design GG9393

Square Footage: 2,317
**Basement Features: Family Room,
2 Bedrooms & Bath (1,475 sq. ft.)**

● A lower-level option turns this tidy
one-story home into a much larger
plan—and accommodates a hillside
nicely. The main level contains the basic
living areas: a great room with a
through-fireplace to the hearth room, a
formal dining room with a bay window
and a kitchen with informal eating space.
The master bedroom, also on this level,
has a wonderfully appointed bath and its
own sitting room. An additional bedroom may serve as a den. The lower
level, when finished, contains space for a
family room with a wet bar and snack
counter, plus two bedrooms and a bath.

Design by
Design
Basics,
Inc.

© design basics inc. 1992

139

Design GG9543 Square Footage: 2,188
Basement Features: Recreation Room, 2 Bedrooms & Bath (1,049 sq. ft.)

● Carriage lamps and brick columns provide a dramatic element to the impressive entry to this one-story traditional. The well-designed floor plan flows nicely. The den is ideally located for use as an office if the need arises. To the left rests the formal living and dining area which provides nearby access to the step-sav-ing kitchen. The family room is separated only by the breakfast nook, which provides access to the rear deck. The master suite, with its tray ceiling and luxurious bath, completes the first floor. The basement contains a recreation room, two secondary bedrooms (one with access to the rear grounds) and a full bath.

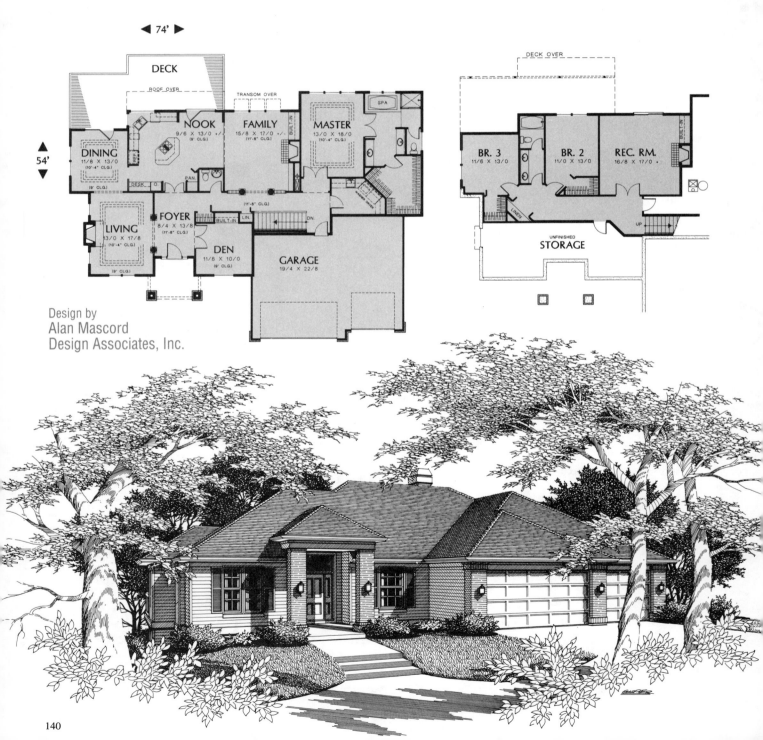

Design by
Alan Mascord
Design Associates, Inc.

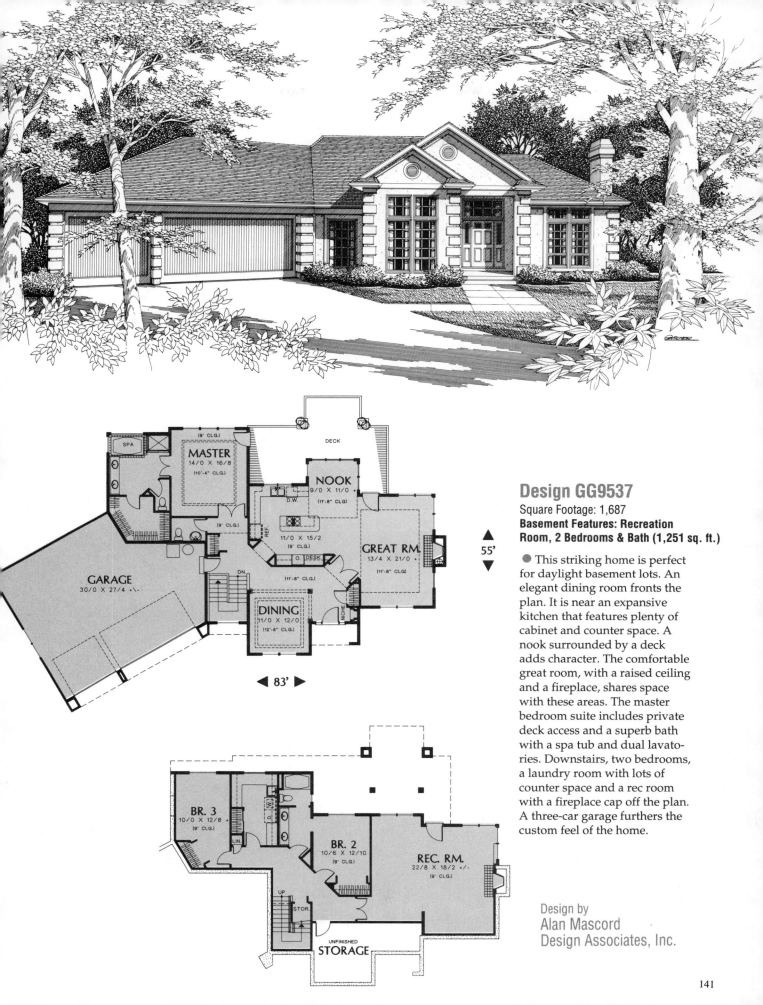

Design GG9537

Square Footage: 1,687
Basement Features: Recreation Room, 2 Bedrooms & Bath (1,251 sq. ft.)

● This striking home is perfect for daylight basement lots. An elegant dining room fronts the plan. It is near an expansive kitchen that features plenty of cabinet and counter space. A nook surrounded by a deck adds character. The comfortable great room, with a raised ceiling and a fireplace, shares space with these areas. The master bedroom suite includes private deck access and a superb bath with a spa tub and dual lavatories. Downstairs, two bedrooms, a laundry room with lots of counter space and a rec room with a fireplace cap off the plan. A three-car garage furthers the custom feel of the home.

Design by
Alan Mascord
Design Associates, Inc.

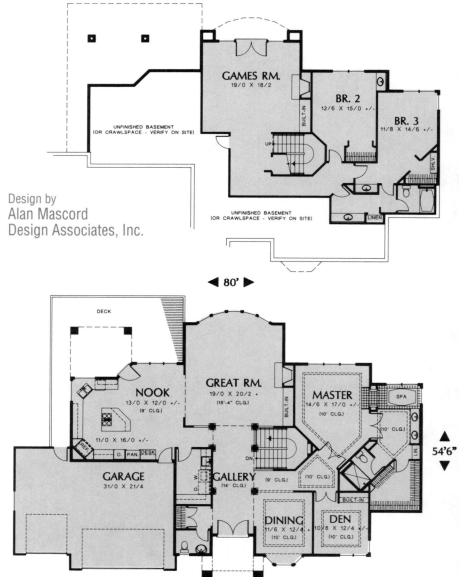

Design by
Alan Mascord
Design Associates, Inc.

Design GG9539

Square Footage: 2,219
Basement Features: Game Room, 2 Bedrooms & Bath (1,324 sq. ft.)

● Sleek lines define the contemporary feel of this home. Double entry doors lead to a columned gallery and an expressive great room. It showcases a fireplace, built-ins and a curving wall of windows. The nearby kitchen utilizes efficient zoning. A nook here opens to a wraparound deck. A dining room and a den finish the first-floor living areas. In the master bedroom suite, large proportions and an elegant bath with a see-through fireplace aim to please. The two bedrooms in the basement have in-room vanities; one has direct access to the compartmented bath. A game room with a fireplace and built-ins leads to outdoor livability.

GAMES RM.
26/8 X 19/0

BR. 2
12/8 X 12/8 +

OPTIONAL
WET BAR

UP

STOR

LINEN

BR. 3
13/0 X 13/0

BR. 4
11/0 X 11/6

◀ 71' ▶

COVERED DECK

DECK

DINING
10/8 X 14/0

LIVING
16/8 X 15/0

BUILT-INS

NOOK
10/0 x 10/4

FAMILY
14/8 X 16/0

MASTER
17/8 X 15/0

BOOKSHELF

SPA

▲
56'
▼

GALLERY

REF. PAN.

DN.

BUILT-IN

GARAGE
32/4 X 23/2 +/-

DEN
12/4 X 14/4 +/-

Design by
Alan Mascord
Design Associates, Inc.

Design GG9417
Square Footage: 2,196
**Basement Features: Game Room,
3 Bedrooms & Bath (1,542 sq. ft.)**

● This refined home is
designed for lots that fall off
toward the rear and works especially well with a view out the
back. The kitchen and eating nook
wrap around the vaulted family
room with its arched transom windows flanking the fireplace.
Directly off the nook is a covered
deck. Don't miss the huge game
room on the lower level.

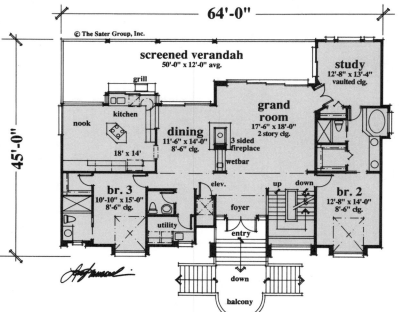

64'-0"

© The Sater Group, Inc.

screened verandah
50'-0" x 12'-0" avg.

grill

kitchen

nook

18' x 14'

dining
11'-6" x 14'-0"
8'-6" clg.

grand
room
17'-6" x 18'-0"
2 story clg.

study
12'-8" x 13'-4"
vaulted clg.

3 sided
fireplace

wetbar

45'-0"

br. 3
10'-10" x 15'-0"
8'-6" clg.

elev.

up   down

br. 2
12'-8" x 14'-0"
8'-6" clg.

utility

foyer

entry

down

balcony

Design GG6620 First Floor: 2,066 square feet
Second Floor: 810 square feet; Total: 2,876 square feet
Basement Feature: Island Basement (1,260 sq. ft.)

● If entertaining's your passion, then this is the
design for you. With a large, open floor plan and
an array of amenities, every gathering will be a
success. The foyer embraces living areas accented
by a glass fireplace and a wet bar. The living and
dining rooms each access a screened entertainment
center for outside enjoyments. The gourmet
kitchen delights with its openness to the rest of the
house. A morning room here also adds a nice
touch. Two bedrooms and a den radiate from the
first-floor living areas. Upstairs—or use the eleva-
tor—is a masterful master suite. It contains a huge
walk-in closet, a whirlpool tub and a private sun
deck. This home is designed with an island
basement.

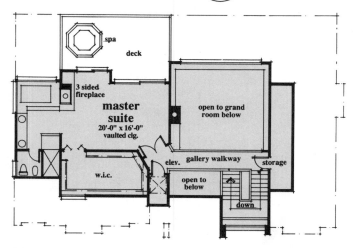

spa

deck

3 sided
fireplace

master
suite
20'-0" x 16'-0"
vaulted clg.

open to grand
room below

gallery walkway

w.i.c.

elev.

storage

open to
below

down

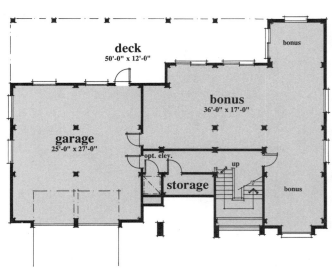

deck
50'-0" x 12'-0"

bonus

garage
25'-0" x 27'-0"

bonus
36'-0" x 17'-0"

opt. elev.

storage

up

bonus

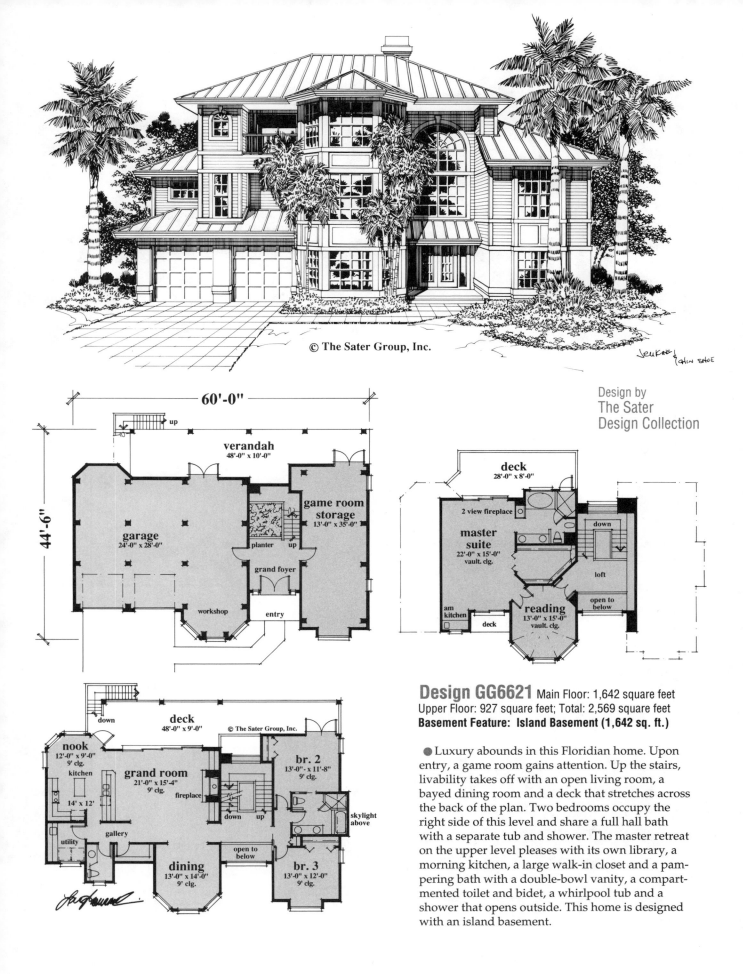

© The Sater Group, Inc.

Jenkins

Design by
The Sater
Design Collection

60'-0"

44'-6"

verandah
48'-0" x 10'-0"

garage
24'-0" x 28'-0"

game room
storage
13'-0" x 35'-0"

planter   up

grand foyer

workshop   **entry**

deck
28'-0" x 8'-0"

2 view fireplace

master
suite
22'-0" x 15'-0"
vault. clg.

down

loft

open to
below

am
kitchen

deck

reading
13'-0" x 15'-0"
vault. clg.

down

deck
48'-0" x 9'-0"

© The Sater Group, Inc.

nook
12'-0" x 9'-0"
9' clg.

kitchen

14' x 12'

grand room
21'-0" x 15'-4"
9' clg.

fireplace

br. 2
13'-0" x 11'-8"
9' clg.

down   up

skylight
above

utility

gallery

open to
below

dining
13'-0" x 14'-0"
9' clg.

br. 3
13'-0" x 12'-0"
9' clg.

Design GG6621 Main Floor: 1,642 square feet

Upper Floor: 927 square feet; Total: 2,569 square feet
Basement Feature: Island Basement (1,642 sq. ft.)

● Luxury abounds in this Floridian home. Upon entry, a game room gains attention. Up the stairs, livability takes off with an open living room, a bayed dining room and a deck that stretches across the back of the plan. Two bedrooms occupy the right side of this level and share a full hall bath with a separate tub and shower. The master retreat on the upper level pleases with its own library, a morning kitchen, a large walk-in closet and a pampering bath with a double-bowl vanity, a compartmented toilet and bidet, a whirlpool tub and a shower that opens outside. This home is designed with an island basement.

Design GG6618

First Floor: 1,944 square feet
Second Floor: 1,196 square feet
Total: 3,140 square feet
Basement Feature: Island Basement (1,940 sq. ft.)

● In the grand room of this home, family and friends will enjoy the ambience created by arches and access to a veranda. Two guest rooms flank a full bath—one of the guest rooms also sports a private deck. The kitchen services a circular breakfast nook. Upstairs, a balcony overlook furthers the drama of the great room. The master suite, with a deck and a private bath opening through a pocket door, will be a pleasure to occupy. Another bedroom—or use this room for a study—sits at the other side of this floor. It extends a curved bay window, an expansive deck, built-ins and a full bath. This home is designed with an island basement.

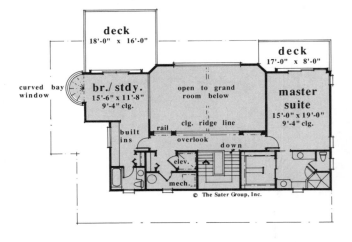

deck
18'-0" x 16'-0"

deck
17'-0" x 8'-0"

curved bay window

br./stdy.
15'-6" x 11'-8"
9'-4" clg.

open to grand room below

master suite
15'-0" x 19'-0"
9'-4" clg.

clg. ridge line

built ins

rail

overlook

down

elev.

mech.

Design by
**The Sater
Design Collection**

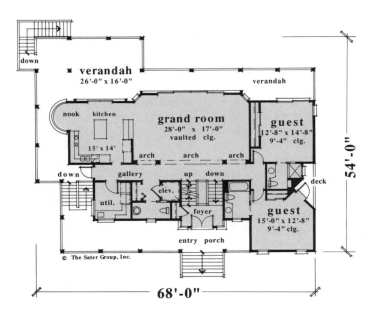

verandah
26'-0" x 16'-0"

verandah

nook   kitchen

15' x 14'

grand room
28'-0" x 17'-0"
vaulted clg.

guest
12'-8" x 14'-8"
9'-4" clg.

arch   arch   arch

down

gallery   up   down

elev.

util.

foyer

deck

guest
15'-0" x 12'-8"
9'-4" clg.

entry porch

54'-0"

68'-0"

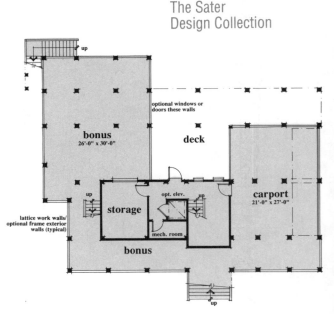

up

bonus
26'-0" x 30'-0"

optional windows or doors these walls

deck

up

opt. elev.

up

storage

carport
21'-0" x 27'-0"

mech. room

lattice work walls/
optional frame exterior
walls (typical)

bonus

146

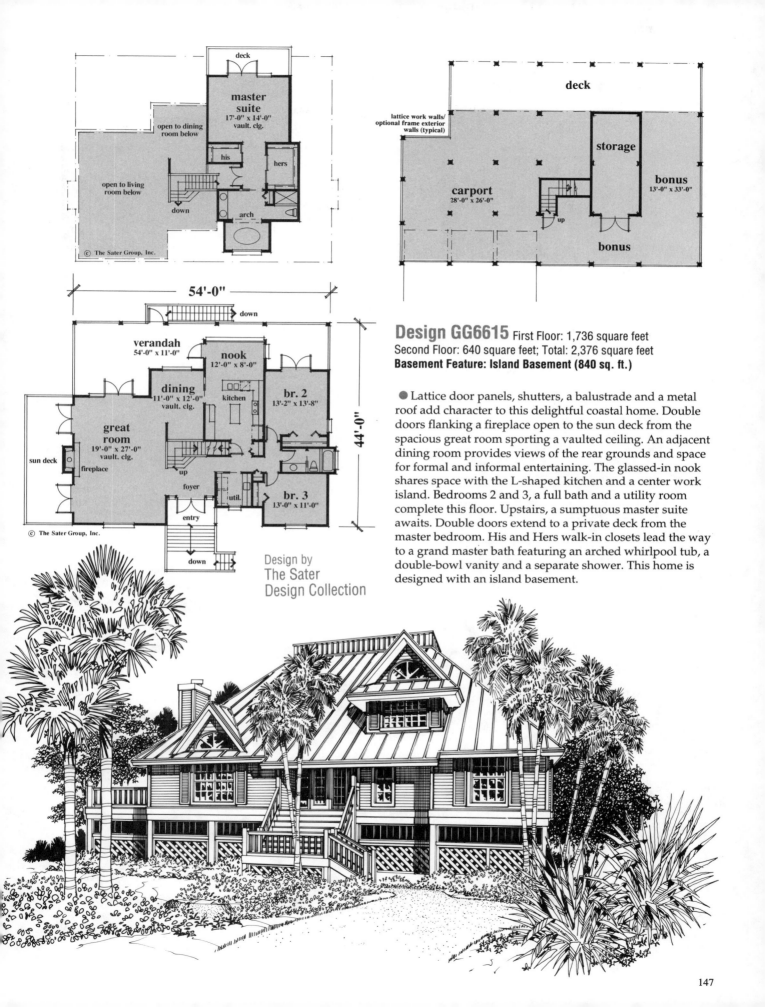

deck

master suite
17'-0" x 14'-0"
vault. clg.

open to dining room below

his

hers

open to living room below

down

arch

© The Sater Group, Inc.

deck

lattice work walls/
optional frame exterior
walls (typical)

storage

carport
28'-0" x 26'-0"

up

bonus
13'-0" x 33'-0"

bonus

54'-0"

down

verandah
54'-0" x 11'-0"

nook
12'-0" x 8'-0"

dining
11'-0" x 12'-0"
vault. clg.

kitchen

br. 2
13'-2" x 13'-8"

44'-0"

great room
19'-0" x 27'-0"
vault. clg.

sun deck

fireplace

up

foyer

util.

br. 3
13'-0" x 11'-0"

entry

down

© The Sater Group, Inc.

Design by
The Sater
Design Collection

Design GG6615 First Floor: 1,736 square feet
Second Floor: 640 square feet; Total: 2,376 square feet
Basement Feature: Island Basement (840 sq. ft.)

● Lattice door panels, shutters, a balustrade and a metal roof add character to this delightful coastal home. Double doors flanking a fireplace open to the sun deck from the spacious great room sporting a vaulted ceiling. An adjacent dining room provides views of the rear grounds and space for formal and informal entertaining. The glassed-in nook shares space with the L-shaped kitchen and a center work island. Bedrooms 2 and 3, a full bath and a utility room complete this floor. Upstairs, a sumptuous master suite awaits. Double doors extend to a private deck from the master bedroom. His and Hers walk-in closets lead the way to a grand master bath featuring an arched whirlpool tub, a double-bowl vanity and a separate shower. This home is designed with an island basement.

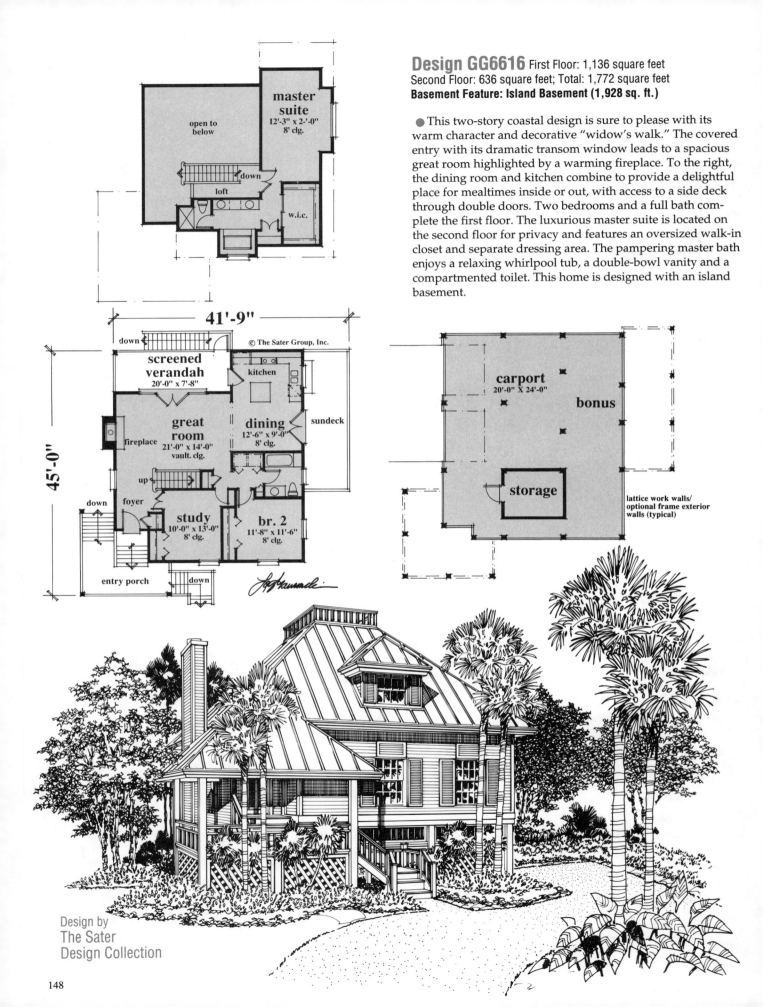

master suite
12'-3" x 2'-0"
8' clg.

open to below

down

loft

w.i.c.

Design GG6616 First Floor: 1,136 square feet
Second Floor: 636 square feet; Total: 1,772 square feet
Basement Feature: Island Basement (1,928 sq. ft.)

● This two-story coastal design is sure to please with its warm character and decorative "widow's walk." The covered entry with its dramatic transom window leads to a spacious great room highlighted by a warming fireplace. To the right, the dining room and kitchen combine to provide a delightful place for mealtimes inside or out, with access to a side deck through double doors. Two bedrooms and a full bath complete the first floor. The luxurious master suite is located on the second floor for privacy and features an oversized walk-in closet and separate dressing area. The pampering master bath enjoys a relaxing whirlpool tub, a double-bowl vanity and a compartmented toilet. This home is designed with an island basement.

41'-9"

45'-0"

down

© The Sater Group, Inc.

screened verandah
20'-0" x 7'-8"

kitchen

great room
21'-0" x 14'-0"
vault. clg.

fireplace

dining
12'-6" x 9'-0"
8' clg.

sundeck

up

foyer

down

study
10'-0" x 13'-0"
8' clg.

br. 2
11'-8" x 11'-6"
8' clg.

entry porch

down

carport
20'-0" X 24'-0"

bonus

storage

lattice work walls/
optional frame exterior
walls (typical)

Design by
**The Sater
Design Collection**

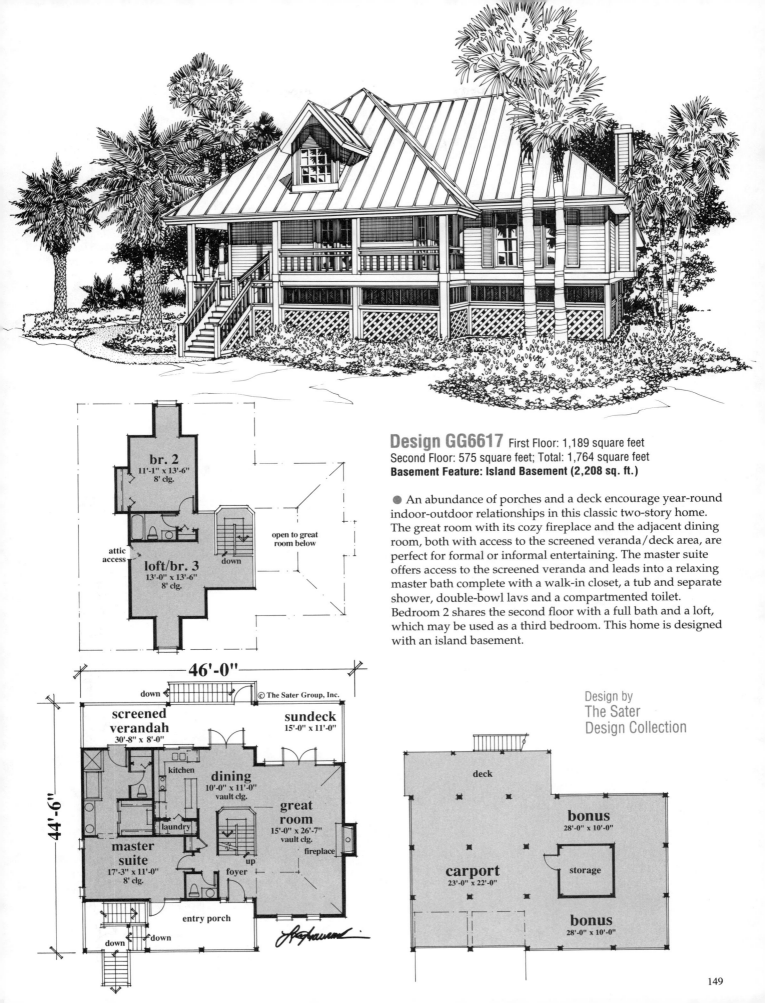

br. 2
11'-1" x 13'-6"
8' clg.

attic access

loft/br. 3
13'-0" x 13'-6"
8' clg.

down

open to great room below

Design GG6617 First Floor: 1,189 square feet
Second Floor: 575 square feet; Total: 1,764 square feet
Basement Feature: Island Basement (2,208 sq. ft.)

● An abundance of porches and a deck encourage year-round indoor-outdoor relationships in this classic two-story home. The great room with its cozy fireplace and the adjacent dining room, both with access to the screened veranda/deck area, are perfect for formal or informal entertaining. The master suite offers access to the screened veranda and leads into a relaxing master bath complete with a walk-in closet, a tub and separate shower, double-bowl lavs and a compartmented toilet. Bedroom 2 shares the second floor with a full bath and a loft, which may be used as a third bedroom. This home is designed with an island basement.

Design by
The Sater
Design Collection

46'-0"

down

© The Sater Group, Inc.

screened verandah
30'-8" x 8'-0"

sundeck
15'-0" x 11'-0"

kitchen

dining
10'-0" x 11'-0"
vault clg.

great room
15'-0" x 26'-7"
vault clg.

fireplace

laundry

up

44'-6"

master suite
17'-3" x 11'-0"
8' clg.

foyer

entry porch

down down

deck

bonus
28'-0" x 10'-0"

carport
23'-0" x 22'-0"

storage

bonus
28'-0" x 10'-0"

© The Sater Group, Inc.

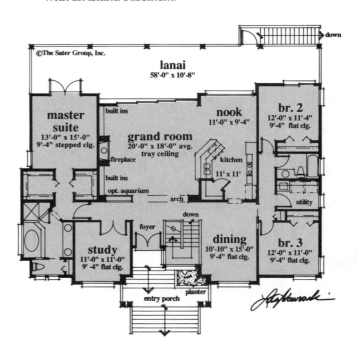

Design GG6622 Square Footage: 2,190
Basement Feature: Island Basement (1,966 sq. ft.)

● A dramatic set of stairs leads to the entry of this home. The foyer leads to an expansive grand room with a fireplace and built-in bookshelves. A lanai opens off this area and will assure outdoor enjoyments. For formal meals, a front-facing dining room offers a bumped-out bay. The kitchen serves this area easily as well as the breakfast room. A study, the master suite and two secondary bedrooms which share a full hall bath make up the rest of the floor plan. A utility area is also nearby. In the master suite, two walk-in closets and a full bath are appreciated features. In the bedroom, a set of French doors offers passage to the lanai. This home is designed with an island basement.

verandah
58'-0" x 12'-0"

recreation
25'-0" x 35'-0"

storage

garage
23'-4" x 24'-0"

up

up

Width 58'
Depth 54'

Design by
The Sater
Design Collection

© The Sater Group, Inc.

lanai
58'-0" x 10'-8"

down

master suite
13'-0" x 15'-0"
9'-4" stepped clg.

built ins

nook
11'-0" x 9'-4"

br. 2
12'-0" x 11'-4"
9'-4" flat clg.

grand room
20'-0" x 18'-0" avg.
tray ceiling

kitchen
11' x 11'

fireplace

built ins

opt. aquarium

arch

utility

down

foyer

study
11'-0" x 11'-0"
9'-4" flat clg.

dining
10'-10" x 15'-0"
9'-4" flat clg.

br. 3
12'-0" x 11'-0"
9'-4" flat clg.

entry porch

planter

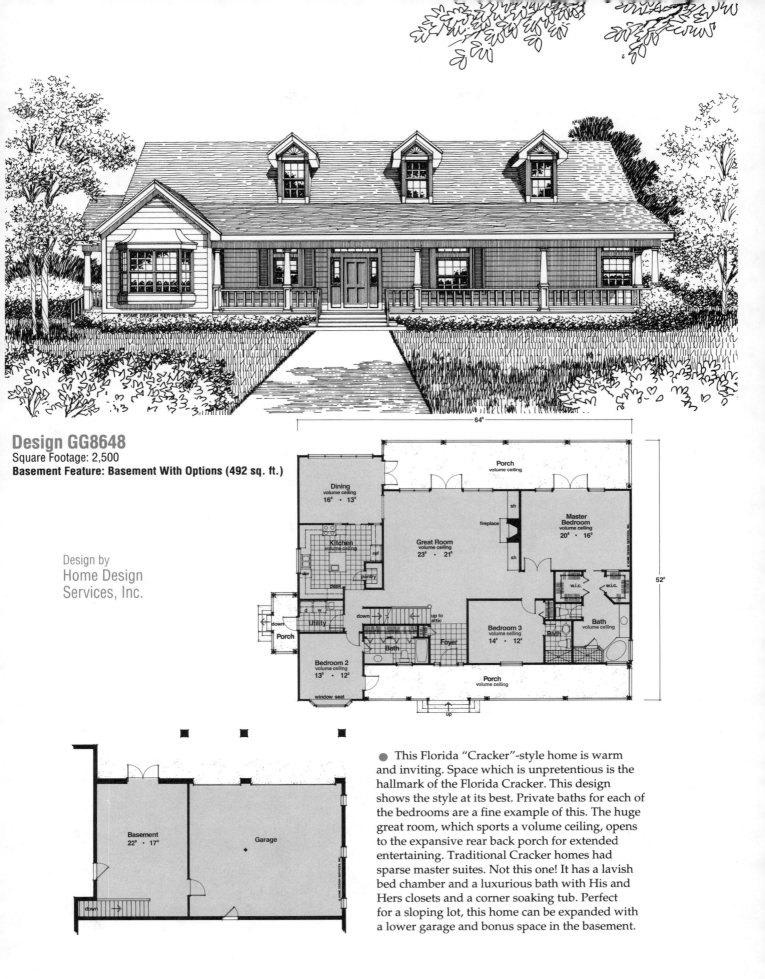

Design GG8648
Square Footage: 2,500
Basement Feature: Basement With Options (492 sq. ft.)

Design by
Home Design
Services, Inc.

Dining
volume ceiling
16⁰ · 13⁴

Porch
volume ceiling

Kitchen
volume ceiling

Great Room
volume ceiling
23⁸ · 21⁰

Master Bedroom
volume ceiling
20⁸ · 16⁰

fireplace

ref

pantry

desk

w.i.c.

w.i.c.

down

d   w

Utility

Porch

down

up to attic

Bath

Bedroom 3
volume ceiling
14⁴ · 12⁴

Bath
volume ceiling

Bath

Foyer

Bedroom 2
volume ceiling
13⁰ · 12⁰

window seat

Porch
volume ceiling

up

64⁰

52⁰

Basement
22⁸ · 17⁰

Garage

down

● This Florida "Cracker"-style home is warm and inviting. Space which is unpretentious is the hallmark of the Florida Cracker. This design shows the style at its best. Private baths for each of the bedrooms are a fine example of this. The huge great room, which sports a volume ceiling, opens to the expansive rear back porch for extended entertaining. Traditional Cracker homes had sparse master suites. Not this one! It has a lavish bed chamber and a luxurious bath with His and Hers closets and a corner soaking tub. Perfect for a sloping lot, this home can be expanded with a lower garage and bonus space in the basement.

BALCONY

UPPER GATHERING RM.

BALCONY

BEDROOM 11⁸x12⁸

BUNK RM. 11⁸x18⁸

LOUNGE 15⁰x6⁰

RAILING

LINEN

CL

BATH

RAILING

UPPER FOYER

DN RAILING

CL

CL

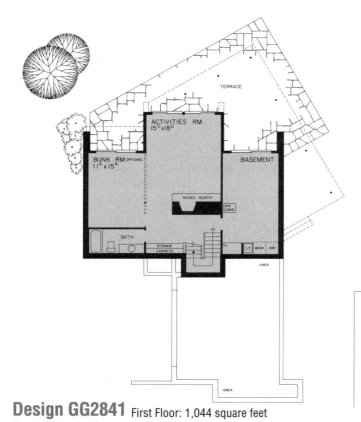

TERRACE

ACTIVITIES RM. 15⁰x18⁰

BASEMENT

BUNK RM. OPTIONAL 11⁴x15⁴

RAISED HEARTH

AIR COND.

BATH

UP

STORAGE CABINETS

CL

LT

WASH. DRY.

UNEX.

UNEX.

44'-0"

DECK

GATHERING RM. 15⁰x18⁰

BALCONY

STUDY/ BEDROOM 11⁸x12⁸

BALCONY ABOVE

DINING RM. 11⁸x10⁰

62'-4"

SNACK BAR

RANGE

KITCHEN 11⁸x11⁰

CL

SEAT

BATH

FOYER

DN

UP

CL

BRM CL

REF'G

D.W.

PORCH

CURB

GARAGE 21⁰x22⁰+ STORAGE

STORAGE

Design GG2841 First Floor: 1,044 square feet
Second Floor: 851 square feet; Total: 1,895 square feet
Basement Features: Activities Room, Bunk Room & Bath (753 sq. ft.)

L

● This spacious tri-level with traditional stone exterior offers excellent comfort and zoning for the modern family. The rear opens to balconies and a deck that creates a covered patio below. A main floor gathering room is continued above with an upper gathering room. The lower level offers an activities room with raised hearth, in addition to an optional bunk room with bath. A modern kitchen on main level features a handy snack bar, in addition to a dining room. A study on main level could become an optional bedroom. The master bedroom is located on the upper level, along with a rectangular bunk room with its own balcony.

Design by
Home Planners, Inc.

Design GG3366 First Floor: 1,638 square feet
Second Floor: 650 square feet; Total: 2,288 square feet
Basement Features: Activity Room & Hobbies/Bedroom (934 sq. ft.)

L

● There is much more to this design than
meets the eye. While it may look like a 1½-story
plan, bonus recreation and hobby space in the
walk-out basement adds almost 1,000 square
feet. The first floor holds living and dining
areas as well as the master bedroom suite. Two
family bedrooms on the second floor are connected by a balcony area that overlooks the
gathering room below. Notice the covered
porch beyond the breakfast and dining rooms.

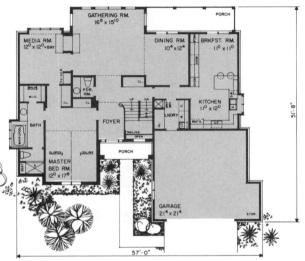

Design by
Home Planners,
Inc.

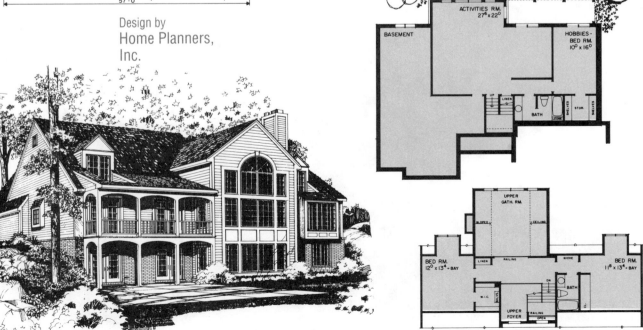

BED RM.
$11^8 \times 13^8$

BALCONY

UPPER GATHERING RM.

BALCONY

BUNK RM.
$11^8 \times 19^0$

BALCONY

RAILING

CL. CL.

BATH

RAILING

UPPER FOYER

DN

CL. CL.

Design GG2511

First Floor: 1,043 square feet

Second Floor: 703 square feet

Total: 1,746 square feet

Basement Features: Activity Room, Bunk Room & Bath (794 sq. ft.)

L **D**

40'-4"

DECK

GATHERING RM.
$15^4 \times 18^4$

BALCONY

STUDY-BED RM.
$11^8 \times 13^8$

DINING RM.
$11^8 \times 11^0$

LINEN CL.

SNACK BAR

BATH

KITCHEN
$11^8 \times 9^8$

FOYER

DN UP

PNTRY REF'G RANGE

52'-0"

CL.

PORCH

ENTRANCE COURT

STORAGE

CARPORT
$11^8 \times 20^0$

TERRACE

ACTIVITIES RM.
$15^4 \times 18^4$

BASEMENT

BUNK RM. OPTIONAL
$11^4 \times 15^8$

RAISED HEARTH

AIR COND

BATH

UP

STORAGE CABINETS

LT WASH. DRY.

CL.

UNEX.

QUOTE ONE™

Cost to build? See page 232 to order complete cost estimate to build this house in your area!

● Study this outstanding multi-level with its dramatic outdoor deck and balconies. This home is ideal if you are looking for a home that is new and exciting. The livability that it offers will efficiently serve your family.

Design by
Home Planners, Inc.

Design by
Home Planners,
Inc.

Design GG2716

First Floor: 1,013 square feet
Second Floor: 885 square feet
Total: 1,898 square feet
**Basement Features: Family Room,
Guest Room & Bath (1,074 sq. ft.)**

L

● Stuck with a hilly site?
If so, this plan may fit right
in. The upper-level master
suite is one highlight. It's
got a huge sitting and
dressing room, as well as a
private balcony. The main
level is a welcome combi-
nation of open floor planning and traditional room
layout. The combo gather-
ing room (which is open to
the upper level) and dining
area total just under 400
square feet; note the
through-fireplace (to a
comfy study off the entry)
and access to the balcony in
back. On the lower level are
a large family room, where
there's another fireplace;
guest bedroom and full
bath; and rear terrace.

Design GG2828

First Floor: 1,078 square feet
Second Floor: 1,066 square feet
Total: 2,144 square feet
Basement Feature: Activities Room (583 sq. ft.)

● The first floor of this contemporary home features an interior kitchen with a snack bar, a living room with raised-hearth fireplace, and a dining room. The first-floor bedroom will make a great guest suite with nearby full bath and terrace access. Upstairs, a large master bedroom is joined by two family bedrooms, one of which

could easily serve as a nursery, office or media room. Also notice the two balconies, three skylights and sewing/hobbies room upstairs. Storage space is available everywhere you look—hall closets on the second floor, in the first floor laundry room and garage, and in the basement plan.

Design by
Home Planners,
Inc.

Design GG2887 First Floor: 1,338 square feet; Second Floor: 661 square feet; Total: 1,999 square feet
Basement Features: Family & Activities Rooms (333 sq. ft.)

● This attractive, contemporary 1½-story will be the envy of many. First, examine the efficient kitchen. Not only does it offer a snack bar for those quick meals but also a large dining room. Notice the adjacent dining porch. The laundry and garage access are also adjacent to the kitchen. An exciting feature is the gathering room with fireplace. The first floor also offers a study with a wet bar and sliding glass doors that open to a private porch. This will make those quiet times cherishable. Adjacent to the study is a full bath followed by a bedroom. Upstairs a large master bedroom suite occupies the entire floor. It features a bath with an oversized tub and shower, a large walk-in closet with built-ins and an open lounge with fireplace. Both the lounge and master bedroom, along with the gathering room, have sloped ceilings. Develop the lower level for additional space.

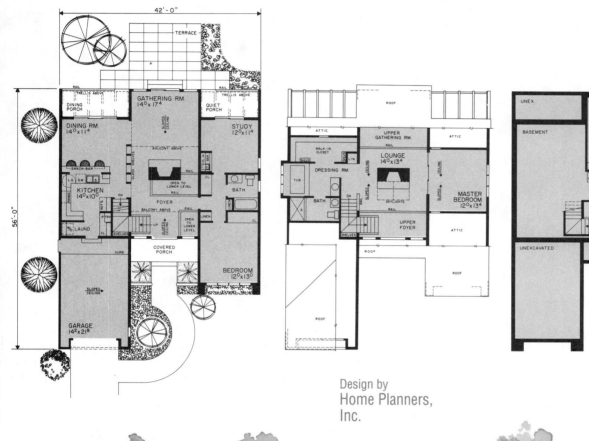

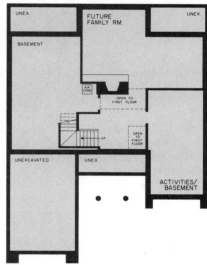

Design by
Home Planners,
Inc.

Design GG2730
Square Footage: 2,490
**Basement Features: Activity Room &
Lounge (1,086 sq. ft.)**

D

● Here is a basic one-story
home that is really loaded
with livability on the first
floor and has a bonus of an
extra 1,086 sq. ft. of planned
livability on a lower level.
What makes this so livable is
that the first floor, adjacent
to the stairs leading below, is
open and forms a balcony
looking down into a dra-
matic planting area. The
first-floor traffic patterns
flow around this impressive
and distinctive feature. In
addition to the gathering
room, study and family
room, there is the lounge
and activity room. Notice the
second balcony open to the
activity room below. The
master bedroom is outstanding with two baths and two
walk-in closets. The attached
three-car garage has a bulk
storage area and is accessible through the service area.

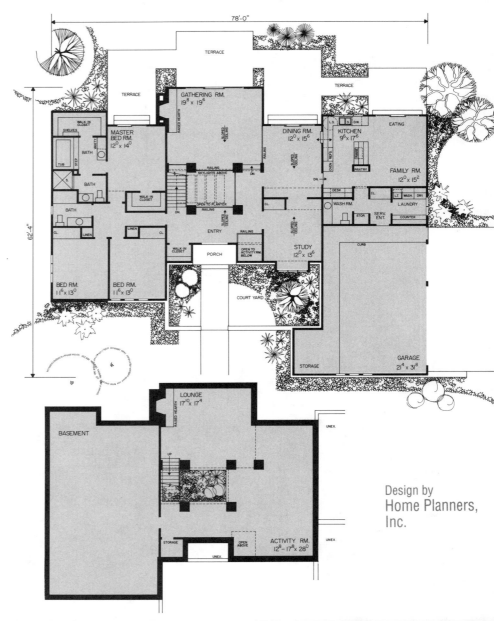

Design by
Home Planners,
Inc.

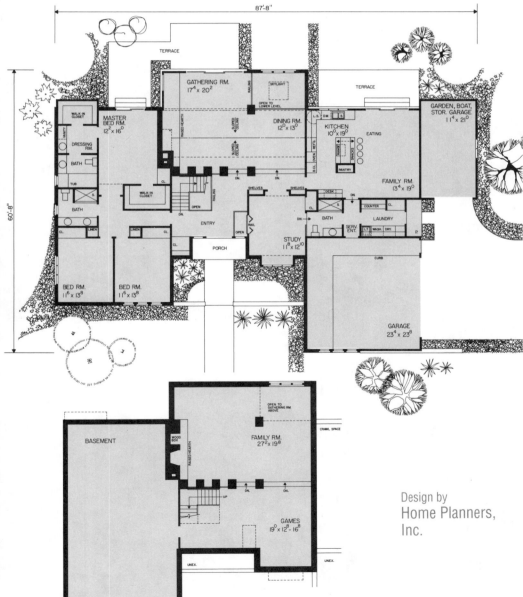

Design GG2721
Square Footage: 2,667
Basement Features: Family Room & Game Room (902 sq. ft.)

● Visually exciting! A sunken gathering room with a sloped ceiling, raised hearth fireplace, corner balcony and skylight . . . the last two features shared by the formal dining room. There's more. Two family rooms . . . one on the lower level with a raised hearth fireplace, another adjacent to the kitchen with a snack bar! Plus a study and game room. A lavish master suite and two large bedrooms. A first floor laundry and reams of storage space, including a special garage for a boat, sports equipment, garden tools etc. There's plenty of space for family activities in this home. From chic dinner parties for friends to birthday gatherings for kids, there's always the right setting . . . and so much room that adults and children can entertain at the same time.

Design by
Home Planners,
Inc.

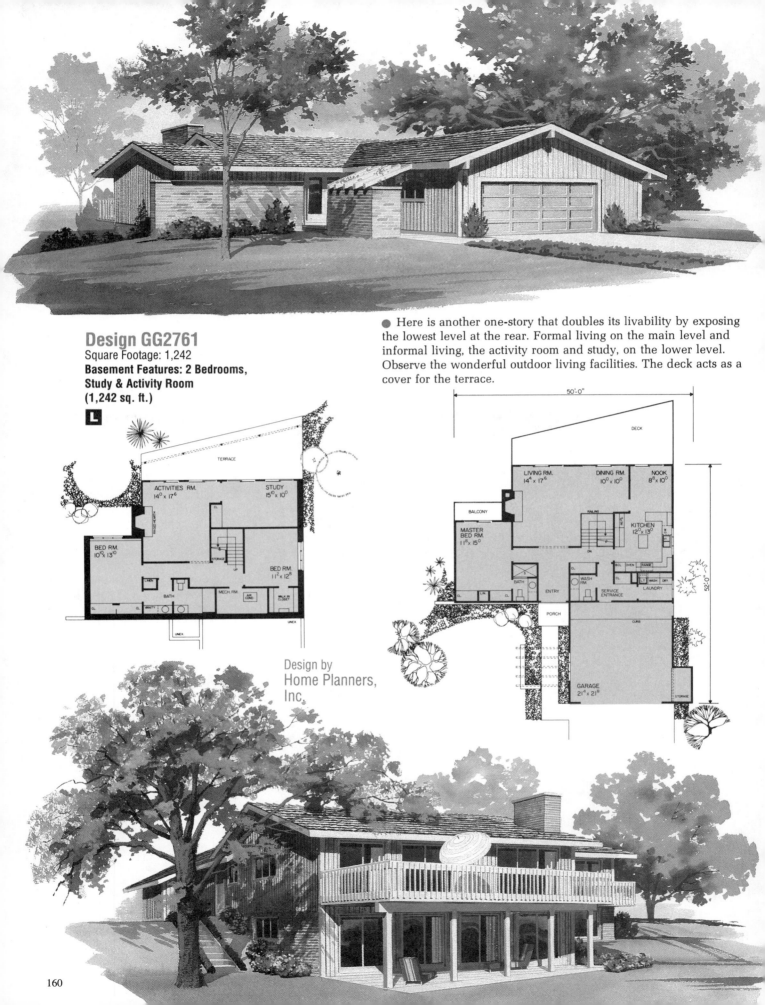

Design GG2761

Square Footage: 1,242
**Basement Features: 2 Bedrooms,
Study & Activity Room
(1,242 sq. ft.)**

● Here is another one-story that doubles its livability by exposing the lowest level at the rear. Formal living on the main level and informal living, the activity room and study, on the lower level. Observe the wonderful outdoor living facilities. The deck acts as a cover for the terrace.

TERRACE

ACTIVITIES RM.
14⁰ x 17⁶

STUDY
15¹⁰ x 10⁰

BED RM.
10⁰ x 13¹⁰

CL

RAISED HEARTH

STORAGE
UP

BED RM.
11² x 12⁸

LINEN

BATH

MECH. RM.

AIR COND.

WALK IN CLOSET

VANITY

CL

UNEX.

UNEX.

50'-0"

DECK

LIVING RM.
14⁴ x 17⁶

DINING RM.
10⁰ x 10⁰

NOOK
8⁸ x 10⁰

BALCONY

RAILING

52'-0"

MASTER BED RM.
11⁸ x 15⁰

DN

KITCHEN
12⁰ x 13⁰

BATH

CL

CL

ENTRY

WASH RM.

SERVICE ENTRANCE

LAUNDRY

OVEN RANGE

PORCH

CURB

GARAGE
21⁴ x 21⁸

STORAGE

Design by
Home Planners,
Inc.

Design GG2769
Square Footage: 1,898
**Basement Features: 2 Bedrooms
& Family Room (1,134 sq. ft.)**

● This traditional hillside design has fine architectural styling. It possesses all of the qualities that a great design should have to serve its occupants fully.

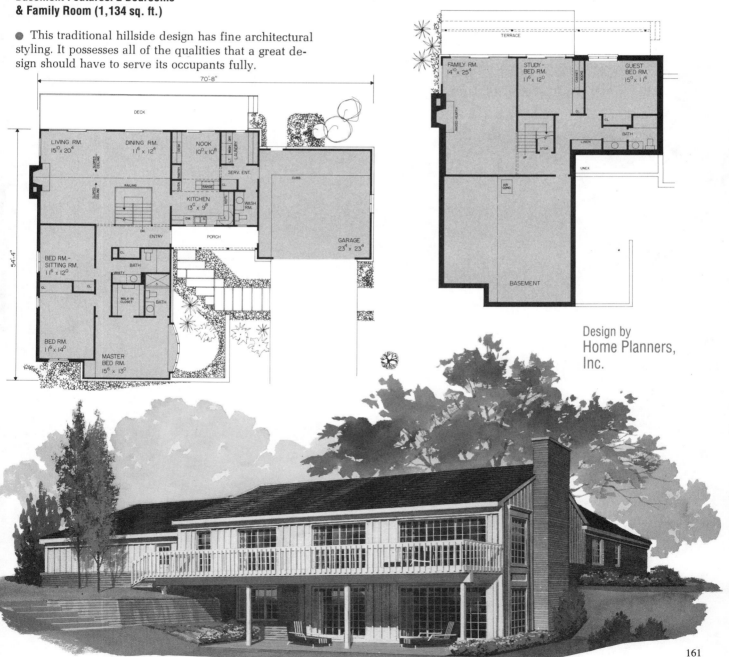

Design by
**Home Planners,
Inc.**

This is an exquisitely styled Tudor tri-level designed to serve its happy occupants for many years. The contrasting use of material surely makes the exterior eye-catching.

Design GG2847
Square Footage: 1,874
Basement Features: Family Room, Bedroom & Sauna (1,131 sq. ft.)

L

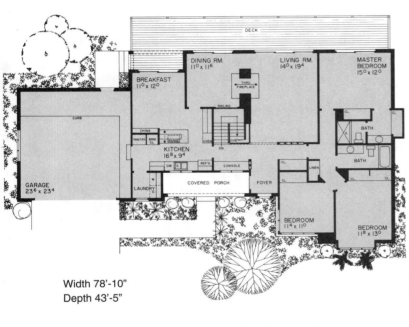

Width 78'-10"
Depth 43'-5"

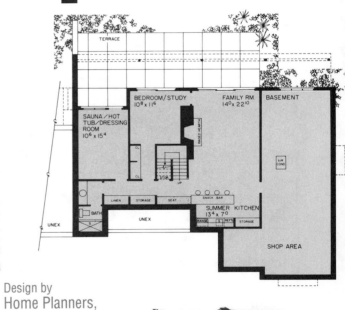

Design by
Home Planners,
Inc.

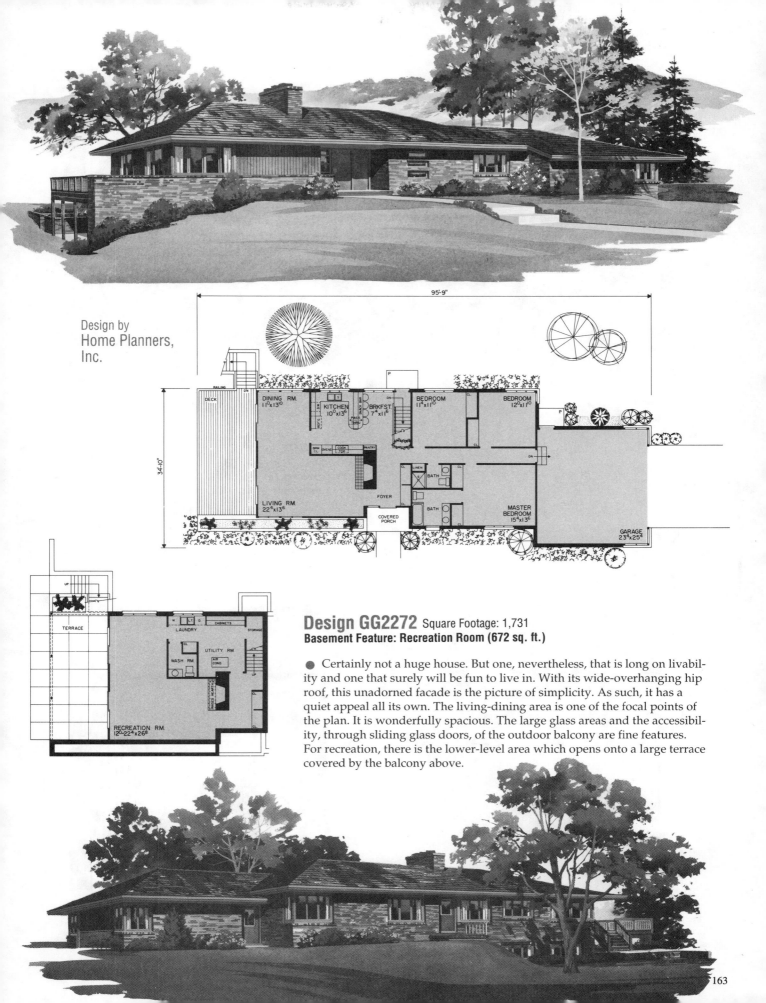

Design by
Home Planners,
Inc.

95'-9"

34'-10"

RAILING

DECK

DINING RM.
11⁰x13¹⁰

KITCHEN
10⁰x13⁶

BRKFST.
7⁴x11⁶

BEDROOM
11⁴x11¹⁰

BEDROOM
12⁰x11¹⁰

OVENS

COOK TOP

PANTRY

BRM CL

LIVING RM.
22⁴x13⁶

FOYER

CL

LINEN

BATH

CL

CL

BATH

COVERED
PORCH

MASTER
BEDROOM
15⁴x13⁶

GARAGE
23⁴x25⁴

UP

TERRACE

LAUNDRY

CABINETS

STORAGE

W   D

CL

WASH RM

UTILITY RM
AIR COND.

CL

RECREATION RM.
12⁰-22⁴x26⁸

Design GG2272 Square Footage: 1,731
Basement Feature: Recreation Room (672 sq. ft.)

● Certainly not a huge house. But one, nevertheless, that is long on livability and one that surely will be fun to live in. With its wide-overhanging hip
roof, this unadorned facade is the picture of simplicity. As such, it has a
quiet appeal all its own. The living-dining area is one of the focal points of
the plan. It is wonderfully spacious. The large glass areas and the accessibility, through sliding glass doors, of the outdoor balcony are fine features.
For recreation, there is the lower-level area which opens onto a large terrace
covered by the balcony above.

Design GG2485

Square Footage: 1,108
**Basement Features: Activities Room,
2 Bedrooms (983 sq. ft.)**

● This hillside vacation home gives the appearance of being a one-story from the road. However, since it is built off the edge of a slope, the rear exterior is a full two-story structure. Notice the projecting deck and how it shelters the terrace. Each of the generous glass areas is protected from the summer sun by the overhangs and the extended walls. The clerestory windows of the front exterior provide natural light to the center of the plan.

Design by
Home Planners,
Inc.

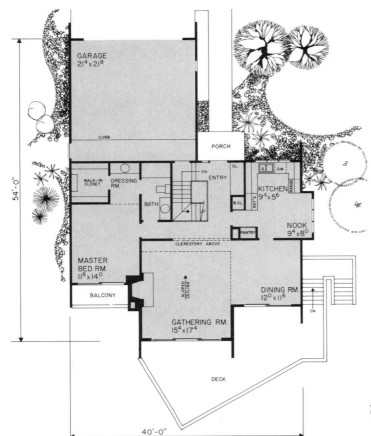

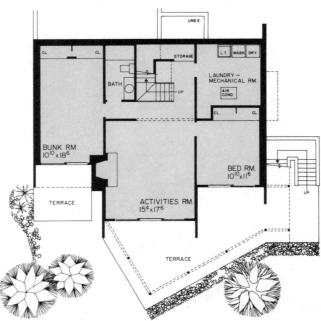

6

FLEXIBLE SPACE DESIGNS

As You Like It

The real advantage of flexible space is the variety of uses it allows. Whether room is needed for a quiet, private area, or a gathering place for the family, it will be available to you when you're ready to use it. Due to the subjective nature of this space, there are no right or wrong choices. The following pages provide floor plans that may serve one function for awhile, and then change to fulfill a completely different need. Designs GG3468 and GG9821 (pages 166 and 179) show how easy this transition can be.

If the second floor is designed with a loft, an easy conversion will transform this space into an office or exercise facility. See Design GG8629 on page 169 for ideas about how to accomplish this with ease.

In some cases, a game room is included in the second-floor designs. When used with an adjacent expandable area, it becomes a zone which is tailor-made for use as a media room. Designs GG8069 and GG8041 on pages 177 and 183 provide shining examples of these possibilities.

Design GG8094 (page 188) contributes an interesting option for the use of flexible space. A well-placed future closet/bath used in conjunction with the game room transforms that area into a spacious guest suite. Making the adjustment is simple.

The following plans with flexible space deal not only with expansion to meet the needs of a growing family, but offer a variety of ideas for the conversion of space that is no longer needed for family members. Once the children leave the nest, space becomes available to convert a bedroom into a sewing room or study that has always been your heart's desire. Homes designed with flexible space offer an array of choices. Using existing rooms that have been modified to be uniquely yours alone—and don't require additional construction costs—is not only budget-smart but meets the challenge for those of us that simply need a change every now and then.

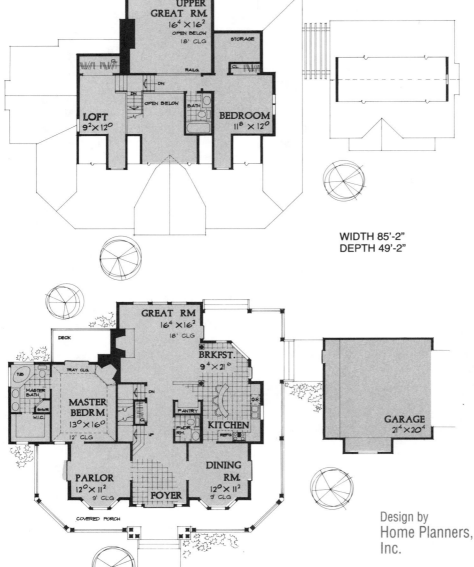

UPPER
GREAT RM.
16⁴ X 16²
OPEN BELOW
18' CLG

STORAGE

RAIL.

CL.

DN

LOFT
9² X 12⁰

OPEN BELOW

DN

BATH

BEDROOM
11⁸ X 12⁰

WIDTH 85'-2"
DEPTH 49'-2"

DECK

GREAT RM.
16⁴ X 16²
18' CLG

TRAY CLG

BRKFST.
9⁴ X 21⁶

TUB

MASTER
BATH

DN

MASTER
BEDRM
13⁰ X 16⁰
12' CLG

PANTRY

KITCHEN

GARAGE
21⁴ X 20⁴

SHWR

W.I.C.

PWDR.
RM.

REFG.

UP

PARLOR
12⁰ X 11²
9' CLG

FOYER

DINING
RM.
12⁰ X 11²
9' CLG

COVERED PORCH

Design by
Home Planners,
Inc.

Design GG3468

First Floor: 1,618 square feet
Second Floor: 510 square feet
Total: 2,128 square feet
Flexible Space: Loft

● There's nothing lacking in this contemporary farmhouse. A wraparound porch ensures a favorite spot for enjoying good weather. A large great room sports a fireplace and lots of natural light. Grab a snack at the kitchen island/snack bar or in the bright breakfast room. The vaulted foyer grandly introduces the dining room and parlor—the master bedroom is just off this room. Inside it: tray ceiling, fireplace, luxury bath and walk-in closet. Stairs lead up to a quaint loft/bedroom—perfect for study or snoozing—a full bath and an additional bedroom. Designated storage space also makes this one a winner.

Design GG3438

First Floor: 1,489 square feet
Second Floor: 741 square feet
Total: 2,230 square feet
Flexible Space: Loft/Studio

L

● A unique farmhouse plan which provides a grand floor plan, this home is comfortable in country or suburban settings. Formal entertaining areas share first-floor space with family gathering rooms and work and service areas. The master suite is also on this floor for convenience and privacy. Upstairs is a guest bedroom, private bath and loft area that makes a perfect studio. Special features make this a great place to come home to.

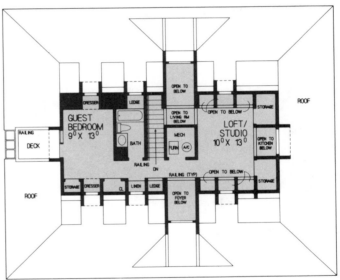

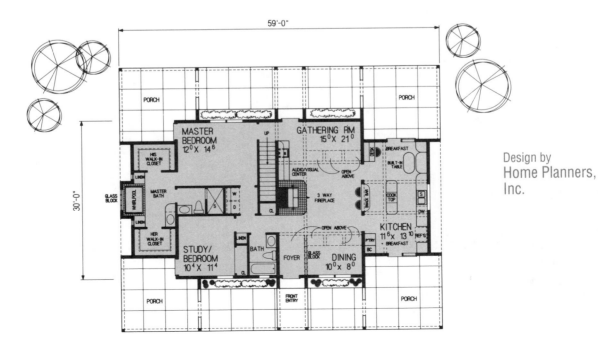

Design by
Home Planners, Inc.

Design GG9673

First Floor: 1,526 square feet
Second Floor: 635 square feet
Total: 2,161 square feet
Flexible Space: Loft/Study & Bonus Room

● This beautiful farmhouse boasts all the extras a three-bedroom design could offer. Clerestory windows with arched tops enhance the exterior both front and back and allow natural light to penetrate into the foyer and great room. A kitchen with island counter and breakfast area is open to the spacious great room through a cased opening with colonnade. The exquisite master suite has a generous bedroom, large walk-in closet and dramatically designed master bath providing emphasis on the whirlpool tub flanked by double columns. Access to the rear deck is possible from the screened porch, master bath and breakfast area. The second level has two bedrooms sharing a full bath and a loft/study area overlooking the great room.

Design by
Donald A. Gardner, Architects, Inc.

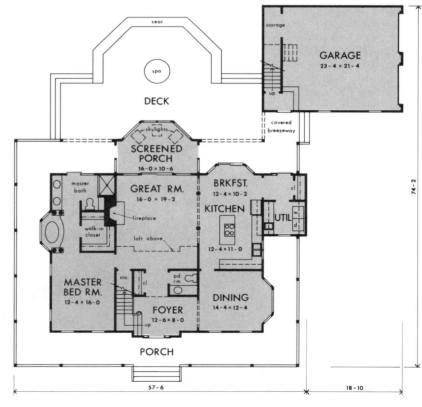

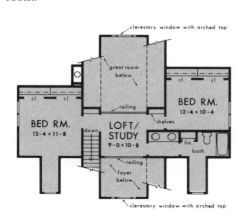

Design GG8629

First Floor: 1,782 square feet
Second Floor: 264 square feet
Total: 2,046 square feet
Flexible Space: Loft

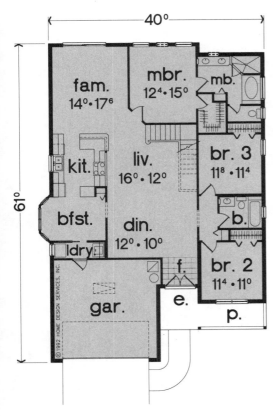

40⁰

61⁰

fam.
14⁰·17⁶

mbr.
12⁴·15⁰

mb.

kit.

liv.
16⁰·12⁰

br. 3
11⁸·11⁴

bfst.

din.
12⁰·10⁰

b.

ldry

f.

gar.

e.

br. 2
11⁴·11⁰

p.

Design by
Home Design
Services, Inc.

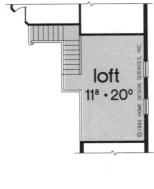

loft
11⁸·20⁰

● This delightful 1½-story plan has a formal living and dining area for evening entertainment and boasts a huge family gathering space. Designed for efficiency, the two secondary bedrooms have private entrances off the formal living area. The master bedroom has all of the features of a larger home including a soaking tub, large walk-in shower and private toilet area. The kitchen is at the heart of the home with a bay-windowed breakfast area adjacent to the efficient laundry room. A loft area on the second floor provides additional space for the growing family. Included in the blueprints are details for two different exteriors.

Design GG9012

First Floor: 1,357 square feet
Second Floor: 1,079 square feet
Total: 2,436 square feet

Flexible Space: Office & Exercise Loft

● An inviting wraparound veranda with delicate spindlework and a raised turret with leaded-glass windows recall the grand Queen Anne-Style Victorians of the late 1880s. Double doors open from the dramatic two-story foyer to a private study with built-in bookcases and a bay window. French doors open from the living room to the front veranda and to the screened porch. A fireplace adds warmth to the breakfast area and the island kitchen. Above the two-car garage is an optional area that is perfect for a home office or guest quarters. Upstairs, the master suite, with His and Hers walk-in closets, leads to a luxurious bath with a garden tub and a glass enclosed shower. An optional exercise loft and plant shelves complete this elegant master bath. Two additional bedrooms, one with a private deck, and the other with a cathedral ceiling, share a dressing area and bath.

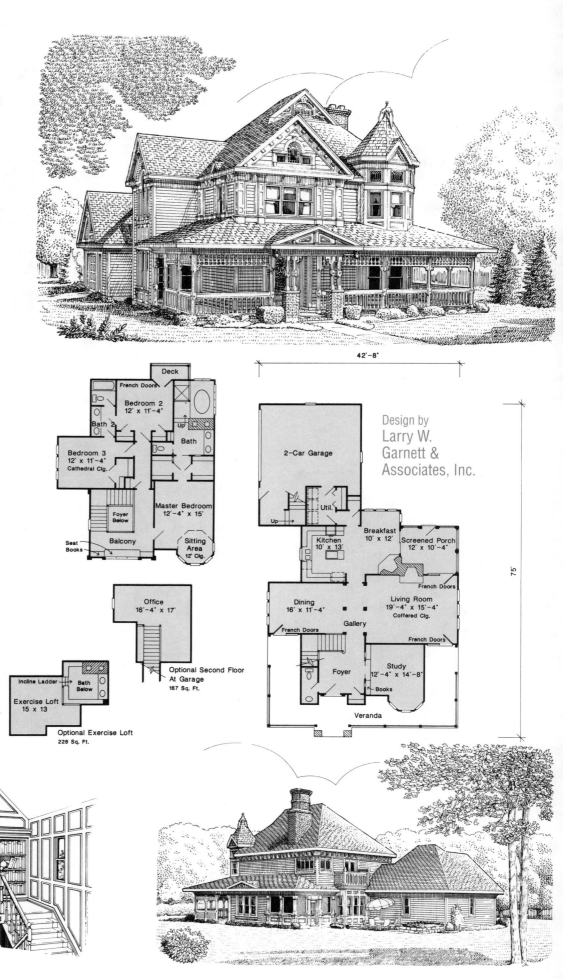

Deck
French Doors
Bedroom 2
12' x 11'-4"
Bath 2
Bath
Up
Bedroom 3
12' x 11'-4"
Cathedral Clg.
Master Bedroom
12'-4" x 15'
Foyer
Below
Seat
Books
Balcony
Sitting
Area
12' Clg.

Office
16'-4" x 17'

Optional Second Floor
At Garage
167 Sq. Ft.

Incline Ladder
Bath
Below
Exercise Loft
15 x 13

Optional Exercise Loft
228 Sq. Ft.

42'-8"

2-Car Garage

Design by
Larry W.
Garnett &
Associates, Inc.

Up
Util.

Breakfast
10' x 12'

Screened Porch
12' x 10'-4"

Kitchen
10' x 13'

French Doors

Dining
16' x 11'-4"

Living Room
19'-4" x 15'-4"
Coffered Clg.

Gallery

French Doors

French Doors

Foyer

Study
12'-4" x 14'-8"

Books

Veranda

75'

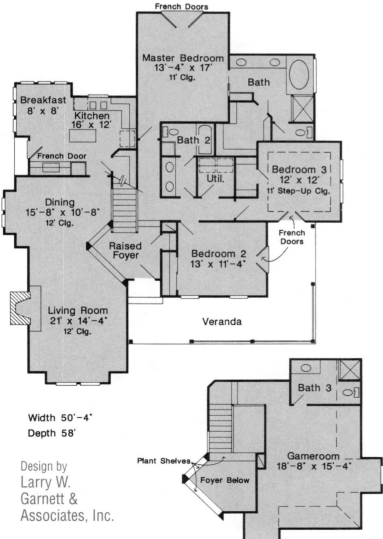

French Doors

Master Bedroom
13'-4" x 17'
11' Clg.

Bath

Breakfast
8' x 8'

Kitchen
16' x 12'

Bath 2

French Door

Bedroom 3
12' x 12'
11' Step-Up Clg.

Util.

Dining
15'-8" x 10'-8"
12' Clg.

Raised
Foyer

French
Doors

Bedroom 2
13' x 11'-4"

Living Room
21' x 14'-4"
12' Clg.

Veranda

Width 50'-4"
Depth 58'

Design by
Larry W.
Garnett &
Associates, Inc.

Plant Shelves

Foyer Below

Bath 3

Gameroom
18'-8" x 15'-4"

Design GG9030

First Floor: 1,837 square feet
Second Floor: 445 square feet
Total: 2,282 square feet
Flexible Space: Gameroom

● A seven-foot wide veranda with ornate fretwork, porch railing and intricate post brackets, along with a copper-topped box window provide this home with old-fashioned charm and romance. Inside, the raised foyer opens into living and dining areas that are perfect for family activities or formal entertaining. Stairs lead to the second floor gameroom and bath. Bedrooms 2 and 3 each have French doors that open to the front veranda. The secluded master bedroom has an eleven-foot ceiling and French doors, while the spacious master bath features a garden tub with adjacent glass-enclosed shower, along with a large walk-in closet. The kitchen combines both form and function with ample cabinet space, a center work island, and a magnificent view through the breakfast area to the rear yard. Plans for a detached two-car garage are included with this design.

Design GG9051

First Floor: 1,604 square feet
Second Floor: 367 square feet
Total: 1,971 square feet
Flexible Space: Loft/Gameroom

● The ornate turned posts at the veranda, along with delicate wood moulding and carved gable brackets give this Queen Anne Style cottage lasting elegance. The dining area features triple French doors and a cathedral ceiling. Bedroom 3 offers a built-in desk, making it a perfect optional study. The master suite has French doors opening to a covered porch, a large bath with a walk-in closet, plenty of linen storage and a glass-enclosed shower. The steep pitched roof offers the opportunity to utilize the attic space for a 14' x 19' bonus room with a half bath. Plans are included for this option, showing a circular staircase located at the foyer closet area. An attached two-car garage is located conveniently just off the handy utility room.

Design by
Larry W.
Garnett &
Associates, Inc.

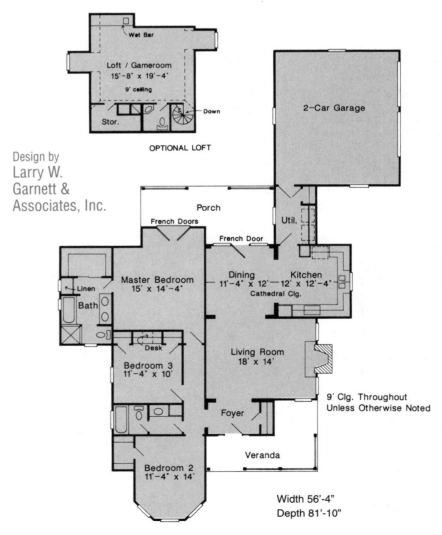

Width 56'-4"
Depth 81'-10"

Design GG9123

Square Footage: 829

Flexible Space: 2 Bedrooms for future use

● Build small, then add on as the family grows or as needs increase. The economical Phase 1 project of this home allows for all the livability of much larger plans: an ample living area, hexagonal dining area, U-shaped kitchen and large bedroom with full bath and huge closet. When you outgrow the Basic Plan, you can add the two additional bedrooms with walk-in closets. The utility room provides adequate space for a washer and dryer. The covered front porch is not only charming, but adds a welcome indoor/outdoor relationship.

PHASE 2
Bedrooms 2 and 3
Adds 355 square feet
to Basic Plan

Bedroom 2
11'-4" x 11'

Bedroom 3
11'-4" x 11'

Bath

Util.

Kitchen

Design by
Larry W.
Garnett &
Associates, Inc.

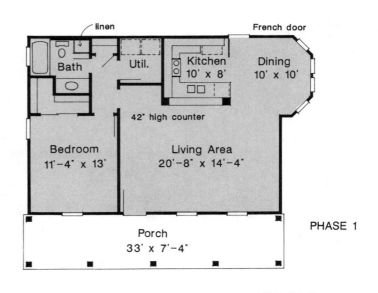

linen

French door

Bath

Util.

Kitchen
10' x 8'

Dining
10' x 10'

42" high counter

Bedroom
11'-4" x 13'

Living Area
20'-8" x 14'-4"

Porch
33' x 7'-4"

PHASE 1

Width 37'-4"
Depth 31'-4"

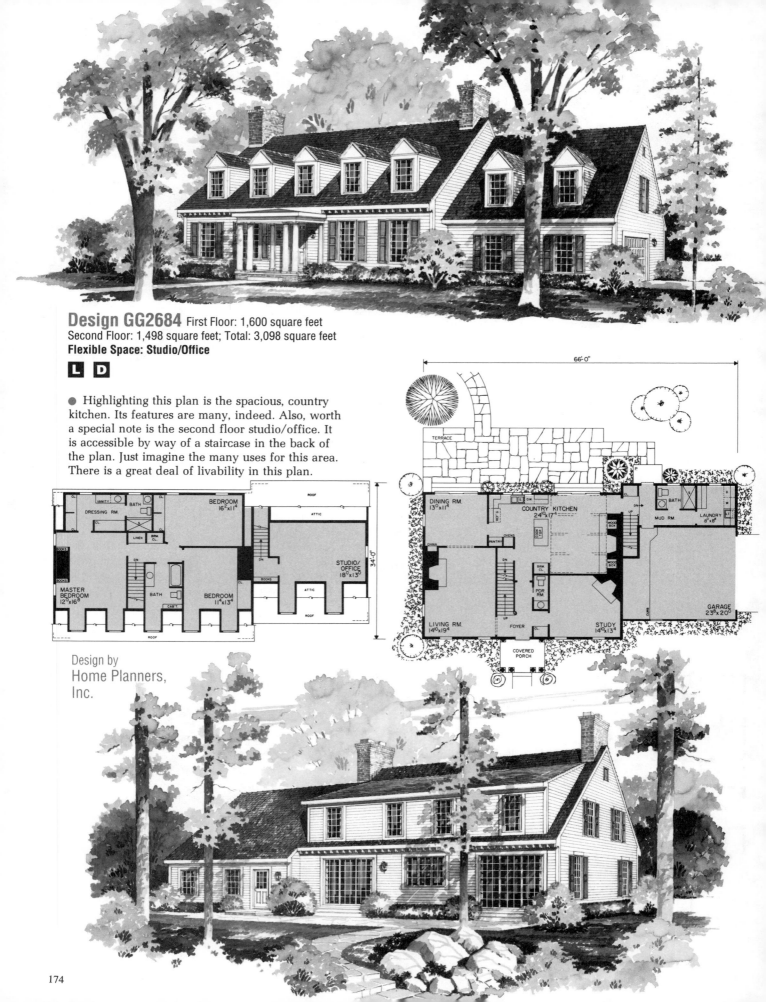

Design GG2684 First Floor: 1,600 square feet
Second Floor: 1,498 square feet; Total: 3,098 square feet
Flexible Space: Studio/Office

L **D**

● Highlighting this plan is the spacious, country
kitchen. Its features are many, indeed. Also, worth
a special note is the second floor studio/office. It
is accessible by way of a staircase in the back of
the plan. Just imagine the many uses for this area.
There is a great deal of livability in this plan.

Design by
Home Planners,
Inc.

Copyright 1992 Stephen S. Fuller, Inc.

Design GG9859

First Floor: 1,333 square feet
Second Floor: 1,425 square feet
Total: 2,758 square feet
Flexible Space: Den & Guest Suite

● This Early American design possesses a rare charm, largely due to its proportions and breezeway. True to tradition are the gambrel roof, brick and siding combination, covered entrance and detailed columns. The main level begins with equally proportioned dining and living rooms framed by columns. The kitchen is large and opens directly onto the breezeway porch, which leads to the two-car garage. The upper level begins with a children's den at the top of the staircase. Just beyond, the private guest bedroom awaits visitors with a complete bath and walk-in closet. The master suite consists of a very large sleeping area with a fireplace, a master bath with a bay window, a separate shower, a water closet and two walk-in closets. This home is designed with a basement foundation.

Width 69'-2"
Depth 46'-10"

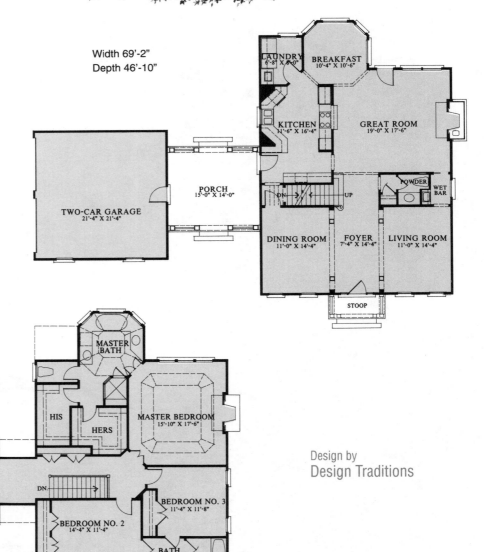

Design by
Design Traditions

175

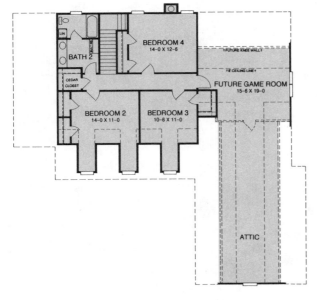

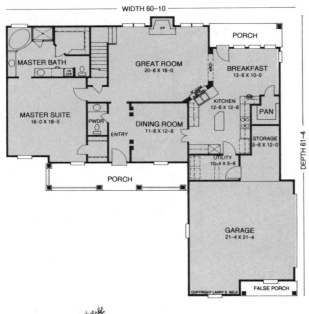

BEDROOM 4
14-0 X 12-6

BATH 2
LIN

↑ FUTURE KNEE WALL ↑

↑ 8' CEILING LINE ↑

CEDAR CLOSET

FUTURE GAME ROOM
15-6 X 19-0

BEDROOM 2
14-0 X 11-0

BEDROOM 3
10-6 X 11-0

ATTIC

WIDTH 60—10

MASTER BATH

FP

PORCH

GREAT ROOM
20-6 X 16-0

BREAKFAST
13-6 X 10-0

KITCHEN
12-6 X 12-6

PAN

MASTER SUITE
16-0 X 18-0

PWDR

DINING ROOM
11-6 X 12-6

ENTRY

STORAGE
15-6 X 12-0

DEPTH 61—4

UTILITY
10-4 X 5-6

PORCH

GARAGE
21-4 X 21-4

FALSE PORCH

COPYRIGHT LARRY E. BELK

Design GG8072 First Floor: 1,638 square feet
Second Floor: 877 square feet; Total: 2,515 square feet
Flexible Space: Future Game Room

● A charming elevation welcomes visitors to this compact four-bedroom home. A roomy front porch provides a great place for relaxing during hot summer evenings. The small porch off the garage is added for decoration and makes a great place for displaying hanging baskets full of blooming flowers. Inside, the entry leads to an oversized great room and a formal dining room with an entrance flanked by square columns. The kitchen features a large breakfast room. The master suite is located downstairs and includes a roomy master bath with corner whirlpool, shower, sitting area and walk-in closet. Upstairs, Bedrooms 2 and 3 are located on the front of the house. A future game room is shown with access to attic space for later expansion. Please specify crawlspace or slab foundation when ordering.

Design by
Larry E. Belk
Designs

COPYRIGHT LARRY E. BELK

COPYRIGHT LARRY E. BELK

BEDROOM 4
14-0 X 12-6

BATH 2

LIN

CEDAR
CLOSET

BEDROOM 2
14-0 X 10-6

BEDROOM 3
11-6 X 10-6

†FUTURE KNEE WALL†

†8' CEILING LINE†

FUTURE GAME RM
14-2 X 17-0

ATTIC
FUTURE EXPANSION
12-2 X 25-6

Width 60'-10"
Depth 58'-4"

MASTER BATH

MASTER SUITE
16-0 X 18-0

PWDR

ENTRY

STOOP

FP

GREAT ROOM
20-6 X 16-0

PORCH

BREAKFAST
13-6 X 10-0

KITCHEN
12-6 X 12-6

PAN

DINING ROOM
11-6 X 12-6

STORAGE
12-0 X 5-6

UTILITY
10-4 X 5-6

GARAGE
21-4 X 21-4

COPYRIGHT LARRY E. BELK

Design by
Larry E. Belk
Designs

Design GG8069

First Floor: 1,638 square feet
Second Floor: 793 square feet
Total: 2,431 square feet
Flexible Space: Future Game Room

● A gambrel roof replete with dormers makes this elevation a stand out from the curb. Inside, the dining room entrance off the entry is flanked by double square columns to add a formal detail. The great room features a large fireplace. The kitchen and breakfast room are entered through an arched opening off the great room. The kitchen is a cook's dream with a large walk-in pantry and a central work island. A desk is provided along with an arched pass-through opening to the great room. The master suite features a fabulous bath with His and Hers vanities, a corner whirlpool tub and a separate shower. Her vanity features a linen cabinet and knee space for sitting. Upstairs, two bedrooms receive lots of light from front dormers. This plan is available with either a crawlspace or slab foundation. Please specify when ordering.

177

OPEN TO BELOW

BEDROOM NO. 3
12'-0" X 11'-6"

DN.

GALLERY

BATH

LOFT
12'-0" X 9'-10"

BEDROOM NO. 2
12'-0" X 12'-0"

Design by
Design Traditions

Design GG9898

First Floor: 2,070 square feet
Second Floor: 790 square feet
Total: 2,860 square feet
Flexible Space: Loft

● Wood shingles are a cozy touch on the exterior of this home; the arched covered front porch adds its own bit of warmth. Interior rooms include a great room with bay window and fireplace, a formal dining room, and study with another fireplace. A guest room on the first floor contains a full bath and walk-in closet. The master bedroom is also on the first floor for privacy. The second floor holds two additional bedrooms, a loft area, and gallery overlooking the central hall. This home is designed with a basement foundation.

DECK

MASTER BEDROOM
13'-4" X 15'-8"

GREAT ROOM
15'-8" X 16'-7"

BREAKFAST
10'-6" X 10'-0"

GUEST BEDROOM
13'-0" X 12'-0"

MASTER BATH

W.I.C.

KITCHEN
10'-6" X 15'-0"

GUEST BATH

UP

DN.

LAUNDRY
6'-4" X 6'-0"

W.I.C.

FOYER
6'-8" X 12'-6"

DINING ROOM
12'-0" X 13'-6"

STUDY
13'-4" X 11'-2"

TWO CAR GARAGE
21'-4" X 21'-4"

Width 57'-6"
Depth 54'

Design GG9821
First Floor: 2,070 square feet
Second Floor: 790 square feet; Total: 2,860 square feet
Flexible Space: Loft

Design by
Design Traditions

● The striking combination of wood frame, shingles and glass create the exterior of this classic cottage. The foyer opens to the main-level layout. To the left of the foyer is a study with a warming hearth and vaulted ceiling. To the right is the formal dining room. A great room with an attached breakfast area is to the rear near the kitchen. A guest room is nestled in the rear of the plan for privacy. The master suite provides an expansive tray ceiling, a glass sitting area and easy passage to the outside deck. Upstairs, two bedrooms are accompanied by a loft for a quiet getaway. This home is designed with a basement foundation.

Width 58'-4"
Depth 54'-10"

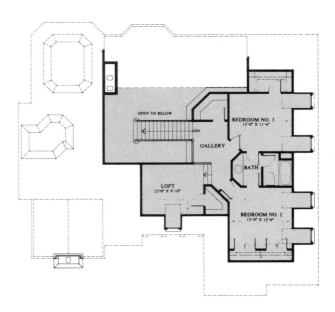

179

COPYRIGHT LARRY E. BELK

Design GG8091

First Floor: 2,087 square feet
Second Floor: 865 square feet
Total: 2,952 square feet
Flexible Space: Future Game Room

● A gable with a Palladian window and a large covered front porch make this home a charming classic. An angled entry opens up the living room and dining room and makes the home feel larger. The master suite is privately located on one side of the home. The kitchen, breakfast room and family room are combined and provide a great, open place for informal gatherings. Bedroom 2 and Bath 2 are nearby. A conveniently located stair originates in the family room. Two bedrooms and a bath are upstairs along with an expandable area to develop as you choose. This plan is available with either a crawlspace or slab foundation. Please specify when ordering.

Design by
Larry E. Belk
Designs

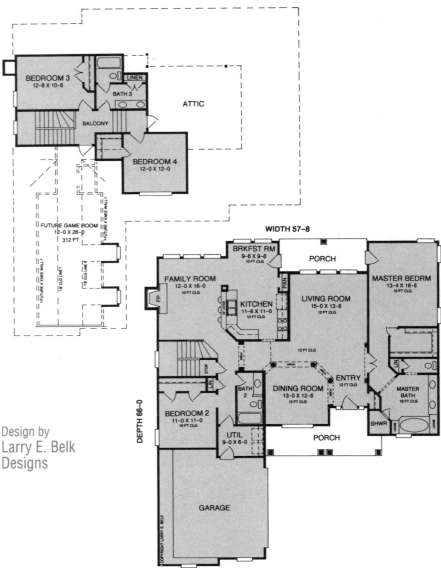

Design GG8092

First Floor: 2,092 square feet
Second Floor: 1,053 square feet
Total: 3,145 square feet
Flexible Space: Future Game Room

● The combination of siding and brick gives this elevation a distinctly homey feeling. Elegant arched openings welcome you upon entering. An open concept is used in the design of the kitchen, breakfast room and keeping room to give the feel of one large area. The master suite has all the extras demanded by today's owner with a sitting area, His and Hers closets and a master bath with a whirlpool tub and a separate shower. Upstairs, Bedroom 3 features its own sitting area. Two other bedrooms—and a bath with private dressing/vanity areas—are also upstairs. A large expandable area is allocated for flexible space. This plan is available with either a crawlspace or slab foundation. Please specify when ordering.

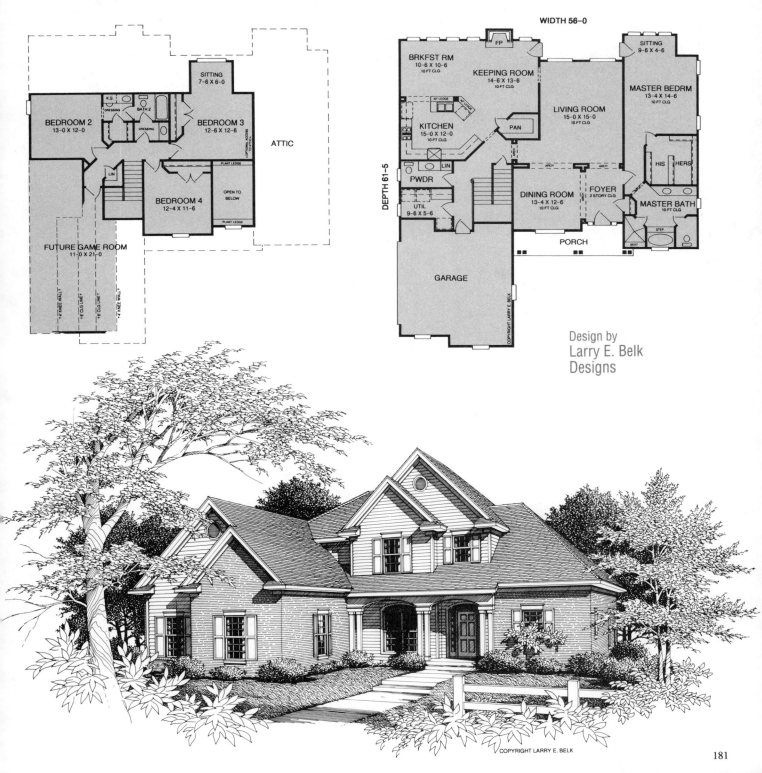

Design by
Larry E. Belk
Designs

COPYRIGHT LARRY E. BELK

WIDTH 67-8

MASTER BATH

COVERED PORCH

BRKFST 12-6 X 10-6

FAMILY ROOM 15-0 X 19-0

MASTER BEDRM 16-0 X 15-4

LIVING ROOM 19-0 X 15-4 VAULTED TO 2 STORY

KIT 12-6 X 15-4

BATH 2

UTIL

STOR

BEDRM 2/STUDY 13-8 X 12-4

FOYER 2 STORY CLG

DINING ROOM 10-8 X 12-6

PWDR

PORCH

3 CAR GARAGE

DEPTH 74-2

Design by
Larry E. Belk
Designs

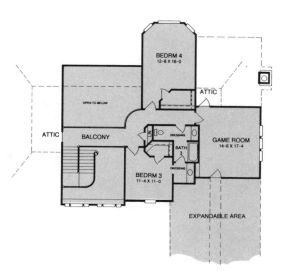

BEDRM 4 12-6 X 16-0

OPEN TO BELOW

ATTIC

ATTIC

BALCONY

DRESSING

GAME ROOM 14-6 X 17-4

BATH 3

BEDRM 3 11-4 X 11-0

DRESSING

EXPANDABLE AREA

Design GG8075 First Floor: 2,469 square feet
Second Floor: 1,013 square feet; Total: 3,482 square feet
Flexible Space: Game Room

● The texture created by the use of stacked stone, siding and brick makes this home a stand out from the curb. Inside, the two-story foyer opens to the vaulted living room and covered porch beyond. The dining room carries a formal flair with square columns defining one wall. The kitchen, with a large work island, the breakfast room and the family room are all conveniently grouped and provide a large area for informal entertaining. The master suite includes a master bath replete with all the amenities including a whirlpool tub, a shower, His and Hers vanities with knee space and His and Hers walk-in closets. A second bedroom is located nearby and is perfect for a nursery, a guest bedroom or a study. Upstairs, two additional bedrooms share a bath designed with a private vanity area for each bedroom. A large game room completes this lovely home. Expandable area is available over the three-car garage and provides a great opportunity to add that in-home office, exercise room or hobby room. Please specify crawlspace or slab foundation when ordering.

Design GG8041

First Floor: 1,937 square feet
Second Floor: 1,215 square feet
Total: 3,152 square feet
**Flexible Space: Game Room &
Expandable Area**

● A massive, stacked-stone gable highlights the entrance to this magnificent European plan. The two-story foyer and the living room—coupled with ten-foot ceilings throughout the remainder of the first floor—provide an open and spacious feeling. The dining room is located to the right of the foyer and is open on two sides. An efficient kitchen with a work island is conveniently grouped with the breakfast room and the family room, sharing a warming fireplace and providing the ideal area for informal gatherings. An adjacent living room provides space for more formal entertaining. The first-floor master suite shares a luxurious master bath with dual vanities, His and Hers walk-in closets and a corner whirlpool tub. Upstairs are three bedrooms, a bath and an oversized game room. In addition, a large area over the garage is available for future expansion, making this a perfect plan for the growing family. This plan is available with either a crawlspace or slab foundation. Please specify when ordering.

Design by
Larry E. Belk
Designs

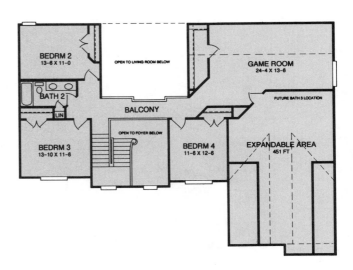

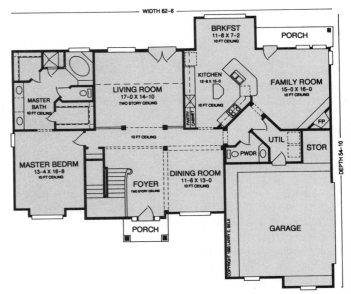

COPYRIGHT 1993 LARRY E. BELK

Design by
Larry E. Belk
Designs

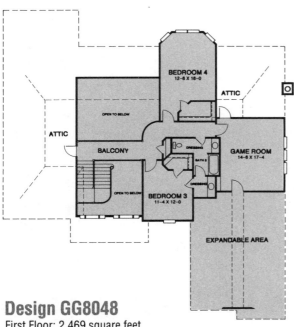

BEDROOM 4
12-8 X 16-0

ATTIC

OPEN TO BELOW

ATTIC

BALCONY

DRESSING

GAME ROOM
14-8 X 17-4

BATH 3

OPEN TO BELOW

BEDROOM 3
11-4 X 12-0

DRESSING

EXPANDABLE AREA

MASTER
BATH

BRKFST
12-6 X 10-6

COVERED PORCH

FAMILY ROOM
15-0 X 19-0

MASTER BEDROOM
16-0 X 15-4

LIVING ROOM
19-0 X 15-4

VAULTED TO 2 STORY

KIT
12-6 X 15-4

UTIL

BATH 2

PWDR

COPYRIGHT 1993

BEDRM 2/STUDY
13-8 X 12-4

FOYER
2 STORY CEILING

DINING ROOM
10-8 X 12-8

3 CAR GARAGE

PORCH

Design GG8048

First Floor: 2,469 square feet
Second Floor: 1,025 square feet
Total: 3,494 square feet
**Flexible Space: Game Room &
Expandable Area**

Width 67'-8"
Depth 74'-2"

● An arresting double arch gives this European-style home a commanding presence. Once inside, a two-story foyer provides an open view directly through the formal living room to the rear grounds beyond. The use of square columns to define the formal dining room adds an air of elegance to the home. A spacious kitchen with a prep island and a bayed breakfast area share space with the family room. A welcoming fireplace is visible to all areas and creates an area for family and informal gatherings. The private master suite features dual lavs, His and Hers walk-in closets, a corner garden tub and a separate shower. A second bedroom, which doubles as a nursery or a study, and a full bath are located nearby. Two bedrooms and a bath, which includes two dressing areas, are located on the second floor. A large game room completes this wonderful family home. Additional expandable space is available over the three-car garage. This plan is available with either a crawlspace or slab foundation. Please specify when ordering.

Design GG8055

First Floor: 1,934 square feet; Second Floor: 807 square feet
Total: 2,741 square feet; **Flexible Space: Game Room**

● A touch of copper renders just the right accent to this traditional brick and stucco exterior. Once inside, a two-story foyer with a plant ledge opens to a formal living room with a coffered ceiling. A see-through fireplace provides a cozy feeling and joins the breakfast room, also highlighted by a coffered ceiling. The large kitchen provides lots of counter space and cabinets for the active cook while a nearby planning desk provides a welcome convenience for use as a computer work station or for organizing records. The gracious master suite with a sitting area and a pampering bath is equipped with a huge walk-in closet, double vanities and a whirlpool tub. The secondary bedroom and full bath located at the front of the home are ideally suited as a private suite or home office. Upstairs, two bedrooms, a full bath and an area allowing for future expansion complete this plan. This plan is available with either a crawlspace or slab foundation. Please specify when ordering.

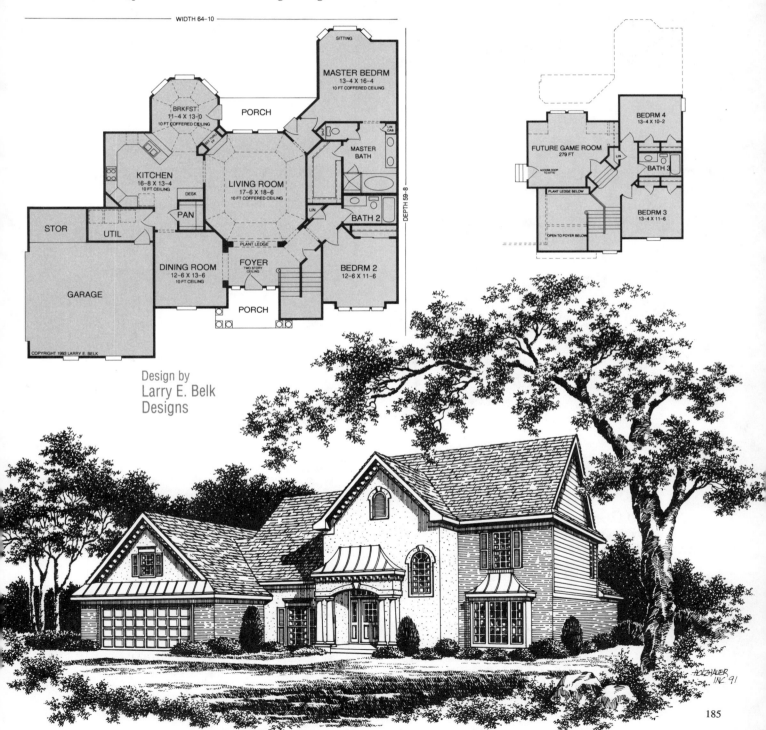

Design by
Larry E. Belk
Designs

185

COPYRIGHT LARRY E. BELK

WIDTH 58-10

MASTER BATH
9 FT CLG
K.S.

LIN
SEAT
PWDR

FP

GREAT ROOM
19-0 X 17-0
VOLUME CLG

←SLOPE TO VOLUME CLG→

PORCH

BRKFST RM
11-6 X 10-0
9 FT CLG

KITCHEN
12-0 X 14-0

FOYER
9 FT CLG

MASTER BEDRM
13-6 X 15-8
9 FT CLG

DINING ROOM
12-6 X 13-6
9 FT CLG

9 FT CLG

DEPTH 59-10

PORCH

PAN

UTIL
9-6 X 6-0

STORAGE

GARAGE

COPYRIGHT LARRY E. BELK

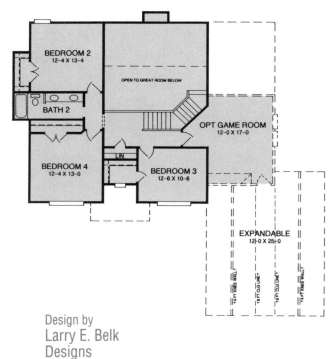

BEDROOM 2
12-4 X 13-4

OPEN TO GREAT ROOM BELOW

BATH 2

OPT GAME ROOM
12-0 X 17-0

BEDROOM 4
12-4 X 13-0

LIN

BEDROOM 3
12-6 X 10-6

EXPANDABLE
12-0 X 25-0

4 FT KNEE WALL
4 FT CLG LIMIT
4 FT CLG LIMIT
4 FT CLG LIMIT
4 FT KNEE WALL

Design by
Larry E. Belk
Designs

Design GG8093

First Floor: 1,635 square feet
Second Floor: 1,331 square feet
Total: 2,966 square feet
Flexible Space: Game Room & Expandable Area

● Twin gables and classic porch details give this home a look that is distinguished, yet warmly inviting. Inside, the floor plan is well-designed with the growing family in mind. A large great room is conveniently located near the kitchen and breakfast room. The kitchen features an abundance of cabinets and a large work island. The master suite is located down-stairs for privacy and features amenities such as the corner whirlpool tub, a separate shower, a double-bowl vanity and a huge walk-in closet. Upstairs, three additional bedrooms share a full hall bath. Additional flexible space is available for future needs. This plan is available with either a crawlspace or slab foundation. Please specify when ordering.

Design GG8049 First Floor: 1,764 square feet
Second Floor: 1,006 square feet; Total: 2,770 square feet
Flexible Space: Game Room

● Two distinctive pop-out dormers provide a chic image for this traditional home. This plan offers a wealth of livability in a compact layout. An efficient, spacious kitchen and breakfast area are located at the front of the house. The kitchen features a large walk-in pantry and a convenient pass-through to the dining room. The two-story great room, with a warming fireplace, is located to the rear of the plan, providing an unobstructed view of the rear grounds. The master bedroom, with large His and Hers walk-in closets, provides a private retreat. The pampering master bath is designed for self-indulgence with a corner whirlpool tub and an oversized shower. A split staircase leads to the second floor which contains two secondary bedrooms and a full bath. Stairs leading to the attic storage area are accessible from Bedroom 2 or the balcony. Area for a future game room with access to Bath 2 is conveniently located off the staircase. This plan is available with either a crawlspace or slab foundation. Please specify when ordering.

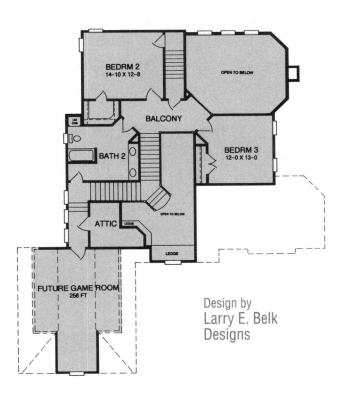

Design by
Larry E. Belk
Designs

COPYRIGHT LARRY E. BELK

Design GG8094

First Floor: 1,701 square feet
Second Floor: 1,122 square feet
Total: 2,823 square feet

Flexible Space: Game Room, Bath & Expandable Area

● Brick arches distinguish the exterior of this lovely traditional home. A large kitchen and breakfast room are located with views to the rear and provide plenty of room for informal family dining. The master suite is notable for its luxury bath with His and Hers walk-in closets, a corner whirlpool tub and a separate shower. The second floor contains three secondary bedrooms and a full bath. A huge gameroom awaits future development as well as a large closet that may be converted to another bath if needed. Additional space over the garage is also available. This plan is available with either a crawlspace or slab foundation. Please specify when ordering.

Design by
Larry E. Belk
Designs

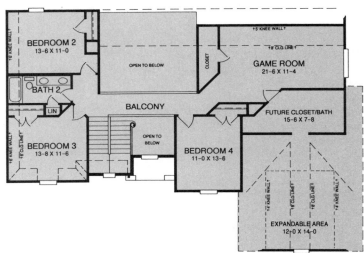

WIDTH 62-6

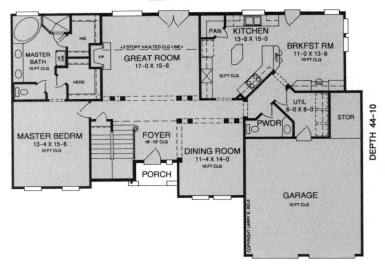

Design GG8010

First Floor: 1,902 square feet
Second Floor: 421 square feet
Total: 2,323 square feet
Flexible Space: Game Room & Expandable Area

● Double French doors with a half-round transom make the entry to this home a real eye-catcher. A bay window on the front—repeating the door treatment—balances this pleasing elevation. Through the entry is the great room with a window wall to the rear yard. The dining room, kitchen and breakfast areas are all conveniently grouped. The kitchen is equipped with a large cooktop island and an eating bar. The corner sink and the windows above make the kitchen bright and add interest to the area. A sun room off the kitchen expands the breakfast area and makes a cozy place for gathering the family. The master bedroom located at the front of the house is notable for its large bay window. Two ample closets and a large master bath complete the master suite. Also included downstairs are two additional bedrooms, Bath 2 and the stairway to the game room upstairs. An expandable area is included for future use. This plan is available with either a crawlspace or slab foundation. Please specify when ordering.

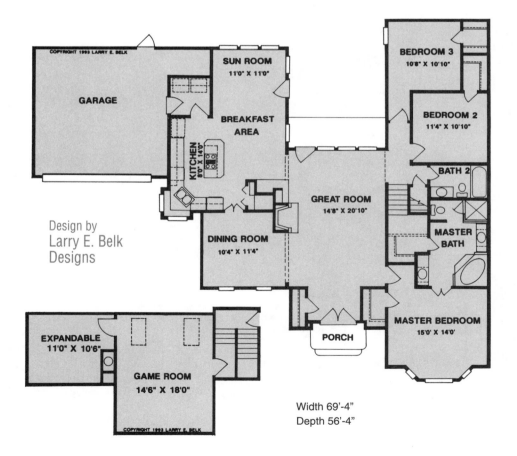

Design by
Larry E. Belk
Designs

Width 69'-4"
Depth 56'-4"

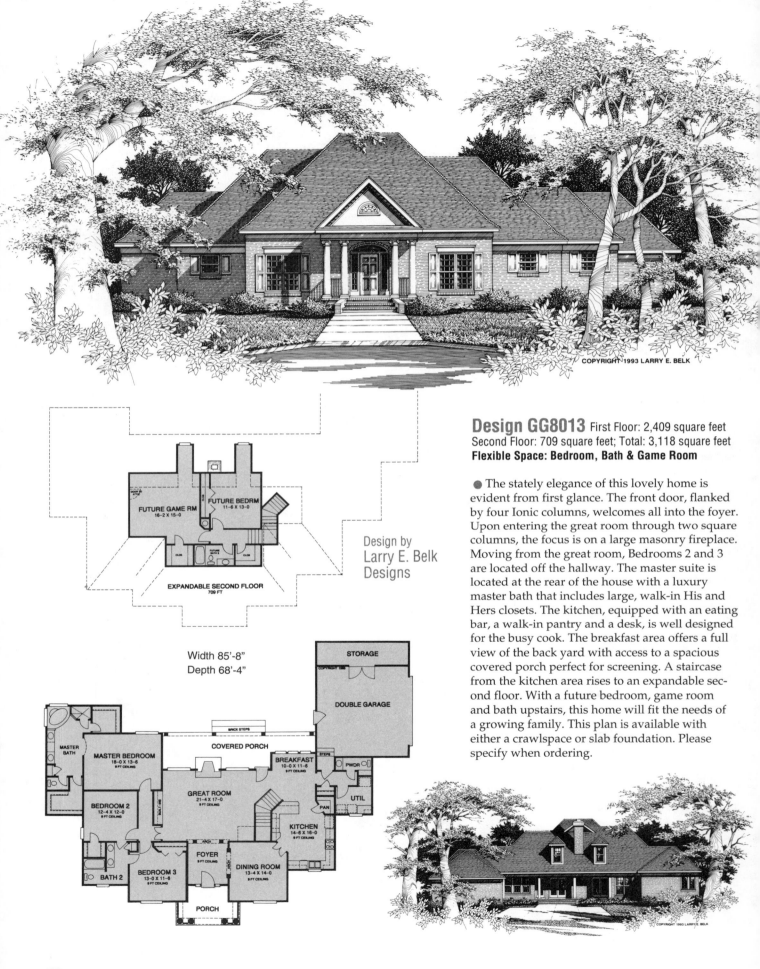

COPYRIGHT 1993 LARRY E. BELK

FUTURE GAME RM
16-2 X 15-0

FUTURE BEDRM
11-6 X 13-0

EXPANDABLE SECOND FLOOR
709 FT

Design by
Larry E. Belk
Designs

Width 85'-8"
Depth 68'-4"

STORAGE

DOUBLE GARAGE

MASTER BATH

MASTER BEDROOM
18-0 X 13-6
9 FT CEILING

COVERED PORCH

BREAKFAST
10-0 X 11-6
9 FT CEILING

PWDR

BEDROOM 2
12-4 X 12-0
9 FT CEILING

GREAT ROOM
21-4 X 17-0
9 FT CEILING

UTIL

PAN

KITCHEN
14-6 X 16-0
9 FT CEILING

BATH 2

BEDROOM 3
13-0 X 11-6
9 FT CEILING

FOYER
9 FT CEILING

DINING ROOM
13-4 X 14-0
9 FT CEILING

PORCH

Design GG8013 First Floor: 2,409 square feet
Second Floor: 709 square feet; Total: 3,118 square feet
Flexible Space: Bedroom, Bath & Game Room

● The stately elegance of this lovely home is
evident from first glance. The front door, flanked
by four Ionic columns, welcomes all into the foyer.
Upon entering the great room through two square
columns, the focus is on a large masonry fireplace.
Moving from the great room, Bedrooms 2 and 3
are located off the hallway. The master suite is
located at the rear of the house with a luxury
master bath that includes large, walk-in His and
Hers closets. The kitchen, equipped with an eating
bar, a walk-in pantry and a desk, is well designed
for the busy cook. The breakfast area offers a full
view of the back yard with access to a spacious
covered porch perfect for screening. A staircase
from the kitchen area rises to an expandable second floor. With a future bedroom, game room
and bath upstairs, this home will fit the needs of
a growing family. This plan is available with
either a crawlspace or slab foundation. Please
specify when ordering.

COPYRIGHT 1993 LARRY E. BELK

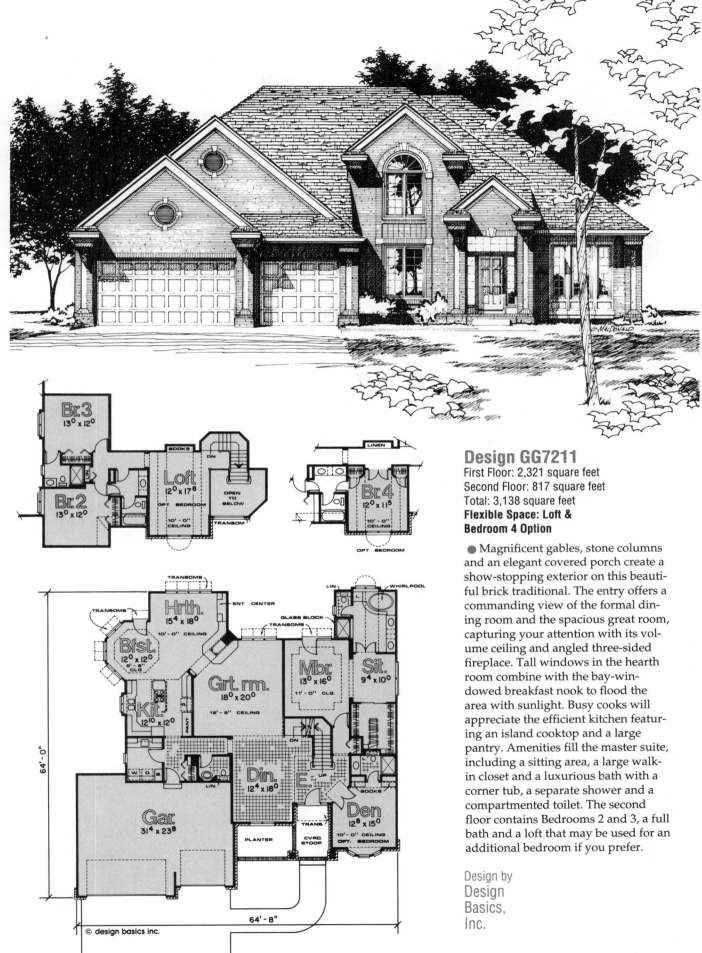

Design GG7211

First Floor: 2,321 square feet
Second Floor: 817 square feet
Total: 3,138 square feet

**Flexible Space: Loft &
Bedroom 4 Option**

● Magnificent gables, stone columns and an elegant covered porch create a show-stopping exterior on this beautiful brick traditional. The entry offers a commanding view of the formal dining room and the spacious great room, capturing your attention with its volume ceiling and angled three-sided fireplace. Tall windows in the hearth room combine with the bay-windowed breakfast nook to flood the area with sunlight. Busy cooks will appreciate the efficient kitchen featuring an island cooktop and a large pantry. Amenities fill the master suite, including a sitting area, a large walk-in closet and a luxurious bath with a corner tub, a separate shower and a compartmented toilet. The second floor contains Bedrooms 2 and 3, a full bath and a loft that may be used for an additional bedroom if you prefer.

Design by
Design
Basics,
Inc.

191

Design by
Design Traditions

GUEST BEDROOM
14'-10" X 10'-0"

BATH

DEN
15'-0" X 10'-0"

MASTER BATH
10'-4" X 10'-6"

BATH   W.I.C.

MASTER BEDROOM
15'-10" X 17'-8"

OPEN TO BELOW

BEDROOM NO. 2
11'-2" X 11'-0"

BEDROOM NO. 3
11'-4" X 12'-0"

Design GG9814

First Floor: 1,370 square feet
Second Floor: 1,673 square feet
Total: 3,043 square feet
Flexible Space: Guest Room & Den

● This English Georgian home features
a dramatic brick exterior. The series of
windows and jack-arch detailing are second only to the drama created by the
porte cochere. The detached garage
allows the home to stretch to the gardens.
Enter into the two-story foyer and the
unusually shaped staircase and balcony
overlook create a tremendous first
impression. Separated only by a classical

colonnade detail, the living and dining
rooms are perfect for entertaining. The
great room features a fireplace on the outside wall. This room opens to the breakfast room and angled kitchen with plenty
of cabinets and counter space. Upstairs is
a guest room, a children's den area, two
family bedrooms and a master suite. Look
for the cozy fireplace, tray ceiling and
sumptuous bath in the master. This home
is designed with a basement foundation.

Width 73'-6"
Depth 49'

LAUNDRY
6'-4" X 8'-0"

BREAKFAST
10'-4" X 10'-6"

DECK

KITCHEN
11'-6" X 11'-0"

GREAT ROOM
19'-0" X 17'-0"

TWO CAR GARAGE
21'-4" X 21'-4"

PORTE-COCHERE
15'-0" X 16'-0"

DINING ROOM
11'-2" X 13'-4"

LIVING ROOM
10'-8" X 14'-6"

FOYER
7'-6" X 17'-6"

CUSTOMIZABLE

Custom Alterations? See page 237 for customizing this plan to your specifications.

Quote One™

Cost to build? See page 232 to order complete cost estimate to build this house in your area!

ROOF

BEDROOM 12⁰ x 10⁰

BATH

BEDROOM 11⁴ x 13⁶

BEDROOM 13⁸ x 13⁴

ATTIC

ROOF

DN

CL

DESK   SHELVES   LIN

ATTIC

DN

RAILING

CL   CL

TUB   BATH   OPEN

ROOF

VANITY

DRESSING RM.

SEAT   LINEN

MASTER BEDROOM 16⁴ x 17²

ROOF

Design by
Home Planners,
Inc.

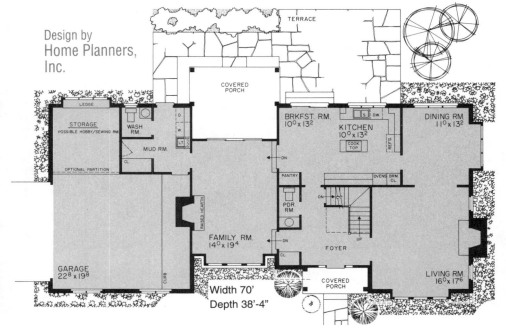

TERRACE

COVERED PORCH

LEDGE

STORAGE
POSSIBLE HOBBY/SEWING RM.

WASH RM.

MUD RM.

OPTIONAL PARTITION

CL

BRKFST. RM. 10⁰ x 13²

KITCHEN 10⁰ x 13²

COOK TOP

DW

REF'S

DINING RM. 11⁰ x 13²

DN

PANTRY

OVENS   BRM. CL.

PDR. RM.

DN

UP

FOYER

GARAGE 22⁸ x 19⁸

RAISED HEARTH

FAMILY RM. 14⁰ x 19⁴

CL

DN

CURB

COVERED PORCH

LIVING RM. 16⁰ x 17⁶

Width 70'
Depth 38'-4"

Design GG2855

First Floor: 1,372 square feet
Second Floor: 1,245 square feet
Total: 2,617 square feet
Flexible Space: Hobby/Sewing Room

L D

● This elegant Tudor house is perfect for the family who wants to move-up in living area, style and luxury. As you enter this home you will find a large living room with a fireplace on your right. Adjacent, the formal dining room has easy access to both the living room and the kitchen. The kitchen/break-fast room has an open plan and access to the rear terrace. Sunken a few steps, the spacious family room is high-lighted with a fireplace and access to the rear, covered porch. Note the optional planning of the storage area located in the garage, perfect as a hobby or sewing room. Upstairs, your family will enjoy three bedrooms and a full bath, along with a spacious master bedroom suite. This is truly a house that will bring many years of pleasure to your family.

● Fluted columns and decorative mouldings at the grand entrance present a stately, dignified exterior. A volume entry with graceful flared staircase opens to the formal dining room and parlor. The comfortable great room with boxed-beam ceiling and a raised-hearth fireplace is brightened by arched transom windows. A strategically located wet bar serves the dining room and the great room. The luxurious master suite includes a large walk-in closet and a spacious bath with whirlpool tub. A spacious media room with a built-in entertainment center is located on the second floor, along with three bedrooms and two full baths.

Design GG9382

First Floor: 1,923 square feet
Second Floor: 1,106 square feet
Total: 3,029 square feet
Flexible Space: Media Room

Design by
Design
Basics,
Inc.

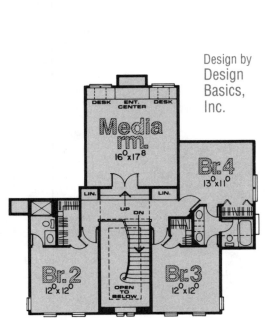

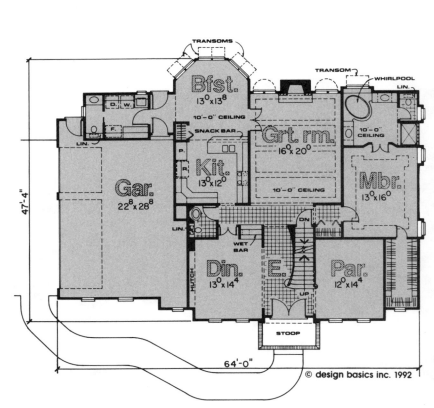

© design basics inc. 1992

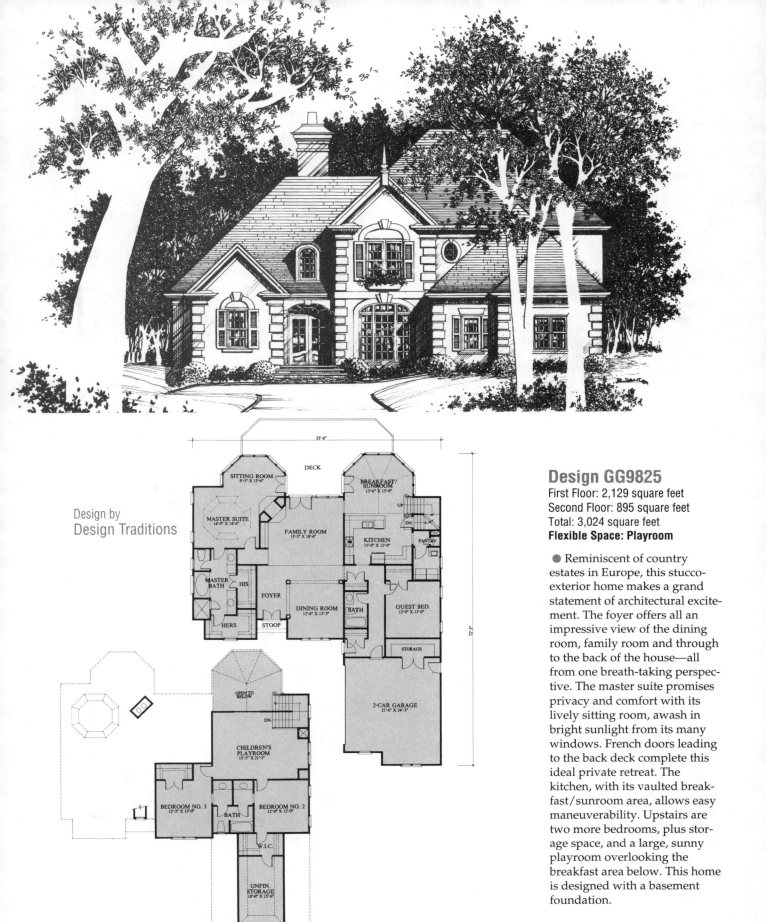

Design by
Design Traditions

Floor plan labels:

55'-6"

SITTING ROOM
9'-3" X 13'-6"

DECK

BREAKFAST/
SUNROOM
13'-6" X 15'-0"

MASTER SUITE
14'-0" X 14'-6"

FAMILY ROOM
15'-3" X 18'-6"

UP

DN.

KITCHEN
15'-0" X 12'-0"

PANTRY

MASTER
BATH

HIS

FOYER

DINING ROOM
12'-6" X 13'-3"

BATH

GUEST BED.
12'-0" X 13'-0"

HERS

STOOP

STORAGE

72'-3"

2-CAR GARAGE
21'-6" X 24'-3"

OPEN TO
BELOW

DN.

CHILDREN'S
PLAYROOM
15'-3" X 21'-3"

BEDROOM NO. 3
12'-3" X 13'-0"

BATH

BEDROOM NO. 2
12'-0" X 12'-0"

W.I.C.

UNFIN.
STORAGE
10'-0" X 15'-6"

Design GG9825

First Floor: 2,129 square feet
Second Floor: 895 square feet
Total: 3,024 square feet
Flexible Space: Playroom

● Reminiscent of country
estates in Europe, this stucco-
exterior home makes a grand
statement of architectural excite-
ment. The foyer offers all an
impressive view of the dining
room, family room and through
to the back of the house—all
from one breath-taking perspec-
tive. The master suite promises
privacy and comfort with its
lively sitting room, awash in
bright sunlight from its many
windows. French doors leading
to the back deck complete this
ideal private retreat. The
kitchen, with its vaulted break-
fast/sunroom area, allows easy
maneuverability. Upstairs are
two more bedrooms, plus storage space, and a large, sunny
playroom overlooking the
breakfast area below. This home
is designed with a basement
foundation.

195

Design GG9134

First Floor: 1,713 square feet
Second Floor: 1,226 square feet
Total: 2,939 square feet
Optional Guest Room: 262 square feet
Flexible Space: Guest Suite & Gameroom

● Large families will appreciate the size and
scope of this grand plan. There are three secondary bedrooms in addition to the first-floor
master suite, plus a guest room with bath over
the garage. The living room has a fireplace and
is complemented by the formal dining room to
the right of the entry foyer. An island kitchen is
served by a breakfast nook and sports a pocket
door to the dining room. Note the large walk-
in closet in the master bedroom and the
window seat and built-in bookcase in the
balcony upstairs.

Design by
Larry W.
Garnett &
Associates, Inc.

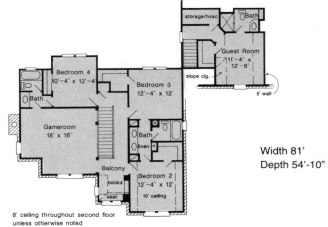

storage/hvac   Bath
Guest Room
11'-4" x
12'-8"
slope clg.
5' wall

Bedroom 4
10'-4" x 12'-4"
Bath
Bedroom 3
12'-4" x 12'
Gameroom
18' x 16'
Bath
linen
Balcony
books
Bedroom 2
12'-4" x 12'
seat
10' ceiling

8' ceiling throughout second floor
unless otherwise noted

Width 81'
Depth 54'-10"

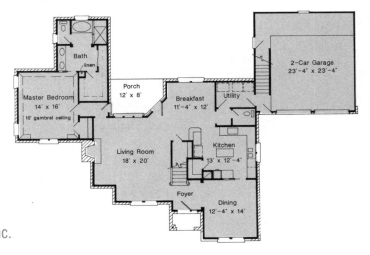

Bath
linen
Master Bedroom
14' x 16'
10' gambrel ceiling
Porch
12' x 8'
Breakfast
11'-4" x 12'
Utility
2-Car Garage
23'-4" x 23'-4"
Living Room
18' x 20'
Kitchen
13' x 12'-4"
Foyer
Dining
12'-4" x 14'

Second Floor

Bedroom 3
11'-8" x 15'-8"

Bath 2

Bedroom 4
12'-8" x 12'

books

4' wall

slope ceiling

linen

Balcony

down

up

Optional Gameroom
18'-8" x 18'-8"

down

slope ceiling

Bedroom 2
15'-8" x 11'-8"

Books

slope ceiling

display ledge

9' x 11'

5' wall

8' ceiling throughout second floor unless otherwise noted

Design by
Larry W.
Garnett &
Associates, Inc.

First Floor

Built-in Breakfast Table

French Door

Breakfast

Linen

Bath

Dining
12'-8" x 11'-4"

Kitchen
10'-8" x 12'

Util.

shelves

Master Bedroom
19' x 15'-8"

Buffet

Pantry

French Doors

French Doors

Living Room
15'-4" x 19'

1/2
Bath

Raised Foyer

Up

2-Car Garage
23'-8" x 21'-4"

52'

57'-8"

9' ceilings throughout first floor

Design GG8927

First Floor: 1,575 square feet
Second Floor: 764 square feet
Total: 2,339 square feet
Optional Gameroom: 468 square feet
Flexible Space: Gameroom

● This stately two-story home is highlighted by interesting multi-pane windows, an arched entry way and a brick exterior. Open floor planning makes this design appear larger than it is. The formal living and dining area combine to create a spacious formal living area. A cheery fireplace and a built-in buffet flank French doors that open onto the side yard. Casual dining is a delight with the built-in breakfast table lit by surrounding windows, perfect for lingering over the morning paper. The master bedroom provides a welcome retreat with its cozy fireplace, huge walk-in closet and pampering bath. Upstairs, Bedrooms 2, 3 and 4 (all with walk-in closets) share a full bath. An optional gameroom provides additional space for indoor recreation and a bookcase to hold books for more quiet times.

Design GG9130
Square Footage: 2,349 square feet
Bonus Room: 398 square feet
Flexible Space: Guest Room or Hobby Room

● Brick arches at the angled front entry along with multiple gables and a bay window give the exterior of this home a comfortable, yet distinctive look. Unique details set this plan apart: angled living room with 10-foot ceiling, fireplace in the master bedroom, octagonal breakfast room. The kitchen features an island and pass-through bar to the breakfast room. The rear covered porch can be accessed through two sets of French doors. Additional space above the garage can be developed as needed for live-in relatives, a college student or for studio or hobby space. There's also convenient storage space in the garage.

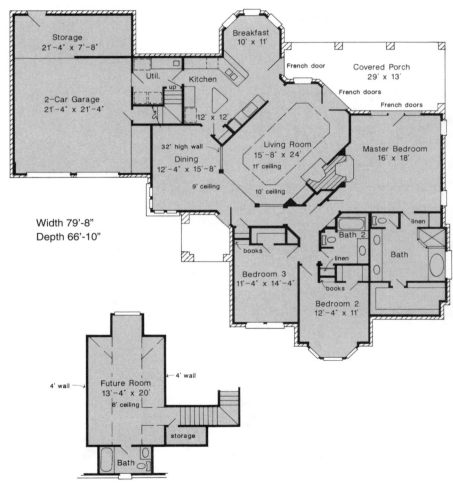

Width 79'-8"
Depth 66'-10"

Design by
Larry W.
Garnett &
Associates, Inc.

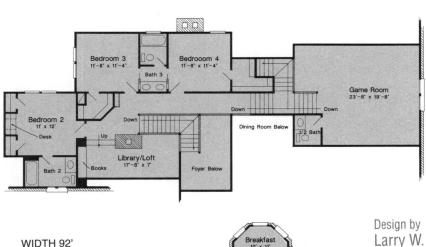

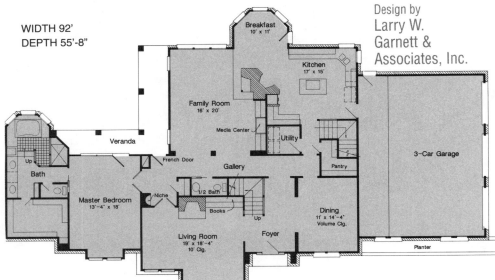

Bedroom 3
11'-8" x 11'-4"

Bath 3

Bedrooom 4
11'-8" x 11'-4"

Game Room
23'-8" x 19'-8"

Bedroom 2
11' x 12'

Desk

Up

Down

Down

Down

Dining Room Below

1/2 Bath

Library/Loft
17'-8" x 7'

Foyer Below

Bath 2

Books

WIDTH 92'
DEPTH 55'-8"

Design by
Larry W.
Garnett &
Associates, Inc.

Breakfast
10' x 11'

Kitchen
17' x 15'

Family Room
16' x 20'

Media Center

Utility

Veranda

French Door

Gallery

Pantry

3-Car Garage

Up

Bath

Niche

1/2 Bath

Master Bedroom
13'-4" x 18'

Books

Up

Dining
11' x 14'-4"
Volume Clg.

Living Room
19' x 18'-4"
10' Clg.

Foyer

Planter

9' Clg. Throughout First And Second Floor
Unless Otherwise Noted

Design GG9152

First Floor: 2,272 square feet
Second Floor: 1,453 square feet
Total: 3,725 square feet
**Flexible Space: Game Room &
Library/Loft**

● Beautiful style reigns both
inside and out for this gracious
two-story design. The facade was
influenced by Tudor homes of the
1930s. The foyer opens to a formal
living room with a fireplace and a
built-in bookcase. The formal dining room has a sloped ceiling with
a balcony above. The kitchen has
an island cooktop and shares a fireplace with the bay-windowed
breakfast area. The master suite
features French doors and a luxurious master bath with a raised
area for a whirlpool tub. The second floor holds three secondary
bedrooms and an optional
gameroom.

Design by
Larry W.
Garnett &
Associates, Inc.

Design GG9124

First Floor: 2,317 square feet
Second Floor: 400 square feet
Total: 2,717 square feet
Flexible Space: Loft

● One-story living makes the most of a high roofline in this delightful plan. The family room dominates the center of the design and has easy access to the formal dining room, the breakfast room with a window seat and the island kitchen. The bedrooms are to the right of the plan with the master suite holding space to the rear. It features a hexagonal sitting area with a gazebo ceiling and a skylit bath. Upstairs is a large loft with ½-bath and wet bar that makes a grand game room, studio or hobby room.

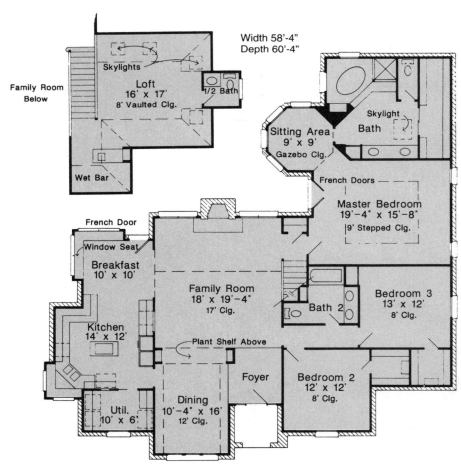

200

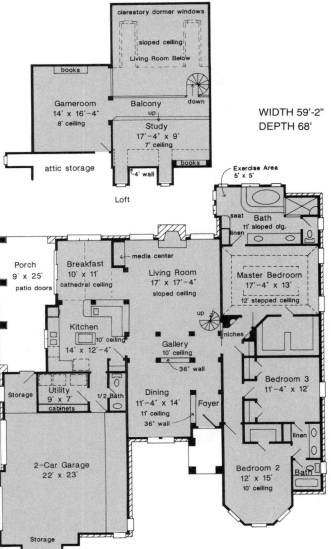

clerestory dormer windows

sloped ceiling

Living Room Below

books

Gameroom
14' x 16'-4"
8' ceiling

Balcony

down

Study
17'-4" x 9'
7' ceiling

up

attic storage

books

4' wall

Loft

Exercise Area
5' x 5'

seat

Bath
11' sloped clg.

linen

Porch
9' x 25'
patio doors

Breakfast
10' x 11'
cathedral ceiling

media center

Living Room
17' x 17'-4"
sloped ceiling

Master Bedroom
17'-4" x 13'
12' stepped ceiling

Kitchen
14' x 12'-4"
10' ceiling

up

Gallery
10' ceiling

36" wall

niches

Storage

Utility
9' x 7'
cabinets

1/2 Bath

Dining
11'-4" x 14'
11' ceiling
36" wall

Foyer

Bedroom 3
11'-4" x 12'

2-Car Garage
22' x 23'

linen

Bedroom 2
12' x 15'
10' ceiling

Bath

Storage

WIDTH 59'-2"
DEPTH 68'

Design GG8922

First Floor: 2,242 square feet
Second Floor: 507 square feet
Total: 2,749 square feet
Flexible Space: Gameroom & Study

● Inspired by the turn-of-the-century homes along the Atlantic Coast, this design features finely detailed brickwork which is accented with shingle siding. The formal dining room is separated from traffic by three-foot walls. The grand two-story living room includes a sloped ceiling, a media center, a fireplace and circular stairs to the second floor. The gourmet kitchen overlooks the living area, breakfast room and a large covered porch. Three bedrooms include a master suite with spacious bath. The second floor offers a gameroom and a cozy study with dormer windows, a sloped ceiling and a built-in bookcase.

Design by
Larry W.
Garnett &
Associates, Inc.

REAR VIEW

Design GG4390

First Floor: 1,507 square feet
Second Floor: 1,086 square feet
Total: 2,593 square feet
Flexible Space: Playroom/Bonus Room

● This plan successfully joins elements of contemporary and traditional design for a thoroughly pleasing result. The unusual set of roof lines creates interesting patterns on the inside on all the first-floor rooms. The second floor has a balcony overlook to the living room below and also contains a bonus room with dormer that would make a great playroom.

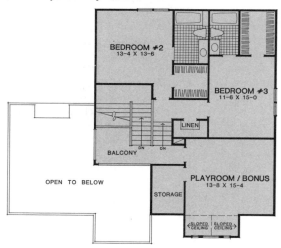

BEDROOM #2
13-4 X 13-6

BEDROOM #3
11-6 X 15-0

LINEN

BALCONY

DN   DN

OPEN TO BELOW

STORAGE

PLAYROOM / BONUS
13-8 X 15-4

SLOPED CEILING   SLOPED CEILING

Design by
Home Planners, Inc.

LIFESTYLE HOME PLANS

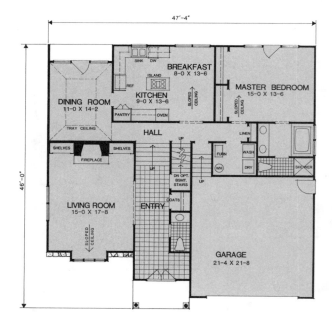

47'-4"

46'-0"

SINK DW

BREAKFAST
8-0 X 13-6

MASTER BEDROOM
15-0 X 13-6

ISLAND

REF

DINING ROOM
11-0 X 14-2

KITCHEN
9-0 X 13-6

SLOPED CEILING

SLOPED CEILING

PANTRY   OVEN

LINEN

TRAY CEILING

HALL

SHELVES   SHELVES

UP

FURN

WASH

FIREPLACE

UP

WH

DRY

SHOWER

DN OPT.
BSMT.
STAIRS

UP

LIVING ROOM
15-0 X 17-8

ENTRY

COATS

GARAGE
21-4 X 21-8

SLOPED CEILING

Photo by Laszlo Regos

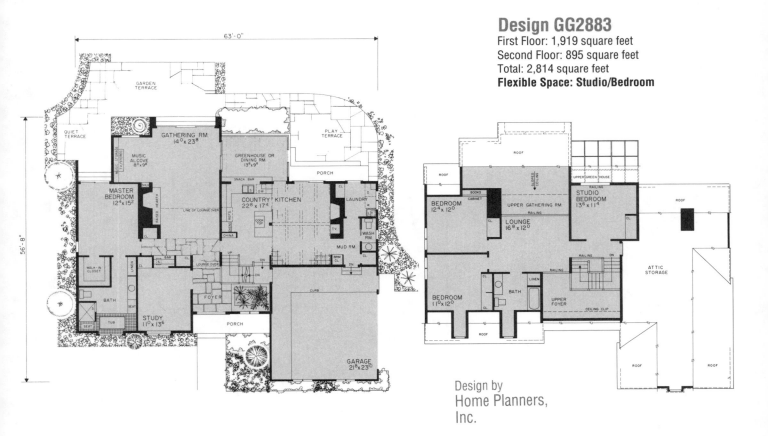

Design GG2883
First Floor: 1,919 square feet
Second Floor: 895 square feet
Total: 2,814 square feet
Flexible Space: Studio/Bedroom

Design by
Home Planners,
Inc.

● A country-style home is part of America's fascination with the rural past. This design's emphasis of the traditional home is in its gambrel roof, dormers and fanlight windows. Having a traditional exterior from the street view, this home also has window walls and a greenhouse, which opens the house to the outdoors in a thoroughly contemporary manner. Like the country houses of the past, it has a gathering room for family get-togethers or entertaining; but the adjacent two-story greenhouse doubles as the dining room and has a pass-through to the country kitchen, which just might be the heart of the house with its work zone and sitting room. There are four bedrooms on the two floors—the master bedroom suite on the first floor and three more on the second floor. A lounge, overlooking the gathering room and front foyer, is also on the second floor.

Design GG2892

First Floor: 1,623 square feet
Second Floor: 160 square feet
Total: 1,783 square feet
Flexible Space: Loft

● What a striking contemporary! It houses an efficient floor plan with many outstanding features. The foyer has a sloped ceiling and an open staircase to the basement. To the right of the foyer is the work center. Note the snack bar, laundry and covered dining porch, along with the step-saving kitchen. Both the gathering and dining rooms overlook the backyard. Each of three bedrooms has access to an outdoor area. The second-floor loft could be used as a sewing room, den or lounge.

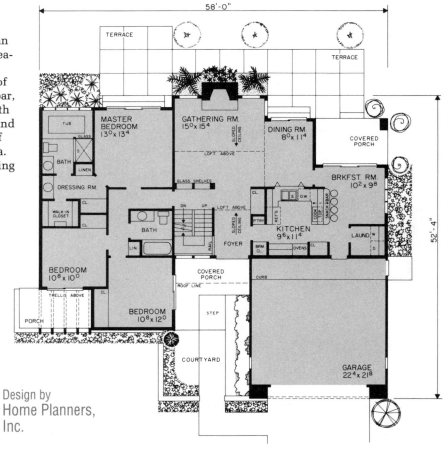

Design by
Home Planners,
Inc.

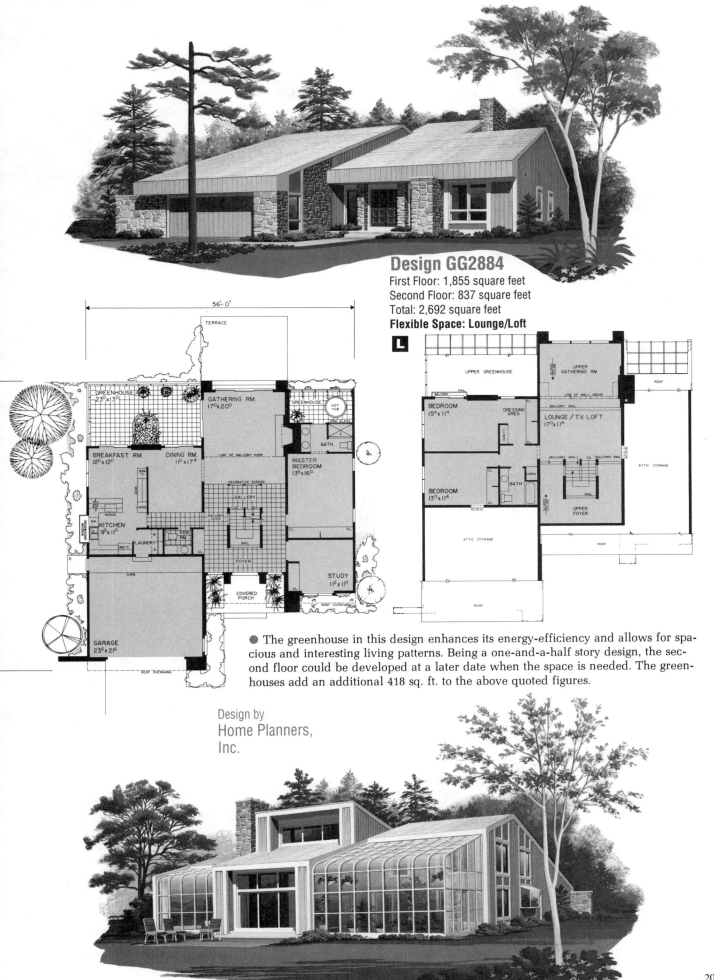

Design GG2884

First Floor: 1,855 square feet
Second Floor: 837 square feet
Total: 2,692 square feet

Flexible Space: Lounge/Loft

● The greenhouse in this design enhances its energy-efficiency and allows for spacious and interesting living patterns. Being a one-and-a-half story design, the second floor could be developed at a later date when the space is needed. The greenhouses add an additional 418 sq. ft. to the above quoted figures.

Design by
Home Planners,
Inc.

Design GG8683 First Floor: 2,254 square feet
Second Floor: 608 square feet; Total: 2,862 square feet
Flexible Space: Loft/Additional Bedroom

● Indoor/outdoor relationships are enhanced by the beautiful courtyard that decorates the center of this home. A gallery provides views of the courtyard and leads to a kitchen featuring a center work island and an adjacent breakfast room offering easy access to the back yard. Combined with the family room, this space will be a favorite for informal gatherings. To the left, the gallery leads to the formal living room and master suite. The secluded master bedroom features a volume ceiling and double doors that lead to a covered patio. Retreat to the master bath, where a relaxing tub awaits to pamper. The second floor contains a full bath shared by Bedrooms 3 and 4 and a loft that provides flexible space for an additional bedroom.

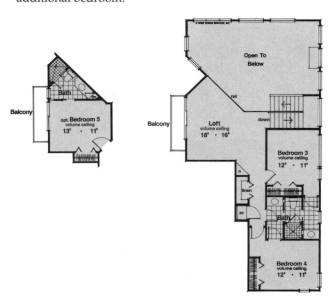

Design by
Home Design
Services, Inc.

206

7

DETACHED-SPACE DESIGNS

So Close, and Yet So Far Away

While the previous chapters focus on expanding and utilizing space in homes originally built, the plans on the following pages are devoted to creating a *separate* space effectively designed and built to enhance a range of exterior styles.

Guest cottages are featured that serve several purposes and offer solutions for a variety of living arrangements. One of the most common of these is the provision of living quarters for family members returning to the nest. Whether they are elderly parents or older children, privacy is a primary consideration. Best of all, this option promises the security of having family close by while retaining independence for everyone. Designs GG9094 and GG8091 on pages 209 and 180 provide charming floor plans with features sure to please both young and old while fulfilling the needs and desires of everyone.

You may choose to exercise your options with a facility devoted to total fitness. Design GGR129 on page 218 is filled with amenities to enhance any workout. These include a mirrored wall and handrail, a separate dressing room and bath, and a sauna and hot tub. To heighten your workouts you may take an invigorating dip in the pool. After all, when it's Summertime, the livin' *should* be easy. Design GGG238 on page 221 works double duty to provide a pool cabana that incorporates a summer kitchen for effortless outdoor meal preparation.

The child in each of us will appreciate the wonderful playhouses represented in this group of plans. The Victorian setting provided by Design GGG228 on page 223 incorporates gracious surroundings that are perfect for a tea party with teddy. Imaginations will soar—and if a child listens, they may hear the thundering hooves of horses crossing the castle drawbridge of Design GGG235 (page 224). Or they may sail off to Never Never Land on Design GGG229 (page 225) where young Captains Courageous and land lubbers alike will have the time of their lives. For those in-between-teens, Design GGR126 on page 227 offers a territory of their own in the form of a multi-use media cottage.

Artists and craftsmen will be inspired by the lighting in Design GGG109 on page 228—an art studio complete with a sun room and work table. The selection of free-to-be spaces just wouldn't be complete without the inclusion of a workshop, and the one featured here is as sturdy and functional as they come! Design GGG111 on page 229 is a winning combination of garage and workshop with lots of wall space for tools, a skylight, and separate storage for lumber or large items—making this an ideal plan for those with special projects in mind.

The structures described are just a few of the outstanding choices offered in this chapter. This portfolio of plans is designed to be useful, imaginative and complementary to the landscape.

Design GG9132

First Floor: 449 square feet
Second Floor: 132 square feet
Total: 581 square feet
Use Of Space: Guest Cottage

Design by
**Larry W.
Garnett &
Associates, Inc.**

● This lovely cottage can serve a variety of lifestyle functions—as a guest house, mother-in-law quarters or as a cozy primary or secondary home for a single or a retired couple. Built-ins maximize the use of space in the living areas. Large windows make the smaller-sized rooms more airy and open. A spiral staircase leads to an upper loft that can be used as an additional bedroom or as office space.

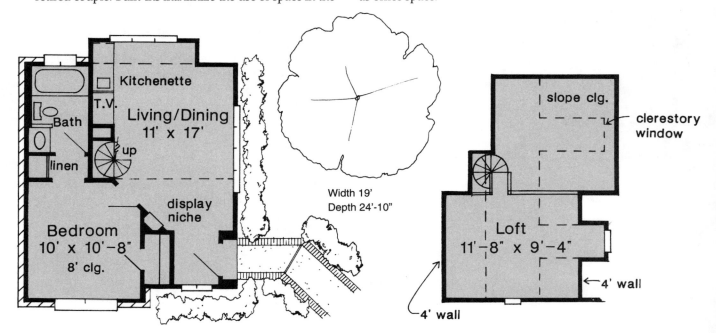

Width 19'
Depth 24'-10"

Design GG9094

First Floor: 627 square feet
Second Floor: 90 square feet
Total: 717 square feet
Use Of Space: Guest Cottage

● Whether you're thinking about a vacation home or a "granny flat" addition to your existing home, this little cottage might be just the alternative you're looking for. The main-level living area provides a full kitchen with the sink in a bay-window area and an attached dining area. A bedroom provides access to a side yard. There is also an abundance of closets. An incline ladder in the living area leads to a loft area overlooking the living room.

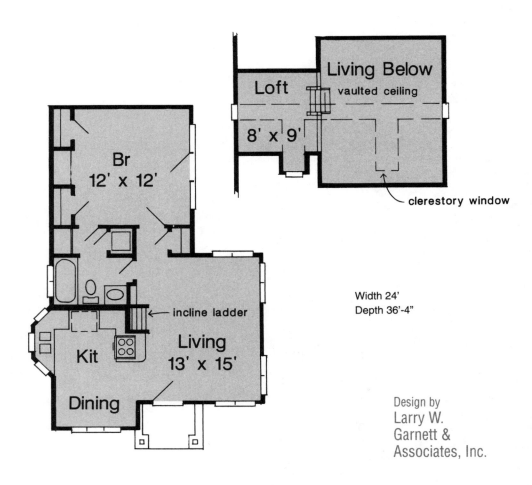

Width 24'
Depth 36'-4"

Design by
Larry W.
Garnett &
Associates, Inc.

Design GG8901

Square Footage: 582
Use Of Space: Guest Cottage

● This charming cottage offers a perfect solution which meets the needs of today's family. Attached to a two-car garage, efficient living quarters provide comfort and ideal livability for weekend guests, children that have returned to the nest for short or extended visits, or use as an in-law suite. Special features include a welcoming covered front porch, a bay-windowed dining room and space for a washer and dryer. If desired, a covered walkway can be extended from the porch to the main house.

Design by
Larry W.
Garnett &
Associates, Inc.

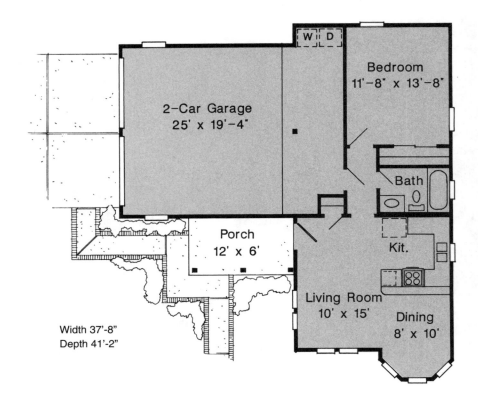

W D

2-Car Garage
25' x 19'-4"

Bedroom
11'-8" x 13'-8"

Bath

Porch
12' x 6'

Kit.

Living Room
10' x 15'

Dining
8' x 10'

Width 37'-8"
Depth 41'-2"

210

Design GG9133

First Floor: 440 square feet
Loft: 126 square feet
Total: 566 square feet
Use Of Space: Guest Cottage

● Charming exterior details make the most of this quaint cottage: dormer windows, covered entry and wood siding. The interior floor plan is perfect for use as a guest house, vacation residence or for comfortably accommodating an extended-stay family. The bay-windowed dinette is complemented by a small kitchen and ample living area. The upstairs loft serves as an additional bedroom or as studio space. A detached two-car garage is included with this plan.

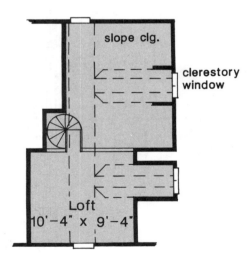

slope clg.

clerestory window

Loft
10'-4" x 9'-4"

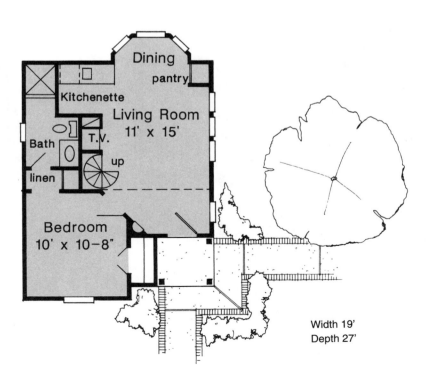

Dining

pantry

Kitchenette

Living Room
11' x 15'

Bath

T.V.

linen

up

Bedroom
10' x 10-8"

Width 19'
Depth 27'

Design by
Larry W.
Garnett &
Associates, Inc.

Design GG8921

Square Footage: 525

Use Of Space: Above-Garage Living Quarters

● The cozy living quarters located above the garage have all the elements of home. Every bit of space in these 525-square-foot quarters is utilized, offering an ideal place for students to live. The kitchen rests to the right of the living area, handy for preparing snacks and taking a break from the books. The bathroom includes a shower and a vanity, providing lots of space to get ready for school in the morning. Plenty of room is supplied in the living area for sleeping and studying.

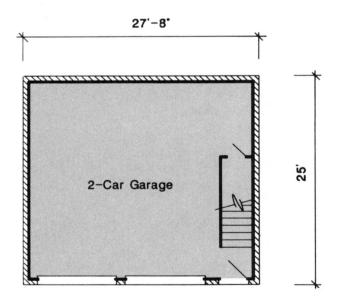

27'-8"

2-Car Garage

25'

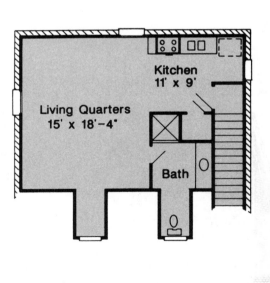

Kitchen
11' x 9'

Living Quarters
15' x 18'-4"

Bath

Design by

Larry W. Garnett & Associates, Inc.

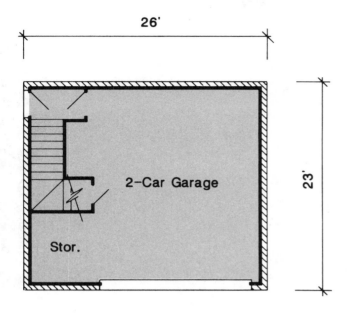

26'

23'

2-Car Garage

Stor.

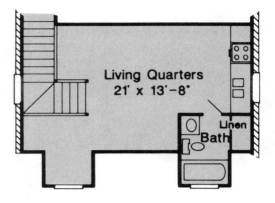

Living Quarters
21' x 13'-8"

Linen
Bath

Design by
Larry W.
Garnett &
Associates, Inc.

Design GG8920
Square Footage: 364
Use Of Space: Above-Garage Living Quarters

● The focal point of the traditional brick exterior is the wood-sided dormers, blending to complement a variety of home styles. Interior stairs lead from the garage to quaint living quarters on the second floor. The living area makes the most of its space, supplying an efficient kitchen on the right side, and a bath nearby. The tub is recessed to utilize space provided by the dormer and the linen cupboard is designed for lots of storage. Plenty of convenience is packed into this 364-square-foot living area, making it the perfect choice for students or children coming back to the nest.

Design GGR128
Use Of Space: Above-Garage Living Quarters

● A garage is just a garage—but a garage topped by a studio apartment can provide a great getaway for children and adults alike. This space also provides the perfect place for private guest quarters or possibly a rental unit for extra income. An arbor leads past the garage and up a stairway to the apartment entrance. The high open living space features a romantic wood stove, a cozy sitting area on one side and a small kitchen and bathroom on the other.

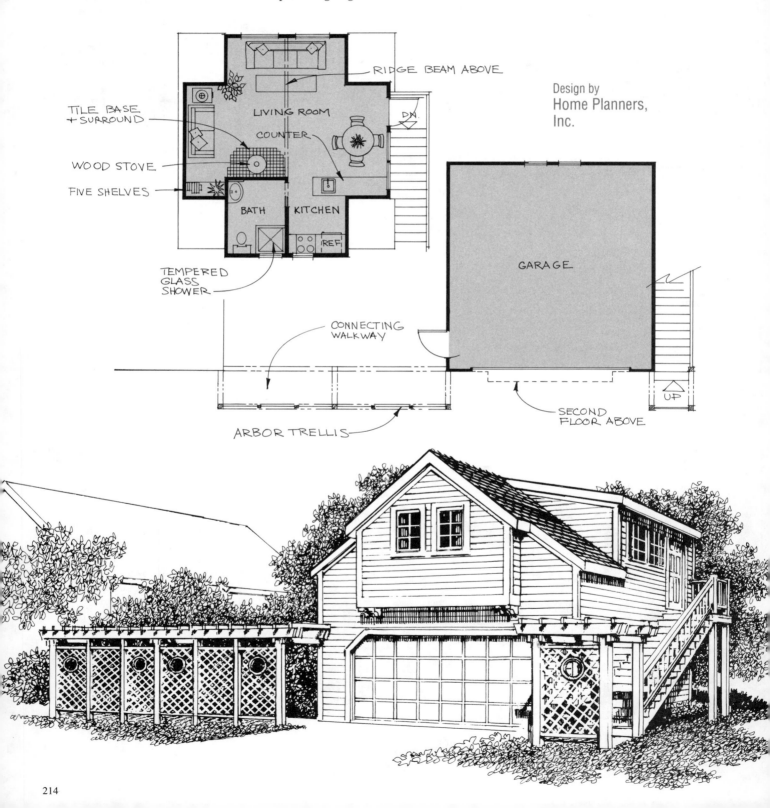

RIDGE BEAM ABOVE

Design by
Home Planners, Inc.

TILE BASE + SURROUND

LIVING ROOM

DN.

WOOD STOVE

COUNTER

FIVE SHELVES

BATH

KITCHEN

REF.

TEMPERED GLASS SHOWER

GARAGE

CONNECTING WALKWAY

SECOND FLOOR ABOVE

ARBOR TRELLIS

UP

Design GGR130
Use Of Space: Guest Cottage

● For families that want to bring parents or children back to the nest, this cozy 530-square-foot cottage offers the perfect opportunity. The recessed corner entry and generous use of windows contribute an extra feeling of spaciousness and light. The front door opens on the living room. To the right, a kitchen equipped with a dishwasher and full-size oven/range shares ample space with the dining room. The bathroom and bedroom are located at the rear and complete this charming plan.

Design by
Home Planners,
Inc.

TEMPERED
GLASS SHOWER

LIN.

BATH

LIVING ROOM

BEDROOM

OVERHEAD
CABINETS

KITCHEN

REF.

COVERED ENTRY

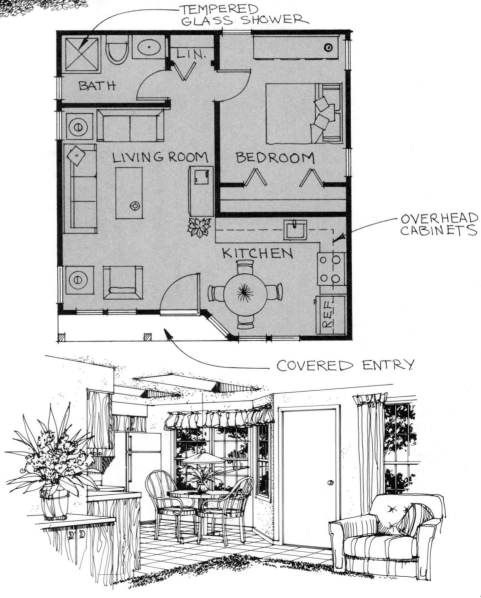

Design by
Home Planners,
Inc.

Design GGG230
Use Of Space: Studio/Guest House

● This versatile design features a unique siding pattern: a little bit of country with a pinch of contemporary sophistication. You can build this 440-square-foot structure on a slab, crawlspace or basement foundation. Planned to take advantage of natural light from all sides, this design will make a perfect studio, game room or office. Or, add a shower in the utility room and it becomes a guest house. Features include a half bath, a 6'x8' kitchen large enough for a stove and refrigerator and a utility room with ample space for a furnace and hot water tank. With all the amenities provided, you could work or relax here for days without ever leaving! The porch area is a charming place to relax and put your feet up as you or your guests contemplate the events of the day or prepare for tomorrow.

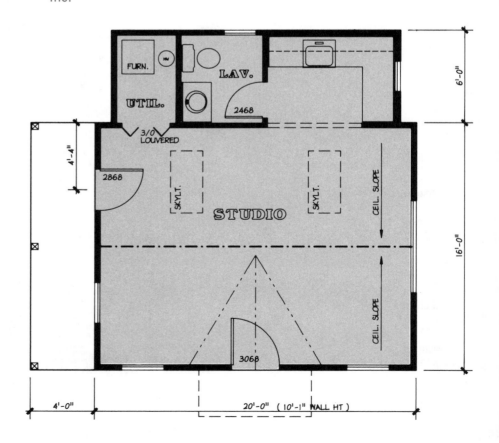

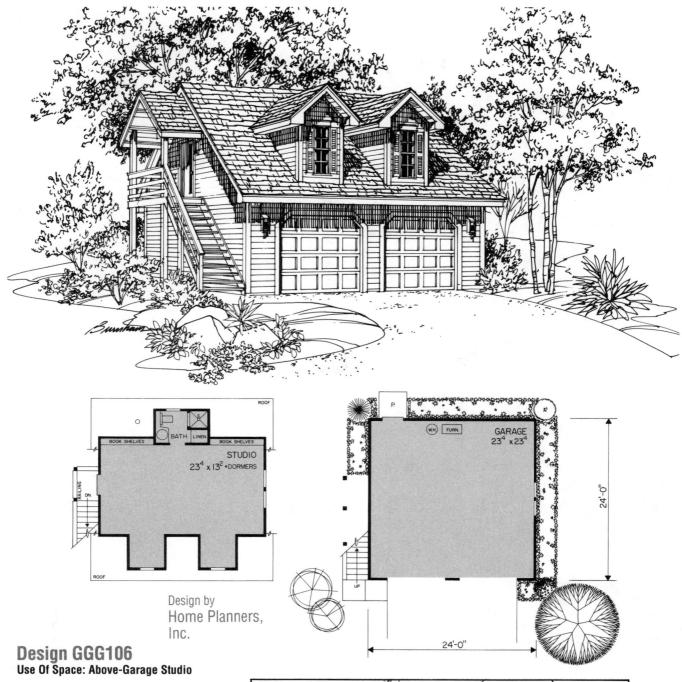

Design by
Home Planners,
Inc.

Design GGG106
Use Of Space: Above-Garage Studio

● Can you top this? Our two-car garage has an artist's studio nestled snugly on the second floor. The Cape Cod-style design, with three dormers, large shutters, paneled doors, and characteristic proportions of roof to floor makes a strong visual statement that would complement a large number of traditional housing styles. An exterior staircase, covered at the top, leads to 300 square feet of fully insulated studio space; adjacent is a full 4x7-foot bath with shower and linen storage.

Design GGR129
Use Of Space: Fitness/Exercise Facility

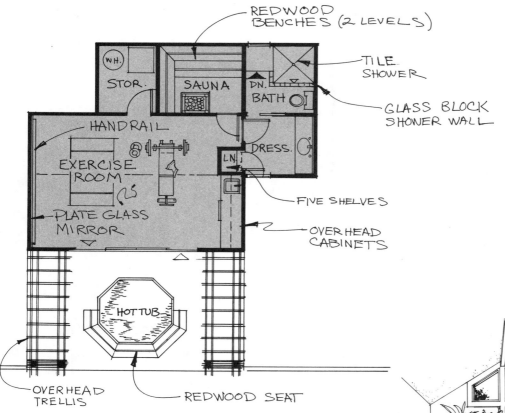

REDWOOD BENCHES (2 LEVELS)

TILE SHOWER

GLASS BLOCK SHOWER WALL

W.H.

STOR.

SAUNA

DN.

BATH

HANDRAIL

EXERCISE ROOM

LN.

DRESS.

FIVE SHELVES

PLATE GLASS MIRROR

OVERHEAD CABINETS

HOT TUB

OVERHEAD TRELLIS

REDWOOD SEAT

● If you're serious about maintaining optimum personal fitness, this free-standing exercise cottage is for you! A wall of mirrors, double-decked windows and sliding doors, vaulted ceilings, plus 250 square feet of floor space provide all the room you need for your workouts. High ceilings accommodate the largest equipment, and features include plenty of storage, a separate dressing room, a mini-kitchen and bathroom facilities with a glass block shower wall. Add a sauna inside, and a hot tub outside, and who could ask for anything more? A ballet bar against the mirrored wall, two-level redwood benches in the sauna and ample storage shelves

Design by
Home Planners, Inc.

and cabinets are additional amenities in this inviting personal gym. Outside, overhead trellises link this gable-roof cottage to your main house and provide added privacy for both the hot tub and exercise areas of this outstanding retreat.

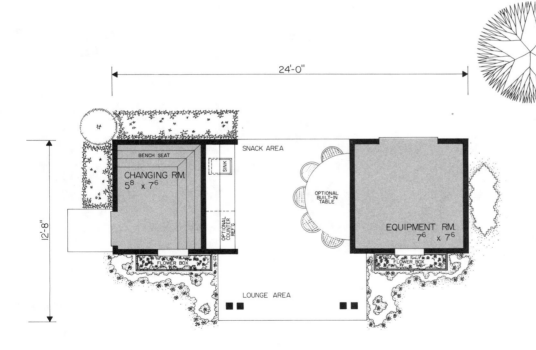

BENCH SEAT

CHANGING RM.
5⁸ x 7⁶

SINK

SNACK AREA

OPTIONAL COUNTER REF'S

OPTIONAL BUILT-IN TABLE

EQUIPMENT RM.
7⁶ x 7⁶

24'-0"

12'-8"

FLOWER BOX

FLOWER BOX

LOUNGE AREA

Design by
Home Planners,
Inc.

Design GGG110
Use Of Space: Pool Cabana

● A mini-kitchen and an optional built-in table tucked in the breezeway of this 250-square-foot double-room unit provide shelter for poolside repasts no matter what the weather. You can enhance both the beauty and function of your pool area with this charming structure. The exterior features include a gable roof with columns in the front, shuttered windows, horizontal wood and shingle siding and decorative flower boxes and a cupola. The two rooms on either side of the breezeway area provide a changing area with built-in seating and a larger area for convenient storage of pool supplies and equipment.

Design GGG239

Use Of Space: Pool Cabana

L

● This structure offers changing room, a bath and an elegant porch for shade. The pool pavilion is designed to provide maximum function in a small area and features built-in benches, shelves, hanging rods and a separate linen closet for towels. The opaque diamond-patterned windows decorate the exterior of the changing area and the mirror-image bath. To enhance the function of the cabana, simply turn the bath into a kitchen and add a sliding window to allow easy passage of refreshments to your family and guests at poolside. When you've had enough sun or socializing, recline in the shade under the columned porch and enjoy a good book or nap.

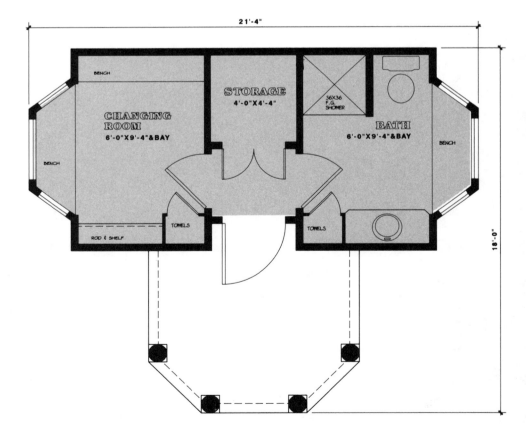

Design by
Home Planners,
Inc.

Design GGG238
Use Of Space: Pool Cabana/Summer Kitchen

● The magic of this design is its flexibility. The side with the changing room includes a built-in bench and private bathroom facilities. The summer kitchen includes a stove, a refrigerator, a food preparation area and a storage pantry. A shuttered window poolside provides easy access to serve your guests across the counter. Linking these two areas is a covered walkway which serves as a shaded picnic area, or a convenient place to get out of the sun. Columns, arches and stained-glass windows provide a touch of grandeur to this fun and functional poolside design.

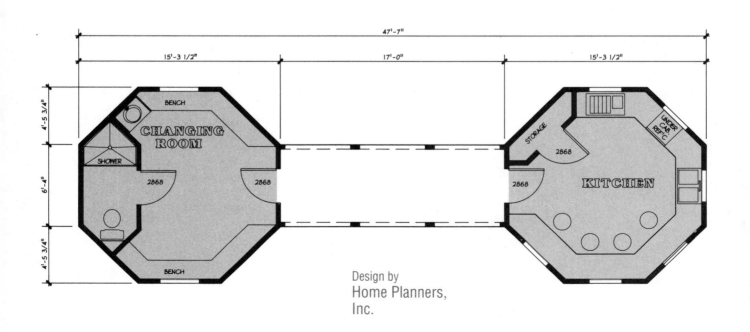

Design by
Home Planners,
Inc.

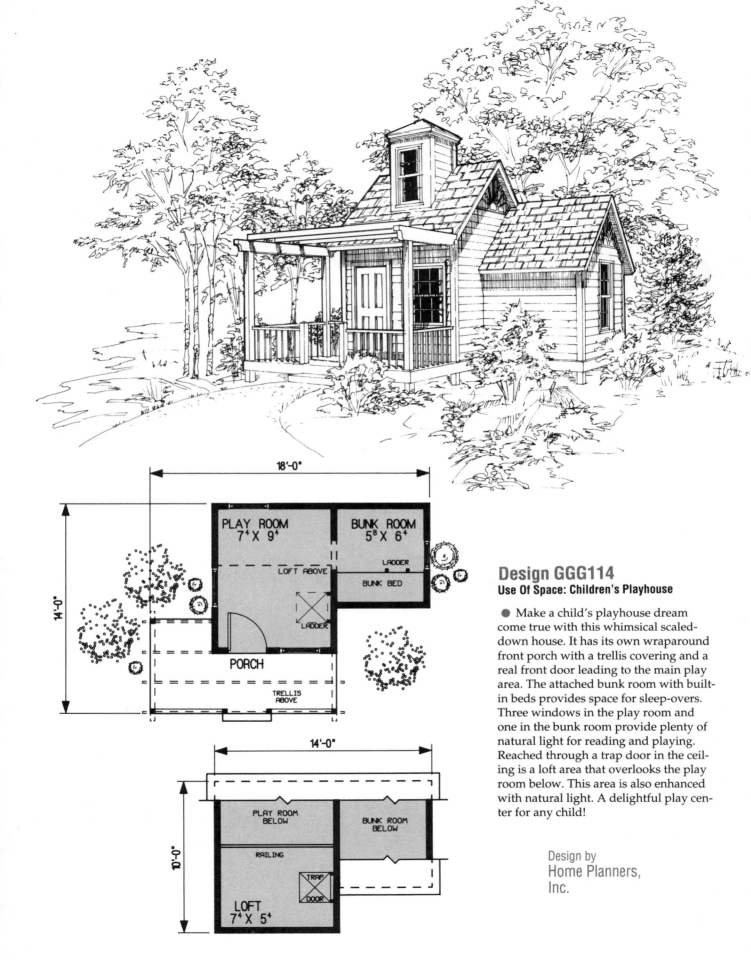

18'-0"

14'-0"

PLAY ROOM
7⁴ X 9⁴

BUNK ROOM
5⁸ X 6⁴

LADDER

BUNK BED

LOFT ABOVE

LADDER

PORCH

TRELLIS
ABOVE

14'-0"

10'-0"

PLAY ROOM
BELOW

BUNK ROOM
BELOW

RAILING

TRAP
DOOR

LOFT
7⁴ X 5⁴

Design GGG114
Use Of Space: Children's Playhouse

● Make a child's playhouse dream
come true with this whimsical scaled-
down house. It has its own wraparound
front porch with a trellis covering and a
real front door leading to the main play
area. The attached bunk room with built-
in beds provides space for sleep-overs.
Three windows in the play room and
one in the bunk room provide plenty of
natural light for reading and playing.
Reached through a trap door in the ceiling is a loft area that overlooks the play
room below. This area is also enhanced
with natural light. A delightful play center for any child!

Design by
Home Planners,
Inc.

Design GGG228
Use Of Space: Children's Playhouse

● This large, 180-square foot, Victorian playhouse is for the kid in all of us. With space enough to hold bunk beds, it is ideally suited for overnight adventures. Young children will spend hours playing in this little house. Older kids will find it a haven for quiet study or a perfect private retreat. Four windows flood the interior with natural light, and a single-door entrance provides access from the porch. The 8'-1" overall height will accommodate most adults and the addition of electricity and water would expand the versatility of this unit.

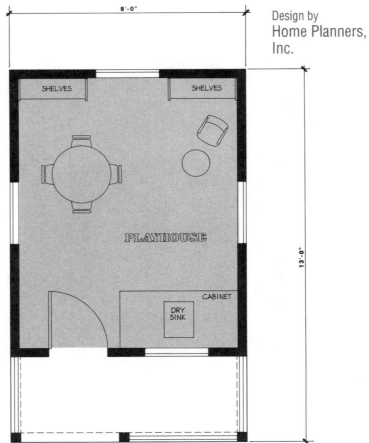

Design by
Home Planners, Inc.

Design GGG235
Use Of Space: Children's Playhouse

● Lords and ladies, knights and evil-doers—this playhouse has everything except a fire-breathing dragon! Your children will spend hours re-enacting the days of Kings and Queens and Knights of the Round Table. Surprisingly easy to build, this play-set—right out of King Arthur's Court—uses standard materials. One corner of the playhouse holds a 4' x 4' sandbox. A stairway leads to a 3' x 3' tower with its own catwalk. The area under the stairway could be enclosed to make a storage room for toys...or a dungeon to hold the captured Black Knight. The double castle doors can be fitted with standard hardware, but wrought-iron hinges will make this innovative playhouse look even more like a castle.

RAMP UP

SAND BOX

10'-0"

4'-0"   4'-0"   3'-0"

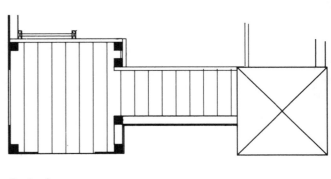

Design by
Home Planners,
Inc.

Design GGG229
Use Of Space: Children's Playhouse

● When it comes to playhouses, it just doesn't get much better than this! Any child's imagination will sail over mysterious unknown seas every time they enter this playhouse. No matter what flag is flown—that of Captain Hook, Davey Jones or Queen Isabella—this playhouse will offer kids years of enjoyment. More than 15' from stem to stern, this unique playhouse is easier to build than it looks. Constructed entirely of standard materials, the design includes a cannon on the Main Deck and gun ports in the hold that pull open to simulate a real Spanish galleon. A concrete foundation is recommended for this structure, due to its overall height—9' 5½" and the number of children who will be sailing off to those creative, wonderful places.

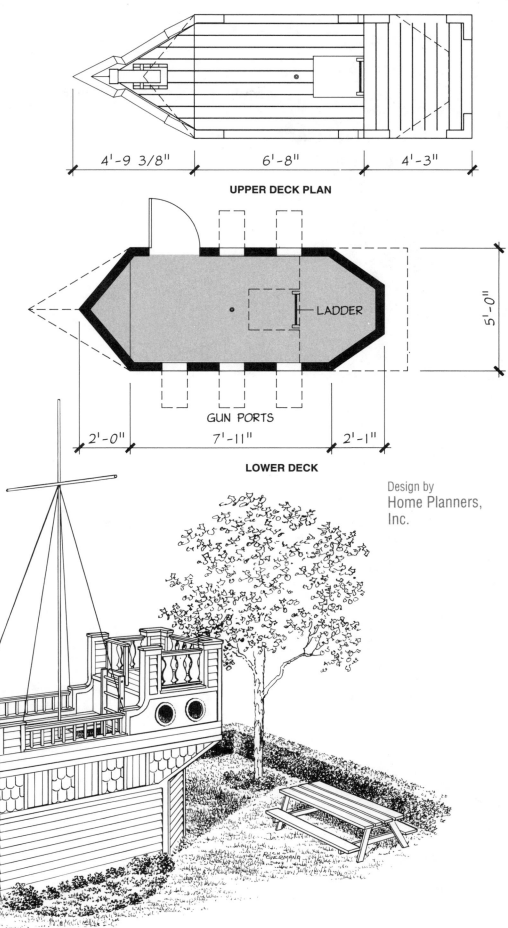

4'-9 3/8"   6'-8"   4'-3"

UPPER DECK PLAN

LADDER

5'-0"

GUN PORTS

2'-0"   7'-11"   2'-1"

LOWER DECK

Design by
Home Planners,
Inc.

Design GGG227
Use Of Space: Shed/Playhouse

● The kids will love this one! This functional, practical shed doubles in design and capacity as a delightful playhouse complete with a covered porch, lathe-turned columns and a window box for young gardeners. The higher roofline on the shed gives the playhouse a two-story effect. The shed is accessed through double doors. The playhouse features a single-door entrance from the porch and three bright windows. The interior wall between the shed and playhouse could be moved another two-and-a-half feet back to make it larger. Or, remove the interior wall completely to use the entire 128-square-foot area exclusively for either the shed or playhouse.

Design by
Home Planners,
Inc.

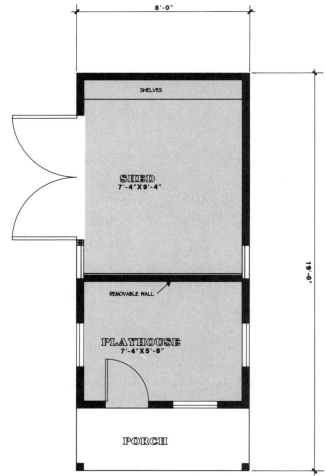

8'-0"

SHELVES

SHED
7'-4"X9'-4"

REMOVABLE WALL

19'-0"

PLAYHOUSE
7'-4"X5'-8"

PORCH

Design GGR126
Use Of Space: Media Retreat for Kids

● Lucky are the teenagers who have the option of staking claim to this private retreat! The overall dimensions of 16' x 22' provide plenty of space for study, TV or just hangin' out. Special features include a raised, carpeted platform in the TV lounge; a comfy window seat for reading; a separate niche for electronic games; and a unique, brightly painted graffiti wall in the entryway. Wired for sound, bright colors and windows in a variety of shapes mark this specially designed, free-standing building as kid territory.

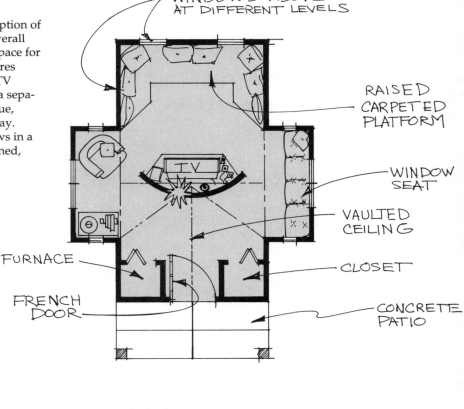

WINDOWS ABOVE AT DIFFERENT LEVELS

RAISED CARPETED PLATFORM

WINDOW SEAT

VAULTED CEILING

FURNACE

CLOSET

FRENCH DOOR

CONCRETE PATIO

TV

Design by
Home Planners,
Inc.

Design by
Home Planners,
Inc.

20'-0"

16'-0"

SUNROOM

DECK

WORK TABLE

UP

Design GGG109

Use Of Space: Studio/Workshop

● This little cottage is both functional and good-looking. Ample counter space and shelving provide plenty of room to spread out materials and tools. Plus, a vaulted ceiling opens up the whole area. Next to the work space is a cozy sunroom. French doors and several windows, including a circle-head version above the doors, bathe the room in sunlight, while overhangs offer adequate shading. To get maximum sun, a south facing for the sunroom is best; it will also provide soft, even illumination for the north-facing work area.

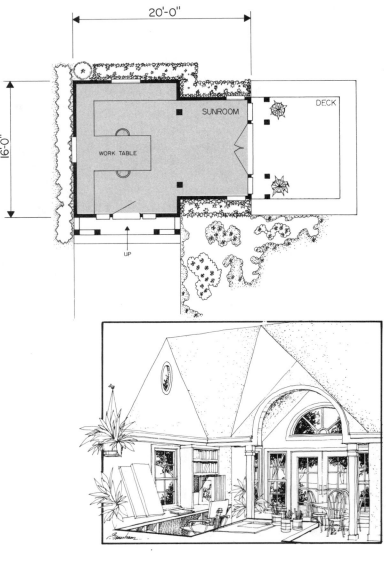

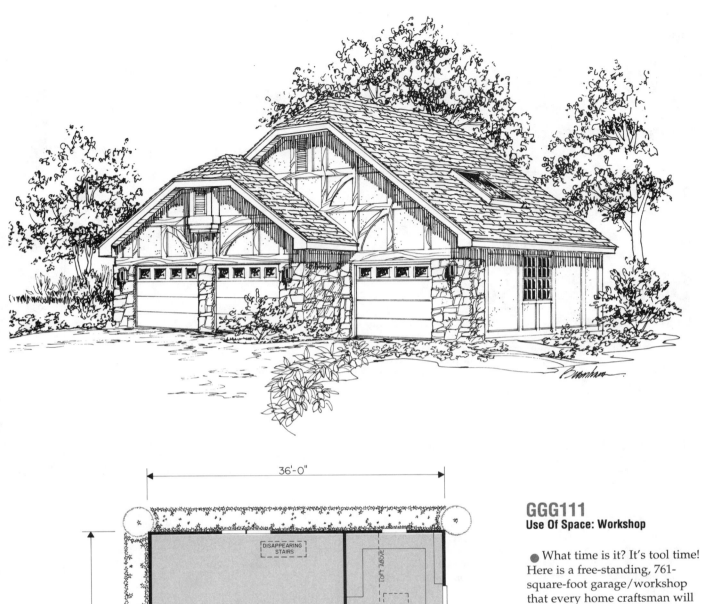

36'-0"

24'-0"

DISAPPEARING
STAIRS

LOFT ABOVE

SKYLIGHT

LADDER

LOFT OPENING

WORKSHOP
11⁸ x 19⁴

GARAGE
23⁰ x 23⁴

GGG111
Use Of Space: Workshop

● What time is it? It's tool time! Here is a free-standing, 761-square-foot garage/workshop that every home craftsman will enjoy. Three garage doors allow for flexible access to the vehicular and workshop areas. A skylight provides an extra measure of natural light for shop projects. A large amount of wall space is provided for handy tool placement above the U-shaped counter surfaces, which also have storage below. For the storage of project lumber, there is an out-of-the-way loft. Around the corner from the shop is a folding stair unit in the garage. This provides access to another generous bulk storage area.

Design by
Home Planners,
Inc.

When You're Ready To Order . . .

Let Us Show You Our Home Blueprint Package.

Building a home? Planning a home? Our Blueprint Package has nearly everything you need to get the job done right, whether you're working on your own or with help from an architect, designer, builder or subcontractors. Each Blueprint Package is the result of many hours of work by licensed architects or professional designers.

QUALITY

Hundreds of hours of painstaking effort have gone into the development of your blueprint set. Each home has been quality-checked by professionals to insure accuracy and buildability.

VALUE

Because we sell in volume, you can buy professional-quality blueprints at a fraction of their development cost. With our plans, your dream home design costs only a few hundred dollars, not the thousands of dollars that custom architects charge.

SERVICE

Once you've chosen your favorite home plan, you'll receive fast, efficient service whether you choose to mail or fax your order to us or call us toll free at 1-800-521-6797.

SATISFACTION

Our years of service to satisfied home plan buyers provide us the experience and knowledge that guarantee your satisfaction with our product and performance.

ORDER TOLL FREE 1-800-521-6797

After you've looked over our Blueprint Package and Important Extras on the following pages, simply mail the order form on page 237 or call toll free on our Blueprint Hotline: 1-800-521-6797. We're ready and eager to serve you.

Each set of blueprints is an interrelated collection of detail sheets which includes components such as floor plans, interior and exterior elevations, dimensions, cross-sections, diagrams and notations. These sheets show exactly how your house is to be built.

Among the sheets included may be:

Frontal Sheet
This artist's sketch of the exterior of the house gives you an idea of how the house will look when built and landscaped. Large ink-line floor plans show all levels of the house and provide an overview of your new home's livability, as well as a handy reference for deciding on furniture placement.

Foundation Plan
This sheet shows the foundation layout includ-

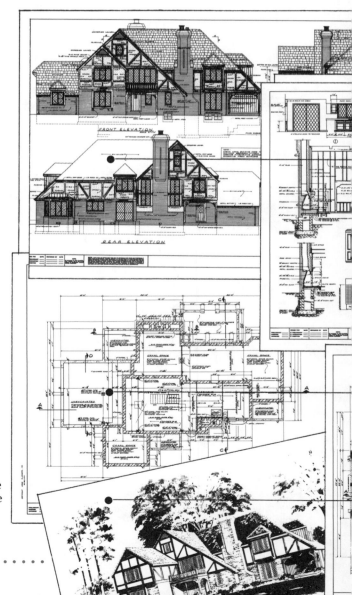

ing support walls, excavated and unexcavated areas, if any, and foundation notes. If slab construction rather the basement, the plan shows footings and details for a monolithic slab. This page, or another in the set, may include a sample plot plan for locating your house on a building site.

Detailed Floor Plans

These plans show the layout of each floor of the house. Rooms and interior spaces are carefully dimensioned and keys are given for cross-section details provided later in the plans. The positions of electrical outlets and switches are shown.

House Cross-Sections

Large-scale views show sections or cut-aways of the foundation, interior walls, exterior walls, floors, stairways and roof details. Additional cross-sections may show important changes in

floor, ceiling or roof heights or the relationship of one level to another. Extremely valuable for construction, these sections show exactly how the various parts of the house fit together.

Interior Elevations

These large-scale drawings show the design and placement of kitchen and bathroom cabinets, laundry areas, fireplaces, bookcases and other built-ins. Little "extras," such as mantelpiece and wainscoting drawings, plus moulding sections, provide details that give your home that custom touch.

Exterior Elevations

These drawings show the front, rear and sides of your house and give necessary notes on exterior materials and finishes. Particular attention is given to cornice detail, brick and stone accents or other finish items that make your home unique.

Sample Package

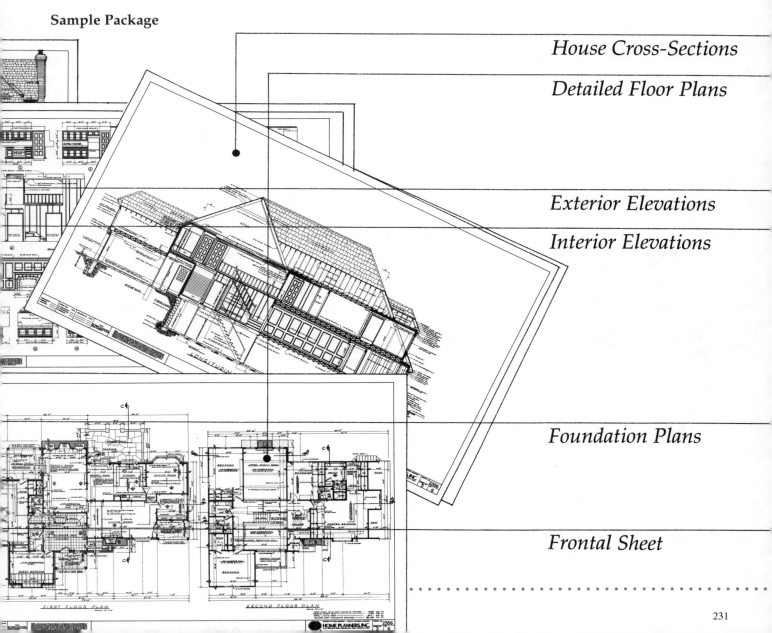

House Cross-Sections

Detailed Floor Plans

Exterior Elevations

Interior Elevations

Foundation Plans

Frontal Sheet

*I*mportant Extras To Do The Job Right!

Introducing eight important planning and construction aids developed by our professionals to help you succeed in your home-building project.

MATERIALS LIST

For many of the designs in our portfolio, we offer a customized materials take-off that is invaluable in planning and estimating the cost of your new home. This comprehensive list outlines the quantity, type and size of materials needed to build your house (with the exception of mechanical system items). Included are:

- framing lumber
- roofing and sheet metal
- windows and doors
- exterior sheathing material and trim
- masonry, veneer and fireplace materials
- tile and flooring materials
- kitchen and bath cabinetry
- interior drywall and trim
- rough and finish hardware
- many more items

(Note: Because of differing local codes, building methods, and availability of materials, our Materials Lists do not include mechanical materials. To obtain necessary take-offs and recommendations, consult heating, plumbing and electrical contractors. Materials Lists are not sold separately from the Blueprint Package.)

This handy list helps you or your builder cost out materials and serves as a ready reference sheet when you're compiling bids. It also provides a cross-check against the materials specified by your builder and helps coordinate the substitution of items you may need to meet local codes.

SPECIFICATION OUTLINE

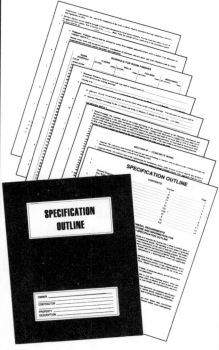

This valuable 16-page document is critical to building your house correctly. Designed to be filled in by you or your builder, this book lists 166 stages or items crucial to the building process. It provides a comprehensive review of the construction process and helps in making choices of materials. When combined with the blueprints, a signed contract, and a schedule, it becomes a legal document and record for the building of your home.

QUOTE ONE™

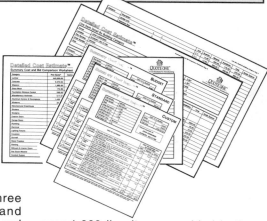

A new service for estimating the cost of building select Home Planners designs, the Quote One™ system is available in two separate stages: The Summary Cost Report and the Detailed Cost Estimate. The Summary Cost Report shows the total cost per square foot for your chosen home in your zip-code area and then breaks that cost down into ten categories showing the costs for building materials, labor and installation. The total cost for the report (including three grades: Budget, Standard and Custom) is just $25 for one home; and additionals are only $15 each. These reports allow you to evaluate your building budget and compare the costs of building a variety of homes in your area.

The Detailed Cost Estimate furnishes an even more detailed report. The material and installation (labor + equipment) cost is shown for each of over 1,000 line items provided in the Standard grade. Space is allowed for additional estimates from contractors and subcontractors. This invaluable tool is available for a price of $100 ($110 for a Schedule E plan) which includes the price of a materials list which must be purchased at the same time.

To order these invaluable reports, use the order form on page 237 or call **1-800-521-6797**.

CONSTRUCTION INFORMATION

If you want to know more about techniques—and deal more confidently with subcontractors—we offer these useful sheets. Each set is an excellent tool that will add to your understanding of these technical subjects.

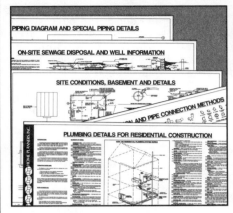

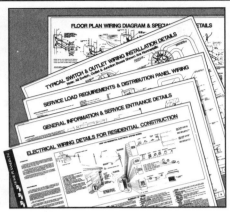

PLUMBING

The Blueprint Package includes locations for all the plumbing fixtures in your new house, including sinks, lavatories, tubs, showers, toilets, laundry trays and water heaters. However, if you want to know more about the complete plumbing system, these 24x36-inch detail sheets will prove very useful. Prepared to meet requirements of the National Plumbing Code, these six fact-filled sheets give general information on pipe schedules, fittings, sump-pump details, water-softener hookups, septic system details and much more. Color-coded sheets include a glossary of terms.

ELECTRICAL

The locations for every electrical switch, plug and outlet are shown in your Blueprint Package. However, these Electrical Details go further to take the mystery out of household electrical systems. Prepared to meet requirements of the National Electrical Code, these comprehensive 24x36-inch drawings come packed with helpful information, including wire sizing, switch-installation schematics, cable-routing details, appliance wattage, door-bell hookups, typical service panel circuitry and much more. Six sheets are bound together and color-coded for easy reference. A glossary of terms is also included.

CONSTRUCTION

The Blueprint Package contains everything an experienced builder needs to construct a particular house. However, it doesn't show all the ways that houses can be built, nor does it explain alternate construction methods. To help you understand how your house will be built—and offer additional techniques—this set of drawings depicts the materials and methods used to build foundations, fireplaces, walls, floors and roofs. Where appropriate, the drawings show acceptable alternatives. These six sheets will answer questions for the advanced do-it-yourselfer or home planner.

MECHANICAL

This package contains fundamental principles and useful data that will help you make informed decisions and communicate with subcontractors about heating and cooling systems. The 24x36-inch drawings contain instructions and samples that allow you to make simple load calculations and preliminary sizing and costing analysis. Covered are today's most commonly used systems from heat pumps to solar fuel systems. The package is packed full of illustrations and diagrams to help you visualize components and how they relate to one another.

Plan-A-Home®

Plan-A-Home® is an easy-to-use tool that helps you design a new home, arrange furniture in a new or existing home, or plan a remodeling project. Each package contains:

- **More than 700 reusable peel-off planning symbols** on a self-stick vinyl sheet, including walls, windows, doors, all types of furniture, kitchen components, bath fixtures and many more.

- **A reusable, transparent, 1/4-inch scale planning grid** that matches the scale of actual working drawings (1/4-inch equals 1 foot). This grid provides the basis for house layouts of up to 140x92 feet.

- **Tracing paper** and a protective sheet for copying or transferring your completed plan.

- **A felt-tip pen**, with water-soluble ink that wipes away quickly.

Plan-A-Home® lets you lay out areas as large as a 7,500 square foot, six-bedroom, seven-bath house.

To Order, Call Toll Free 1-800-521-6797

To add these important extras to your Blueprint Package, simply indicate your choices on the order form on page 237 or call us Toll Free 1-800-521-6797 and we'll tell you more about these exciting products.

House Blueprint Price Schedule and Plans Index

These pages contain all the information you need to price your blueprints. In general the larger and more complicated the house, the more it costs to design and thus the higher the price we must charge for the blueprints. Remember, however, that these prices are far less than you would normally pay for the services of a licensed architect or professional designer. Custom home designs and related architectural services often cost thousands of dollars, ranging from 5% to 15% of the cost of construction. By ordering our blueprints you are potentially saving enough money to afford a larger house, or to add those "extra" amenities such as a patio, deck, swimming pool or even an upgraded kitchen or luxurious master suite.

To use the Index below, refer to the design number listed in numerical order (a helpful page reference is also given). Note the price index letter and refer to the House Blueprint Price Schedule at right for the cost of one, four or eight sets of blueprints or the cost of a reproducible sepia. Additional prices are shown for identical and reverse blueprint sets, as well as a very useful Materials List for some of the plans.

DESIGN	PRICE	PAGE	CALIFORNIA PLANS	CUSTOMIZABLE	QUOTE ONE™	DECK	DECK PRICE	LANDSCAPE	LANDSCAPE PRICE	REGIONS
▲GG1956	A	25			🏠	D117	S			
▲GG1964	C	64								
▲GG1967	B	65								
▲GG2192	D	81				D117	S	L218	Z	1-6,8
▲GG2272	B	163								
▲GG2320	C	24								
▲GG2485	B	164								
▲GG2488	A	38	✔		🏠	D102	Q			
▲GG2490	A	39			🏠					
▲GG2500	B	62				D100	Q	L204	Y	1-3,5,6,8
▲GG2510	A	67				D105	R	L200	X	1-3,5,6,8
▲GG2511	B	154			🏠	D108	R	L229	Y	1-8
▲GG2556	C	82				D103	R			
▲GG2563	B	129			🏠	D114	R	L201	Y	1-3,5,6,8
▲GG2622	A	107			🏠	D103	R	L200	X	1-3,5,6,8
▲GG2633	C	84								
▲GG2659	B	83			🏠	D113	R	L205	Y	1-3,5,6,8
▲GG2665	D	11	✔							
▲GG2682	A	6			🏠	D115	Q	L200	X	1-3,5,6,8
▲GG2684	C	174				D114	R	L204	Y	1-3,5,6,8
▲GG2690	C	79								
▲GG2699	C	63						L211	Y	1-8
▲GG2716	C	155						L229	Y	1-8
▲GG2718	C	66				D105	R			
▲GG2721	C	159								
▲GG2730	C	158				D124	S			
▲GG2761	B	160						L229	Y	1-8
▲GG2769	C	161								
▲GG2774	B	103	✔		🏠	D100	Q	L207	Z	1-6,8
▲GG2822	A	26	✔		🏠			L229	Y	1-8
▲GG2828	B	156								
▲GG2841	B	152						L208	Z	1,2,5,6,8
▲GG2847	C	162						L220	Y	1-3,5,6,8
▲GG2855	B	193			🏠	D103	R	L219	Z	1-3,5,6,8
▲GG2883	C	203								
▲GG2884	B	205						L228	Y	1-8
▲GG2887	A	157								
▲GG2892	B	204								
▲GG2945	B	102								
▲GG2969	C	73				D110	R	L223	Z	1-3,5,6,8
▲GG2970	D	74	✔		🏠			L223	Z	1-3,5,6,8
▲GG2974	A	75	✔		🏠			L223	Z	1-3,5,6,8
▲GG2983	A	8								
▲GG2988	B	86				D120	R	L201	Y	1-3,5,6,8
▲GG3310	C	35			🏠	D111	S	L227	Z	1-8
▲GG3321	C	55				D116	R	L209	Y	1-8
▲GG3323	C	32						L223	Z	1-3,5,6,8
▲GG3330	A	27								
▲GG3347	D	40			🏠			L230	Z	1-8
▲GG3351	C	128				D115	Q	L209	Y	1-6,8
▲GG3366	D	153						L220	Y	1-3,5,6,8
▲GG3382	C	76				D110	R	L202	X	1-3,5,6,8
▲GG3383	C	77				D111	S	L205	Y	1-3,5,6,8
▲GG3386	E	78				D111	S	L216	Y	1-3,5,6,8
▲GG3389	C	72				D115	Q	L205	Y	1-3,5,6,8
▲GG3396	C	54				D111	S	L207	Z	1-6,8
▲GG3403	C	37			🏠			L237	Y	7
▲GG3435	D	30	✔		🏠			L227	Z	1-8
▲GG3437	C	31						L212	Y	1-8
▲GG3438	C	167			🏠			L209	Y	1-6,8
▲GG3441	C	33						L239	Z	1-8
▲GG3450	C	41	✔		🏠	D106	S	L229	Y	1-8
▲GG3455	B	34			🏠	D105	R	L238	Y	3,4,7,8
▲GG3458	C	52			🏠	D105	R	L222	Y	1-3,5,6,8
▲GG3461	B	58			🏠			L204	Y	1-3,5,6,8
▲GG3462	B	57			🏠			L207	Z	1-6,8
▲GG3467	B	53			🏠			L203	Y	1-3,5,6,8
▲GG3468	C	166						L209	Y	1-6,8
▲GG3503	E	80				D108	R	L210	Y	1-3,5,6,8
▲GG3510	C	85								
GG4390	B	202								
GG6615	D	147								
GG6616	D	148								
GG6617	D	149								
GG6618	E	146								
GG6620	E	144								
GG6621	D	145								
GG6622	C	150								
† GG7211	E	191								
† GG7222	E	138								
GG8002	C	105								
GG8010	C	189								
GG8013	D	190								
GG8017	C	68								
GG8025	E	71								
GG8041	D	183								
GG8048	D	184								
GG8049	C	187								
GG8050	C	109								
GG8055	C	185								
GG8069	C	177								
GG8072	C	176								
GG8075	D	182								

House Blueprint Price Schedule
(Prices guaranteed through December 31, 1995)

	1-set Study Package	4-set Building Package	8-set Building Package	1-set Reproducible Sepias
Schedule A	$240	$300	$360	$460
Schedule B	$280	$340	$400	$520
Schedule C	$320	$380	$440	$580
Schedule D	$360	$420	$480	$640
Schedule E	$480	$540	$600	$700

Additional Identical Blueprints in same order ....$50 per set
Reverse Blueprints (mirror image) ....$50 per set
Specification Outlines...$10 each
Materials Lists (for Home Planners', Design Basics', Alan Mascord's, and
Donald Gardner's Plans only):
  ▲ Home Planners' Designs...$40
  † Design Basics' Designs..$75
  ✳ Alan Mascord's Designs...$40
  ◆ Donald Gardner's Designs...$40
If ordering a Matirials List for a Schedule E plan, add $10 to above prices
Exchanges.........................$50 exchange fee for the first set; $10 for each additional set
                      $70 total exchange fee for 4 sets
                      $100 total exchange fee for 8 sets
To Order: Fill in and send the Order Form on page 237—or call us Toll Free 1-800-521-6797.

DESIGN	PRICE	PAGE	CUSTOMIZABLE	QUOTE ONE™	CALIFORNIA PLANS
GG8089	C	22			
GG8090	B	108			
GG8091	C	180			
GG8092	C	181			
GG8093	C	186			
GG8094	C	188			
GG8095	D	70			
GG8629	B	169			
GG8648	C	151			
GG8679	D	36			
GG8681	C	124			
GG8682	C	125			
GG8683	C	206			
GG8901	A	210			
GG8920	A	213			
GG8921	A	212			
GG8922	D	201			
GG8927	D	197			
GG8970	D	12			
GG8981	C	130			
GG9003	C	60			
GG9012	D	170			
GG9030	D	171			
GG9051	B	172			
GG9074	B	59			
GG9081	E	14			
GG9094	B	209			
GG9096	C	21			
GG9120	D	61			
GG9122	D	16			
GG9123	B	173			
GG9124	D	200			
GG9130	D	198			
GG9132	A	208			
GG9133	A	211			
GG9134	D	196			
GG9152	E	199			
GG9159	D	20			
GG9187	C	18			
† GG9206	C	51			
† GG9247	C	50			
† GG9265	C	49			
† GG9316	D	47			
† GG9321	C	28			
† GG9325	D	46			
† GG9339	C	48			
† GG9382	E	194			
† GG9390	E	44			
† GG9393	E	139			
† GG9394	E	45			
✳ GG9400	D	126			
✳ GG9410	D	119			
✳ GG9417	E	143			
✳ GG9420	D	104			
✳ GG9438	E	118			
✳ GG9440	D	120			
✳ GG9478	D	127			
✳ GG9486	C	106			
✳ GG9489	C	42			
✳ GG9498	E	23			
✳ GG9511	C	121			
✳ GG9516	B	56			
✳ GG9537	D	141			
✳ GG9539	D	142			
✳ GG9540	B	43			
✳ GG9541	C	122			
✳ GG9542	D	123			
✳ GG9543	D	140			
◆ GG9606	C	97			
◆ GG9625	C	100			
◆ GG9626	C	101			
◆ GG9644	C	96			
◆ GG9645	C	98			
◆ GG9661	C	92			
◆ GG9673	D	168			
◆ GG9702	D	99			
◆ GG9706	D	94			
◆ GG9709	D	90			
◆ GG9734	C	91			
◆ GG9736	D	93			
◆ GG9738	D	89			
◆ GG9745	D	95			
◆ GG9750	C	88			
GG9804	D	112			
GG9812	C	114			
GG9814	D	192			
GG9821	C	179			
GG9823	C	113			
GG9825	C	195			
GG9831	C	132			
GG9833	D	115			
GG9839	B	136			
GG9840	B	137			
GG9842	C	116			
GG9843	B	133			
GG9844	B	134			
GG9846	C	135			
GG9859	C	175			
GG9870	D	110			
GG9898	D	178			
GG9900	C	117			
GG9909	D	111			
GGG106	$40	217			
GGG109	$40	228			
GGG110	$40	219			
GGG111	$40	229			
GGG114	$30	222			
GGG227	$40	226			
GGG228	$30	223			
GGG229	$40	225			
GGG230	$40	216			
GGG235	$40	224			
GGG238	$50	221			
GGG239	$40	220			
GGR126	$75	227			
GGR128	$85	214			
GGR129	$85	218			
GGR130	$85	215			

Before You Order . . .

Before filling out the coupon at right or calling us on our Toll-Free Blueprint Hotline, you may want to learn more about our services and products. Here's some information you will find helpful.

Quick Turnaround
We process and ship every blueprint order from our office within 48 hours. Because of this quick turnaround, we won't send a formal notice acknowledging receipt of your order.

Our Exchange Policy
Since blueprints are printed in response to your order, we cannot honor requests for refunds. However, we will exchange your entire first order for an equal number of blueprints at a price of $50 for the first set and $10 for each additional set; $70 total exchange fee for 4 sets: $100 total exchange fee for 8 sets. . . *plus* the difference in cost if exchanging for a design in a higher price bracket or *less* the difference in cost if exchanging for a design in a lower price bracket. One exchange is allowed within a year of purchase date. **(Sepias are not exchangeable. No exchanges can be made for the California Engineered Plans since they are tailored to your specific building site.)** All sets from the first order must be returned before the exchange can take place. Please add $10 for postage and handling via ground service; $20 via 2nd Day Air; $30 via Next Day Air.

About Reverse Blueprints
If you want to build in reverse of the plan as shown, we will include an extra set of reverse blueprints (mirror image) for an additional fee of $50. Lettering and dimensions will appear backward. Right-reading reverses of Home Customizer® plans are available. Call 1-800-521-6797, ext. 800 for more details.

Modifying or Customizing Our Plans
With such a great selection of homes, you are bound to find the one that suits you. However, if you need to make alterations to a design that is customizable, you need only order our Customizer® kit or call our Customization representative at 1-800-521-6797, ext. 800 to get you started. We strongly suggest you order sepias if you decide to revise non-Customizable plans significantly.

Architectural and Engineering Seals
Some cities and states are now requiring that a licensed architect or engineer review and "seal" your blueprints prior to building due to local or regional concerns over energy consumption, safety codes, seismic ratings or other factors. For this reason, it may be necessary to talk to a local professional to have your plans reviewed. In some cases, Home Planners can seal your plans through our Customization Service. Call 1-800-521-6797, ext. 800 for more details.

Compliance with Local Codes and Regulations
At the time of creation, our plans are drawn to specifications published by the Building Officials and Code Administrators (BOCA) International, Inc.; the Southern Building Code Congress (SBCCI) International, Inc.; the International Conference of Building Officials; or the Council of American Building Officials (CABO). Our plans are designed to meet or exceed national building standards. Some states, counties and municipalities have their own codes, zoning requirements and building regulations. Before building, contact your local building authorities to make sure you comply with local ordinances and codes, including obtaining any necessary permits or inspections as building progresses. In some cases, minor modifications to your plans by your builder, architect or designer may be required to meet local conditions and requirements. Home Planners may be able to make these changes to Home Customizer® plans providing you supply all pertinent information from your local building authorities.

Foundation and Exterior Wall Changes
Most of our plans are drawn with either a full or partial basement foundation. Depending on your specific climate or regional building practices, you may wish to change this basement to a slab or crawlspace. Most professional contractors and builders can easily adapt your plans to alternate foundation types. Likewise, most can easily change 2x4 wall construction to 2x6, or vice versa. For Home Customizer® plans, Home Planners can easily make the changes for you.

How Many Blueprints Do You Need?
A single set of blueprints is sufficient to study a home in greater detail. However, if you are planning to obtain cost estimates from a contractor or subcontractors—or if you are planning to build immediately—you will need more sets. Because additional sets are cheaper when ordered in quantity with the original order, make sure you order enough blueprints to satisfy all requirements. The following checklist will help you determine how many you need:

_____ Owner

_____ Builder (generally requires at least three sets; one as a legal document, one to use during inspections, and at least one to give to subcontractors)

_____ Local Building Department (often requires two sets)

_____ Mortgage Lender (usually one set for a conventional loan; three sets for FHA or VA loans)

_____ TOTAL NUMBER OF SETS

Toll Free 1-800-521-6797

Normal Office Hours:
8:00 a.m. to 8:00 p.m. Eastern Time
Monday through Friday
Our staff will gladly answer any questions during normal office hours. Our answering service can place orders after hours or on weekends.

If we receive your order by 4:00 p.m. Eastern Time, Monday through Friday, we'll process it and ship within 48 hours. When ordering by phone, please have your charge card ready. We'll also ask you for the Order Form Key Number at the bottom of the coupon.
For Customization orders call 1-800-521-6797, ext. 800.

By FAX: Copy the Order Form on the next page and send it on our FAX line: 1-800-224-6699 or 1-602-297-9937.

Canadian Customers
Order Toll-Free 1-800-561-4169
For faster service and plans that are modified for building in Canada, customers may now call in orders directly to our Canadian supplier of plans and charge the purchase to a charge card. Or, you may complete the order form at right, adding 40% to all prices and mail in Canadian funds to:

The Plan Centre 20 Cedar Street North
Kitchener, Ontario N2H 2W8

By FAX: Copy the Order Form at right and send it via our Canadian FAX line: 1-519-743-1282.

The Home Customizer®

Many of the plans in this book are customizable through our Home Customizer® service. Look for this symbol 🏠 on the pages of home designs. It indicates that the plan on that page is part of The Home Customizer® service.

Some changes to customizable plans that can be made include:

- exterior elevation changes
- kitchen and bath modifications
- roof, wall and foundation changes
- room additions
- and much more!

If the plan you have chosen to build is one of our customizable homes, you can easily order the Home Customizer® kit to start on the path to making your alterations. The kit, priced at only $29.95, may be ordered at the same time you order your blueprint package by calling our toll-free number or using the order blank at right. Or you can wait until you receive your blueprints, spend some time studying them and then order the kit by phone, FAX or mail. If you then decide to proceed with the customizing service, the $29.95 price of the kit will be refunded to you after your customization order is received. The Home Customizer® kit includes:

- instruction book with examples
- architectural scale
- clear acetate work film
- erasable red marker
- removable correction tape
- ¼" scale furniture cutouts
- 1 set of Customizable Drawings with floor plans and elevations

The service is easy, fast and *affordable.* Because we know and work with our plans and have them available on state-of-the-art computer systems, we can make the changes efficiently at prices much lower than those charged by normal architectural or drafting services. In addition, you'll be getting custom changes directly from Home Planners—the company whose dedication to excellence and long-standing professional experience are well recognized in the industry.

Call now to learn more about how simple it can be to have the *custom home* you've always wanted.

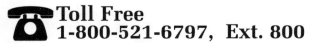

☎ Toll Free
1-800-521-6797, Ext. 800

California Customers!!

For our customers in California, we now offer California Engineered Plans (CEP) and California Stock Plans (CSP) to help in meeting the strict California building codes. Check Plan Index for homes that are available through this new service or call 1-800-521-6797 for more information about the availability of the service and prices.

BLUEPRINTS ARE NOT RETURNABLE

ORDER FORM

HOME PLANNERS, INC., 3275 WEST INA ROAD
SUITE 110, TUCSON, ARIZONA 85741

THE BASIC BLUEPRINT PACKAGE
Rush me the following (please refer to the Plans Index and Price Schedule in this section):

_____ Set(s) of blueprints for plan number(s) _____.	$_____
_____ Set(s) of sepias for plan number(s) _____.	$_____
_____ Additional identical blueprints in same order @ $50 per set.	$_____
_____ Reverse blueprints @ $50 per set.	$_____
_____ Home Customizer® Kit(s) for Plan(s)_____ @ $29.95 per kit.	$_____

IMPORTANT EXTRAS
Rush me the following:

_____ Materials List: $40 Home Planners' Designs (Not available for CEP service); $75 Design Basics' Designs; $40 Alan Mascord's Designs; $40 Donald Gardner's Designs. Add $10 for a schedule E plan. $_____

_____ Quote One™ Summary Cost Report @ $25 for 1, $15 for each additional, for plans _____ $_____

_____ Quote One™ Detailed Cost Estimate @ $100 Schedule A-D; $110 Schedule E for plan_____. $_____
(must be purchased with Blueprints set; Materials List included.)
Building Location: City_____ Zip Code_____

_____ Specification Outlines @ $10 each. $_____

_____ Detail Sets @ $14.95 each; any two for $22.95; any three for $29.95; all four for $39.95 (save $19.85). $_____
❑ Plumbing ❑ Electrical ❑ Construction ❑ Mechanical
(These helpful details provide general construction advice and are not specific to any single plan.)

_____ Plan-A-Home® @ $29.95 each. $_____

DECK BLUEPRINTS

_____ Set(s) of Deck Plan _____.	$_____
_____ Additional identical blueprints in same order @ $10 per set.	$_____
_____ Reverse blueprints @ $10 per set	$_____
_____ Set of Standard Deck Details @ $14.95 per set	$_____
_____ Set of Complete Building Package (Best Buy!) Includes Custom Deck Plan_____ plus Standard Deck Details. (See Index and Price Schedule)	$_____

LANDSCAPE BLUEPRINTS

_____ Set(s) of Landscape Plan _____.	$_____
_____ Additional identical blueprints in same order @ $10 per set.	$_____
_____ Reverse blueprints @ $10 per set	$_____

Please indicate the appropriate region of the country for Plant & Material List. (See Map on page 240): Region _____

POSTAGE AND HANDLING	1-3 sets	4+ sets
DELIVERY (Requires street address - No P.O. Boxes)		
•Regular Service (Allow 4-6 days delivery)	❑ $8.00	❑ $10.00
•2nd Day Air (Allow 2-3 days delivery)	❑ $12.00	❑ $20.00
•Next Day Air (Allow 1 day delivery)	❑ $22.00	❑ $30.00
POST OFFICE DELIVERY	❑ $10.00	❑ $14.00
If no street address available. (Allow 4-6 days delivery)		
OVERSEAS DELIVERY Note: All delivery times are from date Blueprint Package is shipped.	fax, phone or mail for quote	

POSTAGE (From shaded box above) $_____
SUB-TOTAL $_____
SALES TAX (Arizona residents add 5% sales tax; Michigan residents add 6% sales tax.) $_____
TOTAL (Sub-total and tax) $_____

YOUR ADDRESS (please print)

Name _____

Street _____

City _____ State _____ Zip _____

Daytime telephone number (_____) _____

FOR CREDIT CARD ORDERS ONLY
Please fill in the information below:
Credit card number _____
Exp. Date: Month/Year _____
Check one ❑ Visa ❑ MasterCard ❑ Discover Card

Signature _____

Please check appropriate box: ❑ Licensed Builder-Contractor
        ❑ Homeowner

☎ **ORDER TOLL FREE**
1-800-521-6797 or
602-297-8200

Order Form Key

TB40BP

Additional Plans Books

ENCYCLOPEDIA OF HOME DESIGNS Our best collection of plans is now bigger and better than ever! Over 500 plans organized by architectural category. Includes all types and styles. The most comprehensive plan book ever. 352 pages.
$9.95 ($12.95 Can.)
1:EN

THE ESSENTIAL GUIDE TO TRADITIONAL HOMES Over 400 traditional homes in one special volume. American and European styles from Farmhouses to Norman French. Best sellers shown in color photographs and renderings. 304 pages.
$9.95 ($12.95 Can.)
2:ET

THE ESSENTIAL GUIDE TO CONTEMPORARY HOMES More than 340 contemporary designs from Northwest Contemporary to Post-Modern Victorian. Color section of best sellers; two-color illustrations throughout. 304 pages.
$9.95 ($12.95 Can.)
3:EC

AFFORDABLE HOME PLANS For the prospective home builder with a modest or medium budget. Features 430 one-, 1½-, two-story and multi-level homes in a wealth of styles. Cost-saving ideas for the budget-conscious included. 320 pages.
$9.95 ($12.95 Can.)
4:AH

LUXURY DREAM HOMES New Edition! Completely updated with 50% new designs, this exciting collection of 154 designs now contains the home you've been waiting for! 192 pages.
$14.95 ($18.95 Can.)
5:LD2

ONE-STORY HOMES A collection of 470 homes to suit a range of budgets in one-story living. All popular styles, including Cape Cod, Southwestern, Tudor and French. 384 pages.
$9.95 ($12.95 Can.)
6:V1

TWO-STORY HOMES 478 plans for all budgets in a wealth of styles: Tudors, Saltboxes, Farmhouses, Victorians, Georgians, Contemporaries and more. 416 pages.
$9.95 ($12.95 Can.)
7:V2

MULTI-LEVEL AND HILLSIDE HOMES 312 distinctive styles for both flat and sloping sites. Includes exposed lower levels, open staircases, balconies, decks and terraces. 320 pages.
$6.95 ($9.95 Can.)
8:V3

VACATION AND SECOND HOMES 345 idyllic plans make the most of your vacation spot, provide the utmost in retirement or starter-home living. Includes Capes, cottages, and A-frames in one- 1½-, two-story, and multi-level homes. 312 pages.
$7.95 ($10.95 Can.)
9:VH

STARTER HOMES 200 easy-to-build plans—from simple do-it-yourself houses to more stylish contemporary designs. Features the all-new Economy Building Series. 224 pages.
$6.95 ($9.95 Can.)
10:ST

EMPTY-NESTER HOMES Perfect for empty-nesters, retirees and couples without children. These 206 plans feature sophisticated designs and upgraded amenities. 224 pages.
$6.95 ($9.95 Can.)
11:EP

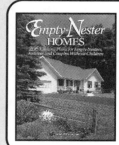
200 FAMILY-FAVORED HOME PLANS Expanded designs for expanding families! Seven top designers present move-up homes combining beautiful styling with more living space. 224 pages.
$7.95 ($10.95 Can.)
12:FF

200 NARROW-LOT HOME PLANS The largest collection ever of homes that meet the unique challenges of today's narrow lots. Up to 3,000 square feet at less than 60-ft. widths! 224 pages.
$7.95 ($10.95 Can.)
13:NL

200 FARMHOUSE AND COUNTRY HOME PLANS Styles and sizes to match every taste and budget, from Classic Farmhouses to Country Capes and Cottages. Expertly drawn floor plans and renderings enhance the sections. 224 pages.
$7.95 ($10.95 Can.)
14:FH

200 BUDGET-SMART HOME PLANS The definitive source for the home builder with a limited budget—have your home and enjoy it too! Amenity-laden homes, in many sizes and styles, can all be built from our plans. 224 pages.
$7.95 ($10.95 Can.)
15:BS

▊ The Landscape Blueprint Package

For the homes marked with an ▊ in this index, Home Planners has created a front-yard landscape plan that matches or is complementary in design to the house plan. These comprehensive blueprint packages include a Frontal Sheet, Plan View, Regionalized Plant & Materials List, a sheet on Planting and Maintaining Your Landscape, Zone Maps and Plant Size and Description Guide. These plans will help you achieve professional results, adding value and enjoyment to your property for years to come. Each set of blueprints is a full 18" x 24" in size with clear, complete instructions and easy-to-read type. To view the designs, call us to order your copy of *The Home Landscaper*, which shows all 40 front-yard designs in glorious full color.

Regional Order Map

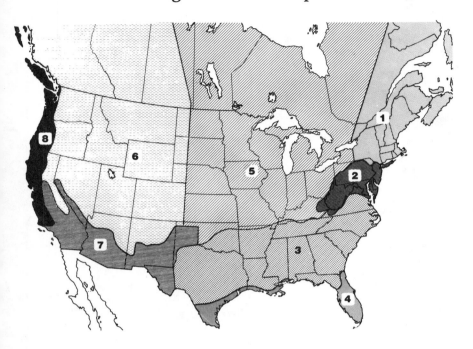

Most of the Landscape Plans shown on these pages are available with a Plant & Materials List adapted by horticultural experts to 8 different regions of the country. Please specify Geographic Region when ordering your plan.

Region	1	Northeast
Region	2	Mid-Atlantic
Region	3	Deep South
Region	4	Florida & Gulf Coast
Region	5	Midwest
Region	6	Rocky Mountains
Region	7	Southern California & Desert Southwest
Region	8	Northern California & Pacific Northwest

▊ The Deck Blueprint Package

Many of the homes in this index can be enhanced with a professionally designed Home Planners' Deck Plan. Those home plans highlighted with a ▊ have a matching or corresponding deck plan available which includes a Deck Plan Frontal Sheet, Deck Framing and Floor Plans, Deck Elevations and a Deck Materials List. A Standard Deck Details Package, also available, provides all the how-to information necessary for building *any* deck. Our Complete Deck Building Package contains 1 set of Custom Deck Plans of your choice, plus 1 set of Standard Deck Building Details all for one low price. Our plans and details are carefully prepared in an easy-to-understand format that will guide you through every stage of your deck-building project. To view all 25 deck designs in our portfolio, call us to order your copy of our *Deck Planner* book.

Deck Plans Price Schedule

CUSTOM DECK PLANS

Price Group	Q	R	S
1 Set Custom Plans	$25	$30	$35
Additional identical sets			$10 each
Reverse sets (mirror image)			$10 each

STANDARD DECK DETAILS

1 Set Generic Construction Details	$14.95 each

COMPLETE DECK BUILDING PACKAGE

Price Group	Q	R	S
1 Set Custom Plans, plus			
1 Set Standard Deck Details	$35	$40	$45

Landscape Plans Price Schedule

Price Group	X	Y	Z
1 set	$35	$45	$55
3 sets	$50	$60	$70
6 sets	$65	$75	$85
Additional Identical Sets			$10 each
Reverse Sets (mirror image)			$10 each

☎ **Toll Free**
1-800-521-6797, Ext. 800